Global Perspectives on Teaching with Technology

Global Perspectives on Teaching with Technology presents a wealth of current research on how teacher education and training programs around the world are preparing teachers to integrate and apply learning technologies across subjects, grade levels, and regions. Digital tools are more integral than ever to an accessible and well-rounded education, although their rapid evolution and proliferation necessitate new guidance into their effective integration and intended outcomes. This book provides graduate students, faculty, and researchers of teacher education, as well as trainers of in-service teachers, with field-tested frameworks, evidence-based theories and models, and real-world examples of the complexities and affordances of teaching with technology. Internationally sourced to reflect today's richly diverse and globalized learner populations, the case studies collected here offer fresh approaches for teacher educators and a springboard for education researchers studying how practitioners can thrive in their classrooms and foster equity among students.

Agnes Chigona is Professor and Head of Research and Postgraduate Studies in the Faculty of Education at Cape Peninsula University of Technology, South Africa.

Helen Crompton is Executive Director of the Research Institute for Digital Innovation in Learning at ODUGlobal and Professor of Instructional Technology at Old Dominion University, USA.

Nyarai Tunjera is Postdoctoral Research Fellow in the Faculty of Education at Cape Peninsula University of Technology, South Africa.

Global Perspectives on Teaching with Technology

Theories, Cases Studies, and Integration Strategies

EDITED BY AGNES CHIGONA, HELEN CROMPTON, AND NYARAI TUNJERA

Designed cover image: © Getty Images / Adene Sanchez

First published 2024
by Routledge
605 Third Avenue, New York, NY 10158

and by Routledge
4 Park Square, Milton Park, Abingdon, Oxon, OX14 4RN

Routledge is an imprint of the Taylor & Francis Group, an informa business

© 2024 selection and editorial matter, Agnes Chigona, Helen Crompton, and Nyarai Tunjera;
individual chapters, the contributors

The right of Agnes Chigona, Helen Crompton, and Nyarai Tunjera to be identified as the authors
of the editorial material, and of the authors for their individual chapters, has been asserted in
accordance with sections 77 and 78 of the Copyright, Designs and Patents Act 1988.

With the exception of Chapter 16, no part of this book may be reprinted or reproduced or utilised
in any form or by any electronic, mechanical, or other means, now known or hereafter invented,
including photocopying and recording, or in any information storage or retrieval system, without
permission in writing from the publishers.

Chapter 16 of this book is available for free in PDF format as Open Access at www.taylorfrancis.
com. It has been made available under a Creative Commons Attribution-Non Commercial-No
Derivatives (CC-BY-NC-ND) 4.0 International license.

Trademark notice: Product or corporate names may be trademarks or registered trademarks, and
are used only for identification and explanation without intent to infringe.

ISBN: 978-1-032-52146-6 (hbk)
ISBN: 978-1-032-52424-5 (pbk)
ISBN: 978-1-003-40663-1 (ebk)

DOI: 10.4324/9781003406631

The Open Access version of chapter 16 was funded by FCDO.

Contents

1 Preparing Teachers to Effectively Integrate Technology in Education 1

HELEN CROMPTON, AGNES CHIGONA, AND NYARAI TUNJERA

2 Educator Integration of Artificial Intelligence Technological Advancements: The Digital Citizenship Framework Model for Professional Development and Wraparound Student Strategic Learning 11

MICHAEL RIBBLE AND N. ANNE GICHURI

3 Exploring the [Surveillant] Impacts of Technology: A Case for Meaningful Integration 26

MORGAN C. BANVILLE

4 Preparation of Future Teachers Teaching with Technology: The Case of Japan 43

TAKAYOSHI MAKI, MASAYASU SAKAGUCHI, NOZOMI SAKATA, AND ASAMI SHIMODA

5 Narratives of Teacher Educators on the Integration of Information and Communication Technologies to Prepare Pre-service Teachers in Specific Subjects 60

THUTHUKILE JITA AND ALICE DHLIWAYO

vi Contents

6 Girls and Computer Science: Professional Development
and Teachers as Role Models 75
JAMES HUGHES AND AGNES CHIGONA

7 Pre-service Teachers' Pedagogical Awareness
of Technology Integration in the Classroom 93
CHIKONDI SEPULA AND CLEMENT SIMUJA

8 Exploration of Foundation Phase: Pre-service Teachers'
Perspectives on Their Abilities to Integrate Technology
in the Classroom 110
CLEMENT SIMUJA

9 Research-Based Teacher Preparation for
Technology-Enhanced Education in Malawi:
A Case Study 127
FOSTER GONDWE

10 Barriers to Self-Directed Learning for Student Teachers
Learning within Asynchronous Online Environments
During Coronavirus-19 Lockdown 142
LUNGI SOSIBO

11 Co-developing Dialogic Teaching with Digital
Technology in Chinese Primary Mathematics Classrooms:
A Design-Based Approach to Lesson Study 160
QIAN LIU

12 Breaking the Digital Divide: How Tech-Enabled
Project-Based Learning Can Level the Playing Field for
Marginalized Learners 179
LIDDY GREENAWAY, NAVYA AKKINEPALLY, HIBA RAHIM, LAUREN LICHTMAN,
AND KARISHMA MHAPADI

13 A Case Study of an Exemplary Grade 5 Teacher's
Experiences When Integrating Technology with
Reading-for-Meaning Strategies in a Meaningful Way 198
JANET CONDY, HEATHER NADIA PHILLIPS, AND CHANTYCLAIRE TIBA

Contents **vii**

14 Effects of a Professional Development Programme for
Teaching and Learning in Digital Environments from the
Perspective of Teachers: Case Study from Finland 214
SINI KONTKANEN, SATU PIISPA-HAKALA, SUSANNA PÖNTINEN,
AND TEEMU VALTONEN

15 What Is Important in Applying ICT to Classroom
Practice in Schools 231
WAKIO OYANAGI

16 A Dialogic Design-Based Research Partnership
Approach: Developing Close-to-Practice Educational
Technology Theory in Kenya 246
LOUIS MAJOR, REBECCA DALTRY, ASAD RAHMAN, DANIEL PLAUT,
MARY OTIENO, AND KEVIN OTIENO

17 Contextualised e-Learning Interventions for HEIs
in Resource-Constrained Environments: The Case
of an African University 265
CAROLINE MAGUNJE

18 Threading Together Digital Technology Integration
Perspectives Across the Globe 281
AGNES CHIGONA, NYARAI TUNJERA, AND HELEN CROMPTON

Contributor Biographies 290

Index 301

Preparing Teachers to Effectively Integrate Technology in Education

1

Helen Crompton, Agnes Chigona, and Nyarai Tunjera

The 21st-century educational landscape has witnessed a profound transformation, primarily driven by the continual march of technological advancements. Digital technology has become an omnipresent fixture in contemporary classrooms, eclipsing traditional instructional tools such as chalkboards and overhead projectors with virtual reality and artificial intelligence. This pervasive digital presence marks the unmistakable advent of the digital age within educational institutions.

Digital technologies, hardware, applications, and supporting infrastructure have been introduced into schools globally. Early reports noted that digital technologies had limited usefulness and usability to meet the aims of educators and schooling systems (Cuban, 2001). As technological options developed, usefulness improved and saw a switch from manual systems for recording to digital systems (Shah, 2014), new options for accessing information and teaching (Albion et al., 2015), learning analytics for policy decisions (Collins & Halverson, 2018), and contextualized, specialized applications for students (Voogt et al., 2018). Technology has ushered in a paradigm shift in pedagogical practices. Students can engage with digital tools, utilizing the tools for research, information access, and collaborative activities. Interactive software platforms have made subjects like mathematics and science more accessible and enjoyable for students. Educators can harness digital tools to globalize their classrooms, enabling students to connect with experts, diverse cultures, and vast information

DOI: 10.4324/9781003406631-1

repositories. Applications designed for students with diverse learning needs offer tailored support, ensuring individualized pathways to success (Starkey, 2020).

In an era of ubiquitous technology, the educational sector stands at a crossroads, where technology's integration presents both immense promise and substantial challenges. This underscores the pivotal role of educators as the mediators between technology and education, entrusted with shaping the learning experiences and empowering the next generation. The need for teachers to use technology to improve teaching practices and student learning has become more and more evident (Bowman et al., 2022). The mere introduction of technology into classrooms can lead to superficial integration if not accompanied by a fundamental shift in pedagogical approaches. The challenge is to ensure that technology serves as a catalyst for innovative teaching strategies, aligning seamlessly with specific learning objectives.

To support educators incorporating technologies in their classrooms, there have been a variety of standards, such as the International Society for Technology in Education standards (Crompton & Sykora, 2021), and frameworks, such as the Technological Pedagogical Content Knowledge (TPACK: Koehler & Mishra, 2008), Substitution, Augmentation, Modification, and Redefinition (SAMR: Puentedura, 2009), and Social Ecological Technology Integration (SETI: Crompton et al., 2023). However, researchers lament that digital competence for pedagogical purposes is poorly integrated into both in-service teacher educational programs (Amhag et al., 2019; Maksimovic & Dimic, 2016) and pre-service teacher programs (Barab et al., 2019).

These calls for educators to be prepared to work in a digital environment have been a concern for many years. Educators typically would choose what digital tools would be used in the classroom and if they were used at all. In recent years, two events have greatly disrupted the traditional educational paradigm in both positive and negative ways. The first was COVID-19, which forced educators across the world to move education into the online space. Educators needed to explore new tools and pedagogies for teaching and learning online as part of Emergency Remote Education (ERE; Crompton et al., 2021a, 2021b). As educators faced the new normal of education post-lockdown, they were then forced to examine the challenge of education with a new wave of generative AI (GenAI) programs.

GenAI programs generate/produce text, images, video, and audio. The most notable advanced GenAI was ChatGPT, which was released to the public in November 2022. As this tool became quickly adopted, the potential for educator and student use to generate text quickly became apparent (Bozkurt et al., 2023). Educators trying to ignore GenAI risk students using these tools to complete the work and may also miss the many innovative ways that these new tools can positively transform education.

About the Book

Therefore, this book was written to share current research on how pre-service and in-service teacher education programs are preparing educators to use and integrate digital technologies, with pedagogies in a meaningful way across subjects and grade levels. Theoretical papers and case studies from across the world provide a snapshot of strategies and practices for technology integration from each author. These 17 chapters provide various viewpoints to highlight different topics, offering different perspectives across 12 countries. Following the introductory chapter, the first two chapters provide a theoretical standpoint on digital citizenship and technological surveillance in educational contexts. This is followed by seven chapters focused on pre-service teacher education, and then seven chapters on in-service teacher education around the globe.

Theoretical Underpinnings

Chapter 2 delineates Ribble's (2023) Digital Citizenship framework. Ribble and Gichuri describe the framework for providing a structured understanding and engagement model for sustainable navigation of this rapidly evolving digital world with a critical awareness of online privacy needs, security issues, essential resources, and requisite responsible use skills. The topic of digital citizenship has been especially important since technologies have provided further access to resources and avenues to communicate with others. The Internet was a large driver in highlighting the need for digital citizenship. Newer GenAI tools such as ChatGPT have renewed that focus on digital citizenship and overarching digital literacy.

In the second theoretical chapter (Chapter 3), Banville discusses the highly debated topic of surveillance technologies for the North American perspective. Surveillance technologies in the education sector include digital technologies that allow people to review student behaviors and collect biometric data, such as proctoring technologies and other general programs. The author notes the increase in the use of surveillance technology during the COVID-19 pandemic. The authors note the connection between digital literacy delineated in Chapter 1 of this book and surveillance as part of digital literacy. The author calls for teacher education to include how surveillance technologies should be used and how technology, care, transparency, and surveillance interact in educational contexts.

Pre-service Teacher Education

The next seven chapters of the book are dedicated to case studies in pre-service teacher education. It is important for the reader to note that while some countries may use the term pre-service, the term Post Graduate Certificate of Education (PGCE) may also be used in some countries described in the book. The length of programs and the time teaching before entering the PGCE may vary from country to country. Maki et al. begin the pre-service teacher education section by offering examples of two teacher education institutions in Japan (Chapter 4). One is a stacked program designed to include Science, Technology, Engineering, Arts, and Mathematics (STEAM) education topics in teacher education. This includes a strong emphasis on technology integration into STEAM education, including artificial intelligence, data science, educational informatics, programming education, program education, and information morality. The second example is on the technical content of designing education using information communication technology (ICT). In examining the two contexts, the authors provide arguments that pre-service teacher training is more than a single course and that teachers should be moved away from a technical and instrumental perspective of ICT to utilizing ICT.

Jita and Dhliwayo's study (Chapter 5) is centered in South Africa, where the investigation focuses on the use of technology in education by pre-service teachers, utilizing the Community of Practice (CoP) framework. The CoP framework consists of three essential components: the domain, the community, and the practice (Wenger-Trayner & Wenger-Trayner, 2015). Within this case study, the authors present narratives that capture the experiences of teacher educators in integrating ICT into a variety of curricular areas. The findings underscore that the modeling of ICT integration for pre-service teachers (PSTs) has the most significant impact on transforming pedagogical practices. The findings consistently highlight the diverse approaches and unique needs of teacher educators as they integrate ICT into their respective subject areas. Additionally, the CoP serves as a safe haven for scholarly reflection on teaching practices and the associated challenges faced by both teacher educators and PSTs.

Moving to Wales in the UK, Hughes and Chigona tell the story of a PGCE study on education, technology, and gender equity (Chapter 6). Specifically, Hughes shares the findings of a study he conducted in a high school to examine female role models in Computer Science. Hughes was concerned to find that females make up only 21% of those taking computer science for their final high school exams. This percentage is particularly concerning with the heightened awareness of gender inequities. The findings of this study report a similar trend to Jita and Dhliwayo's study in Chapter 5 that modeling is essential and, in this case, the findings report on the importance of the teacher as a role model for students. This chapter provides helpful recommendations, such as keeping a focus on positive gender modeling and avoiding stereotypes.

Moving from modeling to the overarching technology integration frameworks, Sepula and Simuja in Chapter 7 and Simuja in Chapter 8 both use the TPACK framework (Koehler & Mishra, 2008) in South Africa with pre-service teachers. Of the three types of knowledge in the TPACK framework (Technology, Pedagogy, and Content Knowledge), Chapter 7 focused on uncovering the pedagogical awareness development of pre-service teachers. Specifically, the goal was to examine the process by which pre-service teachers were able to build pedagogical understanding as they incorporated technology during the teaching practicum. The framework was helpful in developing all TPACK areas. At the conclusion of the study, Sepula and Simuja recommended that pre-service teachers engage in reflective practice, which allows them to dedicate time and space to examine their own pedagogical understanding and use it to enhance their technology integration in teaching practices. Simuja then went on to explore pre-service teachers' perceptions of their ability to incorporate technology into education. The findings revealed that the small group of pre-service teachers interviewed expressed great confidence in their capabilities in technology integration. It is interesting to note that they also placed importance in developing theoretical understandings with frameworks, such as TPACK as well as practical experiences.

In Chapter 9, Gondwe discusses his utilization of the TPACK framework and instructional design frameworks in the challenging low-income setting of Malawi. This case study vividly illustrates Gondwe's endeavors to enhance the authenticity of learning experiences within teacher preparation programs, with a particular emphasis on the integration of technology in education. The teaching perspective often leans heavily towards theoretical learning, with limited connections to practical, real-world learning activities. This chapter offers concrete and direct examples of applying design thinking principles to enhance course quality and effectiveness.

The concluding chapter in the realm of pre-service teacher education delves into the challenges faced during the COVID-19 lockdown period. Sosibo's case study (Chapter 10), set within the South African context, investigates the obstacles encountered by pre-service teachers while engaging in self-directed learning in asynchronous environments. The study illuminated a range of barriers, some stemming from intrinsic factors such as procrastination, lack of motivation, adaptability issues, lack of focus, and poor time management. Additionally, extrinsic barriers, such as shortcomings in course design by teacher educators and a lack of a sense of community, were identified. This information holds significance for both practitioners and the academic community, offering valuable insights into critical areas to address when working with pre-service teachers in similar emergency situations. Furthermore, these findings can serve as a starting point for examining challenges in non-emergency contexts as well.

In-service Teacher Education

The in-service section comprises seven distinct case studies. Building upon the pre-service teacher education section's emphasis on intentional course design, the utilization of technology integration frameworks, the significance of modeling, and the understanding of learner needs, many of these key aspects are carried forward into the in-service chapters.

In Chapter 11, Liu encapsulates several of these critical elements in the process of designing plans for teachers. Specifically, Liu employs design-based research to craft lesson plans for pre-service teachers in China, aimed at fostering dialogic participation and active learning. This case study offers a novel contribution by shedding light on how to develop and execute a viable, effective, and sustainable teacher professional development program for dialogic teaching and technology-integrated pedagogy within the context of Chinese primary education.

Preparing Teachers to Effectively Integrate Technology **7**

To empower teachers to integrate technology seamlessly and effectively into their educational practices, it is imperative that such integration is given equal prominence in the professional development they receive. Liu's study effectively achieves this using two digital platforms that facilitate the exploration of both theoretical and practical considerations in technology integration.

Greenway et al. also developed a learning platform within a low-income context. Chapter 12 delves into the work of Learning Equality and their creation of the Kolibri learning platform. This platform places a strong emphasis on project-based and playful learning approaches, while also incorporating social-emotional learning materials derived from Amal Alliance's Colors of Kindness program. Aligned with the Ugandan curriculum, the case study's findings reveal statistically significant progress among learners in foundational literacy, numeracy skills, and social-emotional competencies.

The collaboration with colleagues adept at digital program development can be highly beneficial. However, it's worth noting that many teacher educators may not have access to such opportunities. Chapter 13, authored by Condy et al., explores an approach for supporting teacher development through the utilization of various digital tools. This study centers on the use of digital tools to equip teachers with classroom literacy instructional practices that promote higher-order thinking skills. The TPACK technology integration framework serves as a guiding lens for technology integration. The study's outcomes have led the authors to provide a set of recommendations, emphasizing the importance of utilizing other tools as necessary, thus shifting the focus away from technology when appropriate.

Technology can be a valuable tool for extending and enhancing the learning experience. However, its effective use requires purposeful, strategic, and careful design, with a strong emphasis on its impact on learning outcomes. In Chapter 14, Sini et al. present a holistic case study focusing on the efficacy of a comprehensive professional development program in Finland, with the goal of enhancing digital teaching practices. The findings underscore the significance of supporting teachers' ongoing learning and active engagement, along with the implementation of activities that promote digital methods for student-centered pedagogies. Chapter 15 offers a glimpse into how Chinese educators incorporate technology into their schools. Specifically, Oyanagi's work sheds light on how ICT and educational data were promoted in Japanese schools during the year 2020, as evident in case reports from Japan. Although this study is based on Japanese cases, it unveils insights into cultural transformations within school environments, the challenges that emerge as the learning landscape evolves, and the advancements made in the process of integrating technology into classrooms.

Major et al., in Chapter 16, have established a novel foundation for applying design-based research (DBR) to enhance integration of educational technology by Kenyan teachers for marginalized learners. The authors have shown how DBR promoted teacher-researcher engagement by adopting a dialogue-informed "intermediate theory building" framework, bridging the theory-practice gap. The final case study in Chapter 17 is situated in Zimbabwe, where Magunje investigates an institution's transition toward technology-enhanced flexible curriculum delivery for practicing teachers. Employing Actor-Network Theory, Magunje examines the roles of senior leadership in advocating for e-learning to provide greater flexibility for both educators and students, while addressing the concerns of instructors who may not be comfortable with this new method. This case study delves into the social-ecological issues that arise, such as the high cost of internet access, and highlights how meeting these needs contributes to the increased acceptance of technology-enhanced education.

It's interesting to observe the common themes that run through these case studies, encompassing frameworks, practices, and considerations. However, it is equally important to acknowledge the contextual nuances that must be taken into account as teachers embark on their journey to master the art of technology integration.

Concluding Statement

The imperative of teacher preparedness to effectively employ technology, encompassing both in-service and pre-service education, cannot be overstated. Passive observation amidst this technological transformation is inadequate. Teachers must actively participate in guiding students through the digital landscape and impart the requisite skills for navigating an increasingly complex and interconnected world. This must be underpinned by teachers having adequate preparation to effectively integrate technology in education. This book explores the profound impact of technology on education and underscores the critical necessity for educators to be adequately prepared, not merely in theory but also in practical terms, to harness technology's potential in their classrooms.

References

Albion, P. R., Tondeur, J., Forkosh-Baruch, A., & Peeraer, J. (2015). Teachers' professional development for ICT integration: Towards a reciprocal relationship between research and practice. *Education and Information Technologies, 20*(4), 655–673.

Amhag, L., Hellstrom, L., & Stigmar, M. (2019). Teacher educations' use of digital tools and the needs for digital competence in higher education. *Journal of Digital Learning in Teacher Education, 35*(4), 203–220. https://doi.org/10.10 80/21532974.2019.1646169

Baran, E., Bilici, S. C., Sari, A. A., & Tondeur, J. (2019). Investigating the impact of teacher education strategies on preservice teachers' TPACK. *British Journal of Educational Technology, 50*(1), 357–370. https://doi.org/10.1111/bjet.12565

Bozkurt, A., Xiao, J., Lambert, S., Pazurek, A., Crompton, H., Koseoglu, S, Farrow, R., Bond, M., Nerantzi, C., Honeychurch, S., & Bali, M. (2023). Speculative futures on ChatGPT and generative artificial intelligence (AI): A collective reflection from the educational landscape. *Asian Journal of Distance Education, 18*(1), 53–130. https://doi.org/10.5281/zenodo.7636568

Bowman, M. A., Vongkulluksn, V. W., Jiang, Z., & Xie, K. (2022). Teachers' exposure to professional development and the quality of their instructional technology use: The mediating role of teachers' value and ability beliefs. *Journal of Research on Technology in Education, 54*(2), 188–204. https://doi.org/ 10.1080/15391523.2020.1830895

Collins, A., & Halverson, R. (2018). *Rethinking education in the age of technology: The digital revolution and schooling in America.* Teachers College Press.

Crompton, H., & Sykora, C. (2021). Developing instructional technology standards for educators: A design-based research study. *Computers and Education Open, 2.* https://doi.org/10.1016/j.caeo.2021.100044

Crompton, H., Burke, D., Jordan, K., & Wilson, S. (2021a). Learning with technology during emergencies: A systematic review of K-12 education. *British Journal of Educational Technology, 52*(4), 1554–1575. https://doi.org/10.1111/ bjet.13114

Crompton, H., Burke, D., Jordan, K., & Wilson, S. (2021b). Support provided for K-12 teachers teaching remotely with technology during emergencies: A systematic review. *Journal of Research on Technology in Education, 54*(3), 473–489. https://doi.org/10.1080/15391523.2021.1899877

Crompton, H., Chigona, A., & Burke, D. (2023). Teacher resilience during COVID-19: Comparing teachers' shift to online learning in South Africa and the United States. *TechTrends.* https://doi.org/10.1007/s11528-022-00826-6 and https://link.springer.com/article/10.1007/s11528-022-00826-6#citeas

Cuban, L. (2001). *Oversold and underused: Computers in the classroom*. Harvard University Press.

Koehler, M. J., & Mishra, P. (2008). Introducing TPACK. In American Association of Colleges for Teacher Education Committee on Innovation & Technology (Ed.), *Handbook for technological pedagogical content knowledge* (pp. 3–29). Routledge.

Maksimovic, J., & Dimic, N. (2016). Digital technology and teachers' competence for its application in the classroom. *Istrazivanja u Pedagogiji, 6*(2), 59–71.

Puentedura, R. (2009, February 4). *As we may teach: Educational technology, from theory into practice* [Blog]. Ruben R. Puentedura's Weblog. http://wwwhiasuscom/rrpweblog/archives/000025html

Ribble, M. S. (2023). *Digital citizenship: Using technology appropriately*. https://www.digitalcitizenship.net/

Shah, M. (2014). Impact of management information systems (MIS) on school administration: What the literature says. *Procedia – Social and Behavioral Sciences, 116*, 2799–2804. https://doi.org/10.1016/j.sbspro.2014.01.659

Starkey, L. (2020). A review of research exploring teacher preparation in the digital age. *Cambridge Journal of Education, 50*, 37–56. https://doi.org/10.1080/0305764X.2019.1625867

Voogt, J., Fisser, P., Pareja Roblin, N., Tondeur, J., & van Braak, J. (2013). Technological pedagogical content knowledge: A review of the literature. *Journal of Computer Assisted Learning, 29*(2), 109–121.

Wanger-Trayner, E., & Wanger-Trayner, B. (2015, June). *Introduction to communities of practice: A brief overview of the concept and its uses*. https://www.wenger-trayner.com/introduction-to-communities-of-practice/

Educator Integration of Artificial Intelligence Technological Advancements

The Digital Citizenship Framework Model for Professional Development and Wraparound Student Strategic Learning

Michael Ribble and N. Anne Gichuri

Introduction

Technological innovations, such as the rapid expansion of generative artificial intelligence (AI) and other emerging technologies, present pressing opportunities and constraining challenges for education (Akgun & Greenhow, 2022; Education Week, 2023; UNESCO, 2023c, July). AI/technology's availability and accessibility in tablet, smartphone, and laptop handheld devices from very young ages make educators' intentional classroom integration decisions and student instruction on responsible use imperative and pressing global human concerns (Heath et al., 2022; Miao et al., 2023; O'Brien & Miller, 2023). This has led to the enactment of new standards, policies, and legal safeguards to sustainably frame AI's transformative societal evolutions, particularly those with a

DOI: 10.4324/9781003406631-2

direct impact on children, which makes educator pre-/in-service professional development training a priority, to guide AI's self-evolving classroom implementation (Cassidy, 2023; Council of Europe, 2023; Miao et al., 2021; UNESCO, 2022).

Insights gained from the forced migration to online teaching and learning during the COVID-19 worldwide lockdown stress the need for educator training on digital learning competencies, such as those offered by the Ribble (2023) Digital Citizenship framework's nine elements, resources, and guided instructional implementation opportunities. The framework enhances effective online and hybrid teaching modalities by equipping educators to address student online safety, privacy, critical analytical thinking, and ethical technology use needs. By informing pre-/in-service professional development training, the framework helps enhance understanding of digital learning integration issues that are critical for sustainable classroom implementation of its nine core elements.

By definition, the framework is a continuous development model of nine core elements centrally organized around progressively spiralling layers of safe, savvy, and social (S3) – essential guiding principles necessary for the appropriate, responsible, and empowered use of technology (Ribble, 2023). The framework is a classroom implementation tool that can help educators promote student critical awareness of online privacy, safety, security, savviness on enduring digital footprints, socio-emotional well-being, intellectual property protections, and responsible use requirements (Floridi et al., 2018; Merod, 2023). The framework was developed in response to our global digital interconnectedness, to address myths and misunderstandings that inhibit true communication and responsible ethical, culturally sensitive, digitally literate, cybersecurity-aware, and globalized interactive collaborations that positively contribute to sustainably inclusive cross-cultural understanding made possible by AI/technological advances that can equalize and multiply constructive opportunities for all (UNESCO, 2022, 2023c, July).

The framework's concept of "citizenship" is therefore expanded beyond traditional definitions that focus on ever-widening concentric circles beginning with self, to extend into new widening spirals of vertical globalized interconnections that require educator instructional competence to aid student learning across ever-evolving increased local-global relationships, ranging from someone down our street, or around the globe, or an AI bot (Education Week, 2023). The framework serves as a critical globally oriented model with a local lens, to help promote student exposure to skills needed to safely navigate fast, seamless AI/technologically interconnected local/global relationships with savviness (Cassidy, 2023). AI/technology advances have resulted in 24/7 connectivity, workload and classroom learning creep into educator and student homes, detractions from intentional awareness, as well as threats to privacy and socio-emotional well-being in unprecedented ways (Kouritzin et al., 2021). Therefore, the framework helps educators intentionally promote student-informed decision-making of when, how, where, and with whom to safely connect online.

This elevates educator instructional abilities beyond traditional roles as holders and dispensers of knowledge, to meet their 21st-century imperative responsibility and role as facilitators transforming student learning mastery of how to safely and ethically locate, consume, generate, and disseminate what is known and how it is known (UNESCO, 2019). Therefore, educators have the ethical obligation and capacity to nurture students' critical and deeper learning across all subjects by leveraging classroom teaching with the framework's skills to promote appropriate AI/technology integration of 21st-century resources for student competence-oriented academic and lifelong success (Heath et al., 2022). The framework aids educator AI/technology integration through guided student instruction on safe, savvy, and socially appropriate user skills that help increase academic productivity, classroom engagement, critical thinking, inclusive communication, efficient organization, and proactive time management skills (Bond & Bedenlier, 2019; Ramirez et al., 2021). Therefore, the framework leverages educator mastery of skills needed to guide students on how, when, who, and where to interact and integrate technological tools into lifelong learning within an ethically nuanced implementation approach formatted to preemptively counterbalance and mitigate AI's inherent risks in a holistic, intentional, and inclusive way.

A single educator creating opportunities to "teach" or model the framework can have an exponential impact on students and can generate significant implications for societal stability and sustainability, given that one educator may connect with a hundred different students in a week. Further, each of those students can in turn have an incalculable potential to reach other peers. Therefore, integration of the framework into pre-/in-service training curriculum is critically important and has to start with policymakers intentionally and systemically embedding it consistently across K–12 and higher education curricular areas. Recent expansion in commercialization of educational technologies further requires intentional short-/long-range focus on educator pre-/in-service instructional skill competencies, to ensure equitable inclusion and ethical sustainable access to quality education by all.

These AI/technological complex realities are often difficult to understand and navigate for adults, but in a daily classroom reality, educators must help students navigate to sustainably master 21st-century learning competencies (O'Brien & Miller, 2023). The interconnected global nature of rapidly evolving AI/technology further compounds the ease with which students share and learn complex unvetted information in words, visual form, and voice with footprint permanency (Merod, 2023). The framework helps advance pre-/in-service educator competence in AI/technology integration for differentiated instruction with the incorporation of classroom safeguards to further enhance students' rigorous mastery of 21st-century essential socio-emotional, creative, critical thinking, adaptability, empathy, ethical collaboration, and digital literacy skills (Battelle for Kids, n.d.; Baysan & Çetin, 2021). Table 2.1 presents the

Table 2.1 The Ribble (2023) Digital Citizenship Framework's Nine Elements and Definitions of Targeted AI/Technology Issues

Digital Citizenship Framework Elements	Definition of Targeted AI/Technology Issues
1. Digital Access	Equitable distribution of technology and online resources
2. Digital Commerce	Electronic buying and selling of goods
3. Digital Communication and Collaboration	Electronic exchange of information, and connection to others
4. Digital Etiquette	Electronic standards of conduct or procedural mores, and focus on thinking of how others may perceive what has been shared
5. Digital Fluency	Process of fully understanding technology and making connections in its best use
6. Digital Health and Welfare	Physical and psychological well-being of users within a digital world
7. Digital Law	Electronic responsibility of technology users, in terms of their actions and deeds
8. Digital Rights and Responsibility	Requirements and freedoms extended to everyone in a digital world, including technology users' considerations for non-digital others
9. Digital Security & Privacy	Electronic precautions technology users need to guarantee short-term and long-term safety

Ribble (2023) framework's nine core elements, each defined in a readily understandable and applicable instructional format that guides educator implementation and outlines how each element's central issue relates to complex AI/technology use.

Safe, Savvy, and Social

The framework organizes these nine foundational core elements into three Safe, Savvy, and Social (S3) essential guiding principles that support and reinforce its curriculum implementation plan through progressive spiralling concentric skill mastery layered targets. For example, the third "Communication and Collaboration" foundational core element tackles the concept of email versus social media platforms by providing three levels of Safe, Savvy, and Social successively complex spiralled discussions of related layered skills and supports, which should begin as soon as children are exposed to their first digital device. The S3 essential guiding principles help educators scaffold student learning awareness of the framework's nine core elements, and allow for a progressively expanded understanding of complex digital citizenship rights and responsibilities necessary to actualize constructive AI/technological advantages while mitigating abuse and misuse constraints.

The framework extends beyond a mere focus on ever-evolving emergent AI/technological tools to instead encompass each curricular area with the S3 essential guiding principles whose skills guide educators in helping students develop resilient salient technological application skills for sustainable use. Therefore, the framework's S3 essential guiding principles should be integrated into the pre-/in-service training curriculum as natural essential learning components necessary across all subjects and grade levels, rather than as a standalone topic/subject. This allows for the framework's S3 essential guiding principles to be woven into lesson activities across all subjects and grade levels to nurture students' progressively widening mastery of AI/technology use, online communications, information literacy, and responsible digital behaviour or netiquette skills (UNESCO, 2023b).

Safety

The framework guides educator classroom implementation starting with safety, the first baseline S3 core guiding principle, which helps promote student foundational skills on how to protect self and others. It helps educators develop student-sustainable AI integration as good stewards and safe, responsible users who can obtain, synthesize, and create information from many different sources and inclusive of diverse perspectives (Payero, 2017). It helps educators critically analyze where and how safeguards should be implemented to safeguard student online safety and socio-emotional learning needs.

For example, the framework helps educators identify crucial safeguards for student data privacy as it relates to their social and emotional safety and sustainable well-being. This requires a collaborative implementation approach involving students and parents by generating a better understanding of how to safely interact online, and the process for resolving issues that arise through ease-of-use pathways for informing proper officials. The framework helps educators foster student online awareness of anti-predatory behaviour, strategies for preemptively protecting personal information, and strategies for safeguarding the security of their user space in online real-life communities to nurture lifelong risk-mitigation capacities (Cassidy, 2023; Merod, 2023).

Its effective implementation requires a comprehensive collaborative approach involving educators, students, and parents. The safety guiding principle allows educators to strengthen the collaborative involvement of parents/guardians early on, which is critical in addressing issues before they reach a crisis point, or before learning gaps compound. Educator skill transfer helps parents support student mastery of critical life skills, through ethical awareness of the need to do the right thing within the digital world contexts seamlessly as they are taught to do offline. The framework helps educators proactively engage parents by deepening knowledge and skills transfer of AI/technology's potential benefits for learning, and context-specific proactive mitigation of negative popular media-identified threats of uncurated student access to sexually explicit content, sharing of private information with strangers, illegal access to entertainment content, cyberbullying, negative body image dystopia, and suicidal ideation.

The framework guides educators on how to adequately plan, communicate, and transfer AI/technology skills mastered to shift parental focus beyond what AI/technology can do, to instead encompass opportunities of "when" and "where" of its appropriate use. This helps to inform parents' purchasing decisions of new digital technology necessary for students to create content, collaboratively interact and learn from peers, and expand project-based learning beyond physical classrooms. Similar to educators, parents need exposure to the framework's resources through workshops and information sessions that help deepen AI/technology understanding of how they are needed to support students' responsible use outside classrooms. Such open communication between educators and parents is critical for student safety from an early age since AI/technology exposure begins from early at-home exposure from infancy, similar to parental early involvement in student comprehension of the alphabet, numbers, and colours (Common Sense Media, 2021; Battelle for Kids, n.d.).

The framework's model supports the formation of campus implementation committees or collaborative teams composed of engaged educators, parents, and students to sustainably, inclusively, and equitably create time, space, and resources for formally promoting ethical, safe, and appropriate integration of AI/technology use in schools (Miao et al., 2021). Teams collaborate to develop school-wide policies, guidelines, and wraparound support initiatives for implementing the framework, with essential assessment instruments incorporated for successive short-/long-term reviews of identification of school and community positive resources, tools, and platforms to scale-up or negative barriers to mitigate, for sustained student development into 21st-century ready societal members. The Los Angeles Unified School District is an example of how a major metropolitan area has adopted and implemented the framework district-wide (Common Sense Media, 2014; Higgin, 2018; Monterosa, 2021).

Savvy

The framework's second essential guiding principle focuses on helping educators develop pathways for students' expanded critical awareness of AI/technology use abilities through progressively spiralled concentric layered understanding and skill awareness built upon the prerequisite safety baseline. The framework aids educator ability to sensitize students on critical socially constructive skills necessary for safe, sustainable AI/technology use and global cyber-connections, through guided proactive skill awareness of safeguards for on/offline privacy, personal information, footprint awareness, anti-predatory mitigation, intercultural competence, socio-emotional well-being, and academic success (Brianza et al., 2022; Davis et al., 2005; Sorensen, 2005).

A direct outcome of the framework's educator skill transfer to students is their active engagement in critical deep learning through interactive participatory analytical activities integral to sustainable 21st-century competence (Mendoza, 2020). The framework helps educators encourage discussions, role-playing, case studies, and real-life scenarios to deepen student understanding of online actions and their implications, crucial for responsible and ethical choices. For instance, through the framework's nine progressive core elements, educators can determine skills to teach at various levels and how to balance AI/technology use with other instructional methods. Similarly, it promotes educator implementation of differentiated instruction to foster student critical thinking skills and ethical decision-making savviness, by exploring diverse digital dilemmas and related on/offline ethical considerations (UNESCO, 2019, 2023a).

The framework helps educators sensitize students on transparency, accountability, and fairness (Akgun & Greenhow, 2022; Education Week, 2023). For example, it emphasizes the importance of considering various ethical implications, such as using AI-created output as one's original work, analyzing AI/technological accessibility by all, and identifying potential biases in the application of AI systems in ways that could exacerbate existing educational and societal inequalities (Heath et al., 2022; Miao et al., 2023; UNESCO, 2022).

The framework guides educators' ability to safely tap and integrate AI/technology to reinforce instructional practices (Ramírez et al., 2021; UNESCO, 2019) by identifying professional development needs, to support their ongoing instructional competence and confidence (UNESCO, 2022). For example, it promotes ethical AI curriculum integration with an emphasis on computational thinking (Grover & Pea, 2018), the importance of ethical considerations on societal impact, emphasis on critical analytical thinking and responsible use, and awareness of potential issues and abuses of AI tools (Gregersen & Bianzino, 2023; Higgin, 2018; UNESCO, 2023a). The framework helps educators generate students' critical awareness of cybersecurity threats such as phishing, identity theft, and cyberbullying and provides strategies for mitigating them through preemptive measures that protect personal information and privacy (O'Brien & Miller, 2023).

The framework emphasizes the need for educators and policymakers to create formalized curricular implementation time and space into daily instructional routines, in addition to embedding robust data protection measures and oversight privacy regulatory compliance processes to safeguard students' sensitive information, integrity of academic/learning processes, and sustainability of critical public schooling infrastructures (Merod, 2023; Miao et al., 2023; UNESCO, 2023b). The framework helps educators address the critical need to ethically gather data for informed decision-making before classroom implementation of AI. The S3 model provides educators the opportunity to determine how, who, where, and when AI/technologies are integrated into classroom routines to enhance student learning and online savviness.

Social

The framework's third essential guiding principle helps educators develop students' AI/technology user skills, which embody the ability to make decisions that exemplify a commitment to ethical respect for self and others. The framework helps educators expand student and parent understanding of AI/technology by advancing awareness of skills necessary to decide what is helpful and necessary versus harmful distractions. It helps educators nurture skills that students need for ethical and safe social interactions, positive digital identity, safety, and savviness on technology user rights versus obligations.

The framework benefits educators' development of students' critical understanding of connections between AI/technology use and their social-emotional well-being by helping to create awareness of threats to self-image dystopia, intellectual property rights, and data privacy protections. It also helps educators critically analyze threats that are eroding sustainable learning environments, for instance, through identification of unethical plagiarism or cheating practices, widening of inequities and learning gaps, as well as learning automation's unintended dehumanization of pedagogy, educator disempowerment, and fragmentation of public education management systems in ways that threaten the sustainability of societal democratic models and local autonomies (Darling-Hammond et al., 2020; Merod, 2023).

The COVID-19 lockdown revealed significant gaps in student access to adequate learning space, technological hardware, and/or internet access outside of school. The framework helps educators identify pathways for fostering sustainable partnerships with community organizations, law enforcement agencies, and industry experts to enhance successful implementation through formal and informal gathering of information and available expertise on AI/technology access gaps in/outside school, and technology access resource capacities within community public and private organizations/businesses to scaffold student learning by bridging identified access gaps – for instance, by opening community libraries evenings and weekends, partnering with community leaders to provide mobile "hotspots" working with telecommunication companies to provide discounted wifi access to families with children, and by creating computer clubs at churches or community social spaces. Such heightened awareness and collaborations are critical and can be sustained by inviting guest speakers and organizing workshops to leverage community resources for students, and for their mastery of real-world social rights and responsibilities implicit in interconnected digital living, learning, and working societal spaces (Floridi et al., 2018; Miao et al., 2023). The framework's outcomes help educators equip students to live inspired, innovative, involved, passionate, reflective, empathetic, informed, savvy, safe, and ethical lives through responsible AI/technology use (Council of Europe, 2023; Haleem, 2022; UNESCO, 2019).

Therefore, the globalized nature of AI/technology beyond traditional physical boundaries allows global connections, communications, and collaborations that create crucial needs for a shared understanding of responsible and ethical use behaviour, and coordinated mitigation of new compounding challenges beyond the reach of existing regulatory structures. The framework helps educators inform students' ability to navigate globalized digital landscapes through preemptive critical awareness, global ethical respect, and inclusive collaborative social engagement. For example, educators can use the framework to incorporate sustainable cross-cultural intra-/inter-regional exchanges from diverse experiential backgrounds into student learning to promote sharing of ideas and collaborations with cultural sensitivity, empathy, and respect for diverging perspectives while recognizing others' rights, privacy, and intellectual property.

This expansion of digital literacy informs educator development of students' ability to find, evaluate, and critically analyze information from various sources, as well as the skills to communicate, collaborate, and create on/offline content (Ohler, 2010; GFC Global, n.d.). The framework helps educators encourage students' ability to think critically about the consequences of online actions and to engage in respectful and constructive online discourse that respects the cultures and laws of diverse users (Ribble et al., 2004). By promoting ethical and inclusive responsible behaviour, the framework helps educators nurture safer, positive, and inclusive learning environments (Council of Europe, 2023). The framework further helps educators expand student learning engagement through globalized collaborative digital advocacy and mobilization of awareness support for critical societal issues such as mitigating the disruptive effects of climate change, protecting endangered species, confronting human smuggling, and crowd-funding responses to traumatic local/global disasters.

Conclusion

The digital citizenship framework helps educators guide student development into active end users of AI/technology as an assistive tool, instead of remaining passive, vulnerable, dependent recipients controlled and harmed through our fragile learning, social, emotional, economic, and physical environments. The framework aims to help educators promote student intentional, critical, sustainable humane AI/technology use as actively engaged informed users conscious of its short-/long-term costs versus benefits (Lynch, 2018).

In closing summary, the digital citizenship framework helps educators:

- Improve pre-/in-service competence training on AI/technology used to promote student sustainable engagement and efficacy within ever-evolving advances.
- Collaboratively engage with policymakers, community members, parents, and students to cater for time and resources needed to implement safety measures and curricular spaces necessary to equitably, inclusively, and ethically meet short-/long-term student educational needs for responsible, safe, socially informed, analytical, savvy, and empowered AI/technology use and well-being.
- Integrate the S3 guiding principles into the curriculum to provide students with the how, who, where, when, and why of skills awareness and ethical perspectives, necessary to securely thrive in an interconnected evolving digital world.
- Engage in pre-/in-service professional development and communication collaborations on the appropriate use of AI/technological advances in and out of the classroom, to generate time and resources needed to limit constraints and transform integration of enabling opportunities for effective, interactive, and safe expansion of learner-centered ideas, abilities, knowledge, and experiential learning facilitated by the educator as a learning "guide on the side," who helps students recognize and efficiently harness the power of AI/technology for the good of self and others.

References

Akgun, S., & Greenhow, C. (2022). Artificial intelligence in education: Addressing ethical challenges in K-12 settings. *AI and Ethics, 2*(3), 431–440. https://doi.org/10.1007/s43681-021-00096-7

Battelle for Kids. (n.d.). *A portrait of a graduate: Your system's vision for 21st century, deeper learning for every student.* https://portraitofagraduate.org/

Baysan, E., & Çetin, Ş. (2021). Determining the training needs of teachers in the ethical use of information technologies. *Kuramsal Eğitimbilim Dergisi [Journal of Theoretical Educational Science], 14*(3), 476–497. https://files.eric.ed.gov/fulltext/EJ1307307.pdf

Bond, M. & Bedenlier, S. (2019). Facilitating student engagement through educational technology: Towards a conceptual framework. *Journal of Interactive Media in Education, 11*(1), 1–14. http://doi.org/10.5334/jime.528

Brianza, E., Schmid, M., Tondeur, J., & Petko, D. (2022). Situating TPACK: A systematic literature review of context as a domain of knowledge. *Contemporary Issues in Technology and Teacher Education, 22*(4). https://citejournal.org/volume-22/issue-4-22/general/situating-tpack

Cassidy, C. A. (2023, July 15). *Misleading AI-generated content is a top concern among state election officials for 2024.* Associated Press. https://www.pbs.org/newshour/politics/misleading-ai-generated

Common Sense Media. (2014, March 20). *Los Angeles unified school district teams with common sense media for the inaugural digital citizenship week.* https://www.commonsensemedia.org/press-releases/los-angeles-unified-school-district

Common Sense Media. (2021). *Teaching digital citizenship in today's world.* https://www.commonsense.org/system/files/pdf/2021-08/common-sense-education

Council of Europe. (2023, May). *Guidelines to support equitable partnerships of education institutions and the private sector.* Steering Committee for Education Policy and Practice. https://rm.coe.int/0900001680a94c1b

Darling-Hammond, L., Flook, L., Cook-Harvey, C., Barron, B., & Osher, D. (2020). Implications for educational practice of the science of learning and development. *Applied Developmental Science, 24*(2), 97–140. https://doi.org/10.1080/10888691.2018.1537791

Davis, N., Cho, M. O., & Hagenson, L. (2005). Intercultural competence and the role of technology in teacher education. *Contemporary Issues in Technology and Teacher Education, 4*(4), 384–394. https://citejournal.org/wp-content/uploads/2016/04/v4i4editorial1.pdf

Education Week. (2023, July 13). *AI in education: Big opportunities, big problems*. https://www.edweek.org/events/k-12-essentials-forum/ai-in-education-big-opportunities

Floridi, L., Cowls, J., Beltrametti, M., Chatila, R., Chazerand, P., Dignum, V., Luetge, C., Madelin, R., Pagallo, U., Rossi, F., Schafer, B., Valcke, P., & Vayena, E. (2018). AI4People – an ethical framework for a good AI society: Opportunities, risks, principles, and recommendations. *Minds and Machines*, *28*(4), 689–707. https://doi.org/10.1007/s11023-018-9482-5

GFC Global. (n.d.). *Being a good digital citizen*. https://edu.gcfglobal.org/en/communicationskills/being-a-good-digital-citizen/1/

Gregersen, H. & Bianzino, N. M. (2023, May 26). AI can help you ask better questions – and solve bigger problems. *Harvard Business Review*. https://hbr.org/2023/05/ai-can-help-you-ask-better-questions-and-solve-bigger-problems

Grover, S., & Pea, R. (2018). Computational thinking: A competency whose time has come. In S. Sentence, E. Barendsen, & C. Schulte (Eds.), *Computer science education: Perspective on teaching and learning in school* (pp. 19–38). Bloomsbury. https://www.researchgate.net/publication/322104135_Computational_Thinking

Haleem, A., Mohd Javaid, M., Qadri, M. A., & Suman, R. (2022). Understanding the role of digital technologies in education: A review. *Sustainable Operations and Computers*, *3*, 275–285. https://doi.org/10.1016/j.susoc.2022.05.004

Heath, M., Asim, S., Milman, N., & Henderson, J. (2022). Confronting tools of the oppressor: Framing just technology integration in educational technology and teacher education. *Contemporary Issues in Technology and Teacher Education*, *22*(4), 754–777. https://citejournal.org/volume-22/issue-4-22/current-practice/confronting-tools

Higgin, T. (2018, July 17). *How to craft useful, student-centred social media policies*. Common Sense Media. https://www.commonsense.org/education/articles/how-to-craft-useful-student-centered

Kouritzin, S., Nakagawa, S., Ellis, T., & Shirzadi, G. (2021, May 30–June 1). *Intersections and atomisation in the academy: Gender, race, and family in academic workload* [Conference presentation]. Canadian Society for the Study of Higher Education Virtual Conference, University of Alberta, Canada. http://www.workloadcreep.ca/

Lynch, M. (2018, April 4). *Does EDTECH reduce the cost of teaching and learning?* The Tech Advocate. https://www.thetechedvocate.org/edtech-reduce-cost-teaching-learning/

Mendoza, K. (2020, July 30). *Quick digital citizenship activities for middle and high school distance learning*. Common Sense Media. https://www.commonsense.org/education/articles/quick-digital-citizenship-activities

Merod, A. (2023, March 29). *Ed-tech experts urge caution on ChatGPT's student data privacy, K-12*. DIVE. https://www.k12dive.com/news/chatgpt-student-data-privacy-concern/646297/

Miao, F., Holmes, W., Huang, R., & Zhang, H. (2021). *AI and education: Guidance for policy-makers*. UNESCO. https://doi.org/10.54675/PCSP7350

Miao, F., Shinohara, K., Vally, Z., & Holmes, W. (2023). *International forum on AI and education: Steering AI to empower teachers and transform teaching*. UNESCO. https://unesdoc.unesco.org/ark:/48223/pf0000381226

Monterosa, V. (2021, January–February). *Digital citizenship for education leaders*. https://leadership.acsa.org/digital-citizenship-for-education-leaders

O'Brien, M. & Miller, Z. (2023, July 21). *White House sets AI safeguard agreements with Amazon, Google, Meta, Microsoft and other tech firms*. Associated Press. https://www.pbs.org/newshour/nation/white-house-sets-ai-safeguard-agreements

Ohler, J. B. (2010). *Digital community, digital citizen*. Corwin Press. https://doi.org/10.4135/9781452219448

Payero, T. (2017, May 22). 5 tips for good digital citizenship. *Teq*. https://www.teq.com/5-tips-good-digital-citizenship/

Ramírez, S., Gana, S., Garcés, S., Zúñiga, T., Araya, R., & Gaete, J. (2021). Use of technology and its association with academic performance and life satisfaction among children and adolescents. *Frontiers in Psychiatry, 12*(764054), 1–12. https://doi.org/10.3389/fpsyt.2021.764054

Ribble, M. S. (2023). *Digital citizenship: Using technology appropriately*. https://www.digitalcitizenship.net/

Ribble, M. S., Bailey, G., & Ross, T. W. (2004). Digital Citizenship: Addressing appropriate technology behaviour. *Learning and Leading with Technology, 32*, 6. https://www.semanticscholar.org/paper/Digital-Citizenship%3A-Addressing

Sorensen, E. K. (2005). Networked learning and collaborative knowledge building: Design and facilitation. *Contemporary Issues in Technology and Teacher Education, 4*(4), 446–455. https://citejournal.org/wp-content/uploads/2016/04/v4i4general3.pdf

UNESCO. (2019). Beijing consensus on artificial intelligence and education. *Proceedings of the International Conference on Artificial Intelligence and Education on Planning Education in the AI Era: Lead the Leap, Beijing, 66720*, 1–70. https://unesdoc.unesco.org/ark:/48223/pf0000368303

UNESCO. (2022). *International forum on AI and education: Ensuring AI as a common good to transform education*. https://unesdoc.unesco.org/ark:/48223/pf0000381226

UNESCO. (2023a). *Ethics of artificial intelligence*. https://www.unesco.org/en/artificial-intelligence/recommendation-ethics

UNESCO. (2023b). UNESCO's *Recommendation on the ethics of artificial intelligence: Key facts*. UNESDOC. https://unesdoc.unesco.org/ark:/48223/pf0000385082

UNESCO. (2023c, July 3). *Generative Artificial Intelligence in education: What are the opportunities and challenges?* https://www.unesco.org/en/articles/generative-artificial-intelligence-education

Exploring the [Surveillant] Impacts of Technology

A Case for Meaningful Integration

Morgan C. Banville

Introduction

During the beginning and throughout the peaks of the COVID-19 pandemic, I was a Ph.D. student in a Rhetoric, Writing, and Professional Communication program in the United States of America. My first time teaching virtual and hybrid undergraduate college courses occurred during the shutdown in the United States that began in March 2020. To provide some context for this chapter and the chosen examples, my experience teaching in private, vocational, and public high schools informed my approach to teaching within higher education, a transition that occurred before the COVID-19 shutdown in 2020. For more information about my time teaching during COVID-19, see the article by Gonzales et al., 2022.

This chapter is situated in the context of United States secondary education and explores examples of the impacts that increased surveillance technology has within the classroom. The chapter is organized by situated global examples and discussion topics and questions, all of which inform an assignment to guide instructors – technical communicators – in critically examining how technological choices impact students within and outside of the classroom. The COVID-19 pandemic shined a light on the lack of accessibility in secondary education. In the hurried response to increased technology in education, instructors need to understand the tools available, how to effectively integrate the technologies into teaching

DOI: 10.4324/9781003406631-3

and learning, and the affordances they can provide beyond the non-digital options. The chapter argues that technical communicators should discuss with students how and why bodies are impacted by surveillance technologies that we choose to introduce in the classroom space.

From my background in secondary and higher education, predominantly teaching students ages 17–22, I gained insight into how some instructors were quick to implement technologies into the classroom without critical examination of potential surveillance impacts. I define surveillance as "the collection of both visible and invisible data/information derived from those being observed, suggesting an application of power over the observed audience, who are often not informed of such collection" (Banville, 2023, p. 32). Globally, instructors (understandably) rushed to move their courses online, and with those courses came an introduction to 'new' applications. For example, many instructors began to implement applications such as Zoom and Cisco WebEx to host their synchronous courses and meet with students. Further, instructors began to increasingly implement invasive remote proctoring technologies such as Proctorio and Respondus to monitor students as they took online exams. This chapter is a response to what I label as the "COVID-19 technological rush." The 'rush' for instructors across the globe to implement technological applications into their classroom spaces created severe consequences. I argue that instructors need to critically examine the applications that they introduce into the classroom space, questioning topics such as intellectual property, privacy, and informed consent as they relate to the opportunity for students to opt in/out of the technology. Through case examples, I question *what are the surveillant impacts of the technologies on students' ethical concerns, particularly the ways that surveillance technologies are not neutral and are discriminatory (see, for example, Noble, 2018; Benjamin, 2019), and applications that were used in the classroom space during the COVID-19 pandemic?*

Throughout the chapter, I'll refer to instructors as *technical communicators*: across levels and subjects, they communicate and negotiate specialized information, especially to and with students. Because technical communicators are "uniquely poised to function as public intellectuals" (Bowdon, 2004, p. 325), teacher-educator programs and educational research would benefit from exploring surveillance studies and emerging technologies through a social justice perspective. I believe that our role as technical communicators is to function as knowledge-makers, influencers, and creators to communicate with audiences. Specifically, this chapter explores how instructors, or technical communicators, may critically examine the technologies and applications that they introduce into the classroom space (whether this is for students or educational programming).

This chapter examines cases in the practice of how popular surveillance technologies were implemented in United States K–12 spaces. Such instances are examined to serve as a cautionary tale for technical communicators across the globe to critically examine the applications and technologies that they introduce into the classroom space. The cases in practice should be integrated by teacher educators and educational researchers into workshop and curriculum design/professional development to prepare teachers not just with the tools to thrive in a digital learning environment, but also to provide equitable strategies for all learners.

Situating within Secondary Education

Many of the technologies, as will be mentioned in the following case examples, proved to be inequitable for many students across the globe. Because technical communicators are advocates (Jones, 2016; Walton et al., 2019), advocating for historically marginalized and multiply marginalized individuals and groups becomes an important part of a technical communicator's teaching. Surveillance systems further disenfranchise students when implemented within the classroom space; technologies, applications, and learning management systems are useful and are often helpful tools, but they must be critically analyzed.

Providing *access* for students, emphasizing *equity* and *collaboration*, and designing technologies and courses to be *diverse* and *just* are ways teacher-educators and researchers may approach technological application evaluation(s). Such principles are replicable; that is, at the core of critical questioning of technologies and their implications, the cases in practice can be transferable to various classroom contexts and levels globally. From my positionality, the specific examples presented explore my role as a university instructor who taught virtual and hybrid during the COVID-19 lockdown; I include lessons learned that inform my approach to developing strategies for pre-service teachers to integrate technologies ethically and efficiently. I also describe a few specific technologies that *were* implemented in my settings and *why* they should have been critically examined before implementation. This practice case could also be used for a teacher professional development workshop to discuss different strategies for in-service teachers to be equipped with skills on effective technology integration into their pedagogy/andragogy.

The cases in the extant literature represented can be critically analyzed through strategies such as *care work* and *transparency*, urging instructors to provide students with opportunities to opt out, reflect, and approach learning with care to integrate technology ethically and efficiently. The following questions may be used as a *guide* to critically examine the lack of 'surveillance apathy' – also known as a shift in attitudes from caring about the impacts of technological implementation on people to the swift implementation of technologies in classrooms for convenience:

- How might the technologies impact the student population?
- Who is this helping? Who is it harming?
- What information does the technology collect and share/distribute? With whom? Who has direct access [to the information, such as instructors, administrators, parent/guardians] and third-party access [companies outside of the immediate institution, and whose information could be found in the Terms of Service and/or Privacy Policies of whichever application you are seeking to introduce into the classroom]?
- Do students have the opportunity to opt out of using the technology/ application? Why or why not?
- How does the technology or application(s) benefit the classroom or institutional space? What is the purpose for the implementation [what purpose does the application serve]?

The bulleted questions are important for instructors, or technical communicators, to ask *themselves*, and are one way to critically examine the applications they introduce for students to use. The questions are only an *entry* point to analyze the applications we, as technical communicators, are intending to implement into our pedagogy. The questions serve as a helpful reminder that although well-intended, we should be careful to critically examine the technologies we introduce into the classroom so as not to require usage of technologies/applications that could cause potential harm to students (i.e., data collection, discrimination, and more). These questions may be applied to a wide range of applications and/or technologies to determine: *what are the surveillant impacts of the technologies and applications that were used in the classroom space during the COVID-19 pandemic?*

30 Morgan C. Banville

Students in secondary education or K–12 are often taught from a young age to follow directions from their instructors (Dunham et al., 2020). Because of this, it is the instructor's responsibility to introduce technologies into the classroom space that are helping students, rather than harming them. Harm can sometimes occur in invisible ways, through data collection and an invasion of privacy. Harm can also occur in very visible ways, through ableist exam proctoring services that fail students because of their hand or eye movements (Brown, 2020). For example, remote proctoring technologies such as Proctorio and Respondus are used for test-taking and collecting biometric information. Biometric information such as facial recognition is collected from students when interacting with such remote proctoring technologies (Burt, 2020). Biometric identification is "any identifier of the body that is collected and used for personal identification (and authentication)" (Banville, 2023, p. 6).

The remote proctoring services measure 'success' through monitoring behavioral regulation or disciplinary power in action (Kaplan, 1995). Students shift their behavior to *comply* with a norm. When technical communicators introduce technologies into the classroom space, they should also address the ways in which emerging and past technologies (digital and not) have become complicit in injustice. For example, materialist arguments note that the body is constituted along specific lines of race, class, gender, and nation, and that "when racialized, classed, gendered, and nationalized bodies lack 'material freedom' to engage in relations with other bodies, the theoretical affection for 'rhizomatic'" becomes problematic (Erevelles, 2011, p. 28). This occurs in the classroom space through the set normalization that is expected from remote proctoring companies (and other third-party applications). As disability activist sarah madoka currie (2023) writes, scholars such as Brier (2021) and Neilson (2021) advocate for the intentional refusal of proctoring and other surveillance practices in the classrooms, or else technical communicators are named complicit in creating a "burnout as destiny" (Neilson, 2021) structure for the most marginalized students in their classes. As currie writes, these students are most likely to be identified as "at risk" or "struggling with resilience" in their relationship to online learning (2023, p. 87). Currie's argument for access is one that technical communicators should engage with:

> When we fail to subvert systems that require students to disclose potentially unsafe work environments, work habits or coping mechanisms in their own work-from-home space using LMS

Exploring the [Surveillant] Impacts of Technology   **31**

analytics and digital proctoring, we consequently make the argument that their work-from-home space is "on campus" through policing it as though we are engaging with them in public space. But that's not public space, and the bodies interacting in that private space are private bodies.

(p. 98)

Such biometric usage in remote proctoring, however, should be noted in its applications in the classroom. We should thus follow Price's (2015) concluding thoughts, to teach students (and ourselves) to move with care. What this means is, according to Price (2015), to give "more when one has the ability to do so, and accepting help when that is needed" as well as care for not "knowing exactly what another's pain feels like," but "respecting each person's pain as real and important" (p. 279). The harm that comes from usage of biometrics may not be understood by everyone, but technical communicators should take care to acknowledge and respect that such harm occurs disproportionately. For example, Smitha Krishna Prasad, a researcher at the Centre for Communication Governance, explained the Aadhaar system in India, which is the largest biometric database in the world. As Prasad notes, the biometric database was introduced with the rationale of "curbing corruption in the provision of social welfare"; however, the biometrics have now become "practically mandatory" for government and private services such as welfare, banking, and education (Mutung'u, 2017). The challenges of biometric databases, whether implemented through remote proctoring in the classroom or as a major database for social welfare and beyond, have global ramifications that became exacerbated during the peak of the COVID-19 pandemic. Some of the challenges with the system in India, for example, include leaks of personal information and the expansion of the use of biometric data beyond the purposes for which the data was collected (Mutung'u, 2017). This should be a concern for many instructors or technical communicators: how do we critically analyze the technologies we introduce into our classroom space? What are the surveillant impacts of the technologies and applications that were used in the classroom space during the COVID-19 pandemic?

Intervention begins in the classroom, and such surveillant harms of technologies should be addressed prior to introducing them within the classroom. Care work must be participatory in nature, that is, "developed through the desires and needs of all participants" (Price, 2015, p. 279). Care work is an important strategy for analyzing the technologies we

32 Morgan C. Banville

introduce in our spaces. Such global examples display how a hasty implementation of technologies during the peak of COVID-19 without critical examination can inform the choices of technologies that technical communicators implement in the classroom space in the *present day.*

An Exigency for Critically Examining Technologies

As the previous section documented, without critically questioning the technologies and applications we use as technical communicators, there can be discriminatory effects for some students. This chapter explores: what are the surveillant impacts of the technologies and applications that were used in the classroom space during the COVID-19 pandemic? To answer this question, I think of the ways in which technical communicators may provide access for students through emphasizing equity and collaboration. Further, the surveillant impacts within the classroom space must be critically examined, especially post peak COVID-19 because of the ways instructors hurried to introduce technologies and applications within the classroom. I am referring to the 'peak' as the major shutdowns that occurred in the United States beginning in March 2020, although there were (and are) certainly higher peaks nationally and internationally. This chapter adds to understandings of how technical communicators may expose students to "everyday issues of injustice that affect students" (Agboka & Dorpenyo, 2022, p. 62). Injustice occurs in often invisible ways: that is, students (and instructors) may not realize the surveillant aspects of the applications they are using. Thus, the hope and goal of this chapter is to act as a foundation for technical communicators across global contexts to critically consider the applications and tools they introduce – or have introduced – into the classroom space. As a reminder, instructors *are* technical communicators because of the ways they negotiate and communicate specialized information.

Approaching the critical examination of technologies through a social justice lens affords both a "practical and applied" stance, not merely "theoretical or ideological stances"; thus, critically analyzing and creating action plans to address emerging technologies is a crucial component of the classroom space and, in turn, the curriculum (Walton & Agboka, 2021). As Gilson (2021) explains, many students will enter professions that help shape who is able to "access, use, enjoy, contribute to, and interact with online material" (p. 179). These same students, and often technical communicators as well, largely view technologies as neutral and unbiased,

Exploring the [Surveillant] Impacts of Technology **33**

which is why curriculum should be developed as a "site for action and an area for enacting theory; it is a nurturing ground for critical, functional, and socially just technical communication" (Agboka & Dorpenyo, 2022, p. 60). No matter the level, technical communicators have an enormous impact on students: the classroom is a site that may engage social justice issues and enable students to critique and address systemic inequalities and disadvantages, especially such systems that continue to surveil and further marginalize. It is important to note that the United States continues to be fraught with its cultural and political decision-making and its impact within the classroom; a more recent example in local legislation is the "Don't Say Gay" bill that was passed in Florida. Curriculum may be developed and adapted based on levels of precarity in geographical locations and identities.

As a case example, let's look at a popular application implemented during the transition to online instruction: Jamboard. The classroom may be viewed as a site of surveillance where technical communicators should *carefully* consider how they introduce technologies, such as Jamboard, into the classroom space. Jamboard is a digital interactive whiteboard developed by Google to work with Google Workspace, formerly known as G Suite. This technology is very popular with technical communicators across the globe and largely familiar to students of varying levels as well. As of October 1, 2024, Google Workspace will no longer house Jamboard and suggests using third-party whiteboard tools such as FigJam, Lucidspark, and Miro. I have not personally used the suggested third-party tools and would caution readers to read through the Terms of Service for the applications. Since students are stakeholders in these systems, conversations about whether or not students have the ability to opt out of using the application is crucial. As technical communicators, we may ask of the application:

- What information does Jamboard, for example, collect?
- Is the information students paste into the whiteboard their own intellectual property [or is it considered Google's property]?
- How does lateral surveillance [peer-to-peer] impact student performance and participation?
- How would giving an opportunity to engage with physical "sticky" notes instead of digital notes contribute to the class dynamic?

This example shows how a critical questioning of a tool implemented during a time when technical communicators didn't have just that [time], can be fruitful for determining which applications are helpful – or potentially harmful – to students.

34 Morgan C. Banville

Surveillance, Care, and Digital Literacy

Critically questioning and examining technologies and subsequent applications is one way instructors, or technical communicators, and students may better develop their digital literacies. Introducing students to issues of surveillance within the classrooms' applications creates an opportunity to reflect, analyze, and interrogate students' digital literacies. Our identities are inextricably linked and tied to the digital age; digital spaces provide for world-making (Muñoz, 2009). Digital literacy is broadly defined as an individual's ability to search, find, evaluate, and compose clear information through typing, writing, tapping, and by using other mediums (i.e., multimedia videos, video calling, and messaging) on various digital platforms, which requires a basic level of computer competency (Bawden, 2008). Digital literacy is important to discuss since our bodies transcend physical boundaries through virtual existences. However, digital spaces can be at times fraught, confusing, or difficult to navigate. These spaces can also be unsafe. As Beck et al. (2021) notes, digital literacy initiatives "foster navigation, examination, searching, composing, remixing, coding, designing, sharing, contributing, and protecting – or the skills needed to enable communication online" (p. 6). Understanding surveillance is *one* form of digital literacy.

As a reminder, this chapter is exploring the global surveillant impacts of the technologies and applications that were used in the classroom space during the COVID-19 pandemic. Surveillance technologies such as biometrics are especially important to review before their usage and implementation in the classroom because of their impact *outside* of the classroom. For example, Leandro Ucciferri, a researcher at Asociación por los Derechos Civiles, described the biometric system in Argentina. The system harbors data from citizens and non-citizens who enter the country: the data is collected for use by the "immigration office, citizens' office, law enforcement, and sub-national agencies with corporate agreements with the national database" (Mutung'u, 2017). Despite varying backgrounds and interests, students may benefit from learning theories and examples that are central to surveillance. If we share with students the ways the applications and technologies we use have global impacts within *and* outside of the classroom space, this is one (of many) means to build digital literacies. How we as technical communicators (instructors) approach implementation of technologies into our classrooms, such as remote proctoring services, is a topic that contends with disability justice.

Exploring the [Surveillant] Impacts of Technology **35**

As Piepzna-Samarasinha (2018) describes, disability justice understands that oppressive forces such as ableism, "racism . . . sexism, and queer- and transphobia" mutually influence and sustain each other (p. 22). Equipping fellow technical communicators with strategies to critically engage technology will in turn challenge students to recognize and attend to diverse and interlocking needs of people globally through deep reflection and discussion.

Layered Surveillance and Transparency as Strategy

In any institution, there is surveillance of instructors by the institution (emails, course content, and so on), instructors surveilling students (participation, attendance, and so forth), and students surveilling one another (peer-to-peer engagement). Other than *care work* as a strategy for critically engaging technologies, we can think of *transparency* as another strategy. Transparency is a strategy that is layered: while as technical communicators we cannot always control what our place of work shares with *us,* we can share with students what we surveil about them and how they also surveil one another (such as with the Jamboard example).

One example of the ways technical communicators, or instructors, may transparently communicate with students is through the example of remote proctoring. Pons and Polak (2008) document how biometrics [in remote proctoring] are used for "associating computer users with their computer behavior, linking employees to their workstation performance, managing user-resource usage and activity, and e-commerce," which are all aspects of students' current and future careers (p. 115). Although Pons and Polak (2008) specifically reference universities, their sentiment can be translated across levels and spaces:

> the students are ultimately customers with a choice, implementations of biometric systems might be met with some level of resistance due to the sensitive nature of identification, storage, and usage of personal data, notwithstanding whether the 'sensitivity' is real or only perceived.
>
> (p. 118)

Further, technical communicators may reflect on the ways in which success is and could be measured in their respective classrooms, especially

36 Morgan C. Banville

through the expectation and choice of technological usage. For example, Rodgers et al. (2022) argue that the way time is regulated and managed is ableist. Time regulation and management fails to account for the crip temporalities by which disabled peoples live their lives. Rodgers et al. (2022) argue that the concept of "crip" and "cripping time" in relation to disabled academics opens new ways of thinking, doing, and being that are not constrained by normative (clock) time that marginalizes disabled academics. The cases in the extant literature, remote proctoring, Learning Management Systems, and classroom applications can be critically analyzed through care work and transparency. How do we make choices about the applications we introduce into the classroom space? Who do they invite in? Who do they leave out? Is there an opportunity to opt out, without consequence(s)? Pre-service teachers, based on the examples, may transfer the questions and subsequent impacts to their own contexts. Surveillance is localized – through our transparency about the technology we use, providing opportunities to opt out, reflect, and approach learning with *care*, teachers can integrate technology *ethically* and efficiently.

A CBP Case for Integration

As previously mentioned, layered surveillance occurs in school systems globally. In the classrooms I have specifically taught in, I found that there was a layered level of *informedness*, as well. That is, as I've argued before (Banville & Sugg, 2021), instructors have a complex understanding of the ways in which the institution surveils them, as well as their own perception of how and why they surveil their students. Surveillance isn't always nefarious! When we implement the strategies of care work and transparency, this looks like a lot of reflection and questioning of norms. Approaching applications through strategies such as care and transparency creates a space where students and technical communicators can respond to surveillance in flux. The ways we ethically and responsibly implement technologies should respond to and adjust "for the space, place, and time in which it is occurring and the bodies with whom it is engaging" (Gilson, 2021, p. 189).

The following assignment helps us to consider my guiding question: what are the [global] surveillant impacts of the technologies and applications that were used in the classroom space during the COVID-19 pandemic? I include an example assignment adopted from Monahan (2022) that could be revised to fit either a professional development workshop or even a case scenario for teacher-educators to use in a course to introduce students to research strategies and critical tools for analyzing technological ethics. The assignment can be adopted depending on the context and audience.

Keyword Report Assignment

Instructors (or students) will select one concept, keyword, or application to further explore (examples could include surveillance, privacy, algorithms, terms of service, a specific application, and more).
The report must:

- Define the concept/keyword/application
- Provide an example of how it could be applied [*transparent about its uses and impacts on people*]
- State how it relates to the class [*How does this concept/keyword/application approach care work? How does it approach ethical implementation of technology, accessibility, and so on?*]
- Provide a full citation [*for students to engage in citation practice*]
- Include a multimodal component [*an audio description, visual, etc. This could be for the instructor to introduce the concept/keyword/application, or it could be part of the student project*]

Here's a partial example of a keyword report: biometrics.

Defining

From the previous example about biometrics as a surveillant tool used in the classroom, I mentioned how biometric identification usually focuses on facial, iris, and keystroke recognition (to name a few) in remote proctoring. I define and view biometric identification and technologies as unique identifiers of the body used for personal identification (and authentication).

Example Usage

One of the most common forms of identification and verification on the retail market and for corporate entities are facial recognition devices. Because faces are, in theory, an identifier of the body, I consider documents such as passports and driver's licenses biometric identification. And the United States Customs and Border Patrol (CBP) does too. As of September 2022, the CBP's website has boasted how they are "leading the way in creating a more seamless, secure – and safer – travel experience" through increased use of facial recognition (Customs and Border Protection, 2023). What you'll notice reading through the website is that the CBP, like other times in United States history, is implementing the technology during a time of crisis. For example, biometric implementation became more apparent and normalized in discourse post-September 11, 2001 (9/11), when biometrics (such as facial recognition) circulated as the solution to prevent "another 9/11." What was once introduced as a safety and security measure has become normalized as a means to surveil and control bodies within the state.

In this specific example, biometric technology has been around for decades, but the increased presence is due to the COVID-19 pandemic. The CBP states that this technology is "hands-free" and therefore "it helps to prevent the spread of germs. So, it's also a better public health option" (Customs and Border Protection, 2023). While the technology is "hands-free," this is a classic example of biometrics being implemented during times of fear (fear of health/safety from COVID-19), and further, it helps guide my definition of what biometrics are. Because facial recognition is used instead of the presentation of a passport, and then further compared against an existing passport or visa photo, this suggests that the CBP believes facial identification is sufficient verification. There are substantial issues with this line of thinking; however, the parameters (employed by CBP at present) are helpful for the purposes of defining biometrics. Interestingly enough, the CBP claims that "All traveler photos of U.S. citizens are deleted, and no photos are ever shared with industry partners" (Customs and Border Protection, 2023). A few thoughts arise here:

- When are the photos deleted? ["CBP retains U.S. citizen photos for no more than 12 hours after identity verification, and only for continuity of operations purposes"]
- Where are they stored? ["Hosted within a secure cloud-based environment"]
- And what if you are not a "U.S. citizen"?

Relation to the Class and Critical Examination

What is fascinating is how the CBP frames biometrics as technologies that are not for surveillance. I explicitly label biometrics as surveillance technologies. Because the CBP associates the term surveillance with "hidden" or "out of sight," they frame the technology as not surveilling. What's interesting is how the CBP mentions that passengers and travelers are "informed about the process and technology" (Customs and Border Protection, 2023). The truth is, the signage in the airports isn't always clear, accessible, or available. In fact, CBP does offer travelers a "choice" in opting out, but this is in fine print at the bottom of a sign off to the side of the biometric identification line. And for international travelers? CBP agents walk up to you, ask for your boarding pass, and then take a picture. No notification of the ability to opt out is given. CBP mentions that "Surveillance programs, on the other hand, involve cameras that are hidden and out of sight, capturing video of people when they are in public spaces and completely unaware or informed" (Customs and Border Protection, 2023). Biometric identification certainly is prevalent in public spaces, and the large majority of people are very uninformed as to the extent of the privacy they are swapping in return for "security."

This example in the mock keyword report gives technical communicators an opportunity to consider how the technologies we implement in the classroom also have impact outside of the space. We can equip ourselves and our students to consider the many impacts of the technologies, carefully and critically, we use within and outside of the classroom space.

Concluding Thoughts and Implications

With the shift to hybrid and virtual during the COVID-19 pandemic, a mass rush to innovate new platforms, applications, and technologies emerged. Many of the 'innovations' were implemented or introduced within classrooms across the globe *without* being critically evaluated for their surveillant impacts. Further, students experienced hyper-surveillance outside of the classroom: biometric technologies, for example, severely influenced disciplinary regulation, with students being required to allow remote proctoring services to access their homes, faces, irises, and more.

40 Morgan C. Banville

This created not just an invasion of privacy, but also severe discriminatory impacts for students who were deemed 'non-compliant' because the biometric technologies could not scan their faces, nor account for other instances where their keyboard strokes or irises acted outside of the 'norm.'

The purpose of including the global examples of surveillance usage, along with the keyword assignment, is to showcase how the technologies we implement in the classroom space can be and are used for often nefarious measures inside/outside the space. From my own experience teaching with technology, I noticed that successful and effective technological implementation was based on researching the technology and/or application I was intending to implement within the classroom, approaching lesson planning with care, and being transparent with my colleagues and students.

Effectiveness, in this example, is/can be measured by student impact and minimal harm through data mining from surveillant applications, and minimal privacy invasion. Based on the situated examples, specific cases in practice, and assignments, as technical communicators we can critically examine how the choice of technology impacts students within and outside of the classroom space. More importantly, through care work and transparency, we can learn how to *effectively* integrate technologies into teaching and learning. We should all consider the tools and technologies we bring into the classroom: what are the global surveillant impacts of such applications, and what are their impacts on technical communicators and students?

References

Agboka, G. Y., & Dorpenyo, I. K. (2022). Curricular efforts in technical communication after the social justice turn. *Journal of Business and Technical Communication, 36*(1), 38–70. https://doi.org/10.1177/10506519211044195

Banville, M. C. (2023). *Am I who I say I am? the illusion of choice: Biometric identification in healthcare* (Order No. 30603350). ProQuest Dissertations & Theses Global (2830119112). https://www.proquest.com/dissertations-theses/am-i-who-say-illusion-choice-biometric/docview/2830119112/se-2

Banville, M. C., & Sugg, J. (2021, October 12–14). *"Dataveillance" in the classroom: Advocating for transparency and accountability in college classrooms.* The 39th ACM International Conference on Design of Communication (SIGDOC 21), Virtual Event, ACM, New York. https://doi.org/10.1145/3472714.3473617

Bawden, D. (2008). Origins and concepts of digital literacy. In C. Lankshear & M. Knobel (Eds.), *Digital literacies: Concepts, policies and practices* (Vol. 30, pp. 17–32). Peter Lang Publishing.

Beck, E., Goin, M., Ho, A., Parks, A., & Rowe, S. (2021). Critical digital literacy as method for teaching tactics of response to online surveillance and privacy erosion. *Computers and Composition, 61.* https://doi.org/10.1016/j.compcom.2021.102654

Benjamin, R. (2019). *Race after technology: Abolitionist tools for the new Jim code.* Polity Press.

Bowdon, M. (2004). Technical communication and the role of the public intellectual: A community HIV-prevention case study. *Technical Communication Quarterly, 13*(3), 325–340. https://doi.org/10.1207/s15427625tcq1303_6

Brier, E. (2021). Pandemic pedagogy: Practical and empathetic teaching practices. *Spectra, 8*(2), 31–37. https://doi.org/10.21061/spectra.v8i2.180

Brown, L. (2020). *How automated test proctoring software discriminates against disabled students.* Center for Democracy and Technology. https://cdt.org/insights/how-automated-test-proctoring-software-discriminates-against-disabled-students/

Burt, C. (2020). *Concerns about biometric online proctoring expressed by students in Australia, U.S. and Canada.* Biometric Update. https://www.biometricupdate.com/202007/concerns-about-biometric-online-proctoring-expressed-by-students-in-australia-u-s-and-canada

currie, s. m. (2023). *The mad manifesto.* University of Waterloo. https://uwspace.uwaterloo.ca/bitstream/handle/10012/19689/Currie_Sarah.pdf?sequence=3

Customs and Border Protection (CBP). (2023). *Introducing biometric facial comparison.* United States Customs and Border Protection. Retrieved January 15, 2023, from https://biometrics.cbp.gov/

Dunham, S., Lee, E., & Persky, A. M. (2020). The psychology of following instructions and its implications. *American Journal of Pharmaceutical Education, 84*(8), ajpe7779. https://doi.org/10.5688/ajpe7779

Erevelles, N. (2011). *Disability and difference in global contexts: Enabling a transformative body politic.* Palgrave.

Gilson, O. A. (2021). An intersectional feminist rhetorical pedagogy in the technical communication classroom. In R. Walton & G. Y. Agboka (Eds.), *Equipping technical communicators for social justice work: Theories, methodologies, and pedagogies* (pp. 178–194). University Press of Colorado.

Gonzales, L., Lockett, A., Foung, D., & Banville, M. (2022, May 12). A constellation of crises: Teaching with technology curing COVID. In *Constellations: A cultural rhetorics publishing space.* https://constell8cr.com/issue-5/a-constellation-of-crises-teaching-with-technology-during-covid/

Jones, N. N. (2016). The technical communicator as advocate: Integrating a social justice approach in technical communication. *Journal of Technical Writing and Communication, 46*(3), 342–361. https://doi.org/10.1177/0047281616639472

Kaplan, M. (1995). Panopticon in Poona: An essay on Foucault and colonialism. *Cultural Anthropology, 10*(1), 85–98. https://www.jstor.org/stable/656232

Monahan, T. (2022). *Technology & social justice course syllabus.* Personal communication.

Muñoz, J. E. (2009). *Cruising utopia: The then and there of queer futurity.* New York University Press.

Mutung'u, G. (2017). Biometrics and identity in the Global South. *Geneva Internet Platform DigWatch.* https://dig.watch/event/12th-internet-governance-forum/biometrics-and-identity-global-south-ws282

Neilson, S. (2021). The problem with "burnout": Neoliberalization, biomedicine, and other soul mates. In *The Routledge companion to health humanities* (1st ed.). Routledge.

Noble, S. U. (2018). *Algorithms of oppression.* New York University Press.

Piepzna-Samarasinha, L. L. (2018). *Care work: Dreaming disability justice.* Arsenal Pulp Press.

Pons, A. P., & Polak, P. (2008). Understanding user perspectives on biometric technology. *Communications of the ACM, 51*(9), 115–118. https://doi.org/10.1145/1378727.1389971

Price, M. (2015). The bodymind problem and the possibilities of pain. *Hypatia, 30*(1), 268–284. https://doi.org/10.1111/hypa.12127

Rodgers, J., Thorneycroft, R., Cook, P. S., Humphrys, E., Asquith, N. L., Yaghi, S. A., & Foulstone, A. (2022). Ableism in higher education: The negation of crip temporalities within the neoliberal academy. *Higher Education Research & Development,* 1–14. https://doi.org/10.1080/07294360.2022.2138277

Walton, R., & Agboka, G. (2021). *Equipping technical communicators for social justice work: Theories, methodologies, and pedagogies.* Utah State University Press.

Walton, R., Moore, K., & Jones, N. (2019). *Technical communication after the social justice turn: Building coalitions for action.* Routledge.

Preparation of Future Teachers Teaching with Technology 4

The Case of Japan

Takayoshi Maki, Masayasu Sakaguchi, Nozomi Sakata, and Asami Shimoda

Japan is an arch-shaped island country in East Asia, with an area of approximately 378,000 square metres and 120 million inhabitants. As part of the Pacific Rim orogenic belt, it is rich in volcanoes, hot springs, and groundwater. The natural environment is harsh, with typhoons, torrential rains, and landslides in summer and snowfall in winter (Japan Institute of Country-ology and Engineering, n.d.). There have been many natural disasters, such as the Great East Japan Earthquake (March 2011), followed by another earthquake and an unprecedented torrential downpour – the Kumamoto Earthquake (April 2016) and Rainstorm (July 2020), respectively. It has been indicated that 'Japanese people' have had a patient temperament based on their living experiences in this harsh natural environment (Watsuji, 1961). This may be linked to the so-called Japanese spirit of always seeking better beyond the current situation, as symbolised by the word *kaizen* (Imai, 2010), partly contributing to the country's world-renowned manufacturing industry, including the automobile industry and general electronics manufacturers. It also wields considerable soft power, such as the spirit of *Omotenashi* (hospitality), which has begun to attract attention since the recent Tokyo Olympics, as well as *anime*, *manga*, and *otaku* culture, and the focus on Japanese food as people become more health conscious.

DOI: 10.4324/9781003406631-4

44 Takayoshi Maki et al.

Regarding the human resources supporting these manufacturing and soft power industries, the National Institute for Educational Policy Research announced that the results of the Programme for International Student Assessment (PISA) 2018 indicated Japan's rank among the top countries worldwide, except for reading comprehension (National Institute for Educational Policy [NIER], 2019). The high quality of Japanese school education has, therefore, attracted attention from abroad. In 2018, the Ministry of Education, Culture, Sports, Science, and Technology (MEXT) launched the Public-Private Joint Platform for Overseas Development of Japanese-style Education (EDU-Port Nippon), which aims to develop Japanese educational practices, such as classroom research and school cleaning (special activities) (Sugimura, 2019). The KOSEN, National Institute of Technology, education model has been introduced and implemented in Mongolia, Vietnam, and Thailand with the aim of industrial human resource development (Shimoda, 2023).

Japanese education is attracting attention overseas owing to its high scores on international achievement tests. However, the preparation of teachers who can teach lessons using information and communication technology (ICT) has just begun. Studies on the integration of ICT into pre-service teacher education reveal issues such as a single ICT subject being offered in the curriculum in extreme cases (Kay, 2006). Thus, it is important to understand the role of ICT in the pre-service teacher education curriculum (Tondeur et al., 2012, 2013). Additionally, regarding ICT-enhanced teaching, 'These studies may indicate the importance of pre-service teachers' understanding with regards to technology: pre-service teacher education should focus on how to use technology and how technology can be used for teaching and learning' (Tondeur et al., 2012, p. 135). Using ICT can be an end in itself; it is a tool used for effective teaching. Therefore, it is important to determine whether the aims and objectives of ICT subjects in pre-service teacher education courses utilise ICT or whether they differ. This chapter examines a flagship teacher education university in Japan, concerning the aforementioned aspects and diagnosing the situation in the early stages of setting up pre-service teacher education that incorporates ICT.

Present and Future of Education in Japan

This section introduces the current state of school education and its future as a background for flagship teacher education universities to assume a leading role in teacher education reforms in Japan.

School Education in Japan Today

Japan's modern school education system celebrated its 150th anniversary in 2022. The current school system takes the form of 6–3–3, single-line, co-educational, with a decentralised educational administration system for managing and supervising schools through boards of education established by local governments. Pre-service teacher education is provided by universities, and any university faculty member can organise teacher education programs (Japan International Cooperation Agency, 2004).

The purpose of education in Japan is stipulated in Article 1 of the Fundamental Law of Education, known as the Constitution of Education. Namely, 'Education shall be conducted with the aim of perfecting the personality and fostering healthy nations, both physically and mentally, with the necessary qualities to form a peaceful and democratic state and society'. In addition, under this objective, Article 2 stipulates five goals: in particular, the first paragraph stipulates that 'the children shall acquire a wide range of knowledge and culture, develop an attitude of seeking the truth, cultivate rich sentiments and moral values, and develop a healthy body' (MEXT, 2020a). It comprehensively defines what is considered 'knowledge, virtue, and body'.

To raise children with a good balance of 'knowledge, virtue and body', the Japanese curriculum is set out in the (legally binding) 'Courses of Study' (MEXT, n.d.a). MEXT examines the textbooks used in schools to ensure that they are consistent with the Courses of Study. The curricula in Japan comprise two main areas: academic and non-academic. Subjects such as the Japanese language, mathematics, science, social studies, music, technology, home economics, and physical education are relatively common in other countries.

A major change in recent years has been the compilation of textbooks on moral education, which used to be a non-subject area, as a 'special subject'. This change was fully implemented in primary and junior high schools in 2018 and 2019, respectively. In addition, since 2020, English has been taught as a foreign language activity in Grade 3 in primary schools and as a foreign language study in Grades 5 and 6. In extracurricular areas, special activities, including school cleaning, project-based learning, and exploration during integrated learning times, are likely to occur. Programming education has become compulsory for primary and junior high schools in 2020 and 2021, respectively (Kaneko, 2022).

Future of School Education in Japan

Japan has taken measures to reform education in line with the times, while maintaining the basic structure of objectives, content, and systems outlined in the previous section. On 1 May 2019, the emperor's throne was succeeded, and Japan entered a new era called 'Reiwa'. Reflecting on this break, several government policies bearing the title of 'Society 5.0' were approved by the Cabinet. For example, on 21 June 2019, four guidelines were laid down for the Basic Policies for Economic and Fiscal Management and Reform 2019 – New Era of 'Reiwa': the Challenge of 'Society 5.0', Growth Strategy Action Plan, Growth Strategy Follow-up, and Comprehensive Innovation Strategy 2019. These include the development of an ICT environment, use of digital textbooks, and programming education. Since 5 December 2019, in the 'Comprehensive Economic Measures for a Secure and Growing Future', as part of developing a personalised learning environment in primary and secondary education and, particularly, at the compulsory education stage by 2023, the development of a high-speed, large-capacity network environment (school LAN) in schools has been promoted. The aim is to create an environment in which each pupil in all grades has a terminal and can fully utilise it. In response, MEXT decided to establish headquarters for the realisation of global and innovation gateways for all (GIGA) schools on 19 December 2019. Coincidentally, the confirmation of COVID-19 at the end of 2019 and the subsequent pandemic (Iwabuchi et al., 2021) provided a tailwind, and the development of 'one device and high-speed network per person', that is, the GIGA school concept, was accelerated.

In January 2021, the Government of Japan presented a vision for a new era of school education (Japanese-style school education in Reiwa), aiming to realise it throughout the 2020s, that is, the realisation of individual-optimal and collaborative learning that leaves no one behind in consideration of the diversity of children's backgrounds. Simultaneously, six directions of reform were presented to realise these learnings (Central Council for Education, 2021): (1) improve the quality, diversity, and inclusiveness of school education and realise equal opportunities in education; (2) realise school management through collaboration and sharing of responsibilities; (3) realise the optimum combination of existing teaching practices and newly installed ICT; (4) combine the principles of completion and acquisition; (5) ensure learning in the case of infectious diseases and outbreaks; and (6) realise sustainable and attractive school education regarding social structures.

In addition to these reform directions, one chapter of the report focuses on the basic concept of ICT use. Specifically, concerning ICT teaching skills, 'new subjects should be established so that students can acquire ICT teaching skills common to each subject in a general way before learning about the use of ICT as teaching methods for each subject' (Central Council for Education, 2021, p. 87). Regarding this, on 4 August 2021, the 'Notification of the enforcement of the Ministerial Ordinance partially amending the Techers' License Law' was issued, and 'Theories and Methods of Education Using ICT' was newly established in the matter of 'subjects related to subjects and teaching' from 2022 (MEXT, 2021).

In December 2022, a report was issued on the ideal state of pre-service education, recruitment, and in-service education for teachers who would lead Japanese-style school education in Reiwa (MEXT, 2022). The report stated that teachers and teaching staff groups who would lead Japanese-style school education in Reiwa should have the ability to (1) accept changes in the environment positively and continue to learn throughout their teaching careers; (2) fulfil their role as teachers to maximise each child's learning; (3) support children's independent learning; and (4) accompany children in their independent learning. The school created a high-quality teaching staff group by securing diverse human resources and improving the qualifications and skills of teachers, who are managed under the leadership of the principal in cooperation with families and the local community, working as a team with diverse staff, and so on. Additionally, the creative and attractive nature of teaching is reaffirmed. The number of applicants is increasing, and teachers are motivated and proud of their work. Moreover, the required qualifications and competencies were reorganised into the following five qualities: (1) teaching; (2) learning; (3) student guidance; (4) handling children who need special consideration and support; and (5) using ICT, information, and educational data.

The Fourth Basic Plan for the Promotion of Education was submitted in March 2023 (MEXT, 2023). This plan included the promotion of learning and exchange planning using ICT. It specifically highlights the improvement of accessibility and the promotion of educational digital transformation (DX) to promote education towards the realization of 'Society 5.0', that is, a symbiotic society where no one is left behind and everyone's potential is drawn out. In addition to the GIGA school initiative, the plan also included the analysis and utilisation of educational data, as observed in the new subjects of flagship teacher education universities in the subsequent section.

This section indicates that the transition to the new era of Reiwa was an opportunity for new approaches to school education and teaching staff under the new social vision of 'Society 5.0'. Using ICT and technology has been incorporated into several proposals and policies, and institutional foundations are generally in place, as evidenced by the revision of the Teachers' Licence Law.

Based on these policies, researchers in the field have stated that with the implementation of the new Courses of Study in a per-pupil device environment, it is crucial for teachers to acquire these 'specialisations' to provide STEAM education, and updating the content of training, teaching, and pre-service teacher education programs is a challenge for the 'creation of a new learning foundation' (Kitazawa & Akabori, 2020, pp. 297–298). Additionally, as a way of addressing these problems, immediate training and other measures in the field of education are essential; however, from a future-oriented perspective, it is necessary to address these issues at the pre-service teacher education stage. Thus, as a pre-service teacher education university, it is necessary to provide instruction that corresponds to future forms of learning using one device per student and high-speed, high-capacity communications, as typified by the GIGA school concept. (Ogura et al., 2021, p. 1). Thus, realising the GIGA school concept, which utilizes STEAM education and one-per-pupil devices, requires corresponding pre-service teacher education.

Flagship Teacher Education Universities

Project Overview of Flagship Teacher Education Universities

The flagship teacher education universities discussed in this section are the result of recommendations by the Education Revitalization Executive Council established during the Second Abe Administration (Eleventh Recommendation: Innovation in Education in Response to Technological Progress and the Reform of Upper Secondary Schools for a New Era, 2019, May 17).

Under the Prime Minister's Office-led and government-led reform, the Central Council for Education examined the specifics of the proposal and compiled a final report on 23 January 2020, on 'The ideal flagship teacher education university that leads teacher education in the Society 5.0 era' (MEXT, 2020b). The report recognises that with the rapid development of technologies such as artificial intelligence (AI), robotics, big data, and the Internet of Things, the 'Society 5.0' era is expected to arrive, in which the very nature of society will change so dramatically that it can be described as 'discontinuous'. School education is expected to respond to these changes, and the roles and skills required of teachers are also expected to change. Thus, universities are expected to change the nature of teacher education.

The report also identified three major roles for flagship teacher education universities: (1) lead the transformation of teacher education in Japan in a new direction; (2) play a central role in Japan's teacher education network; and (3) contribute to addressing problems in school education and making policy recommendations. Emphasis was placed on the research and development of leading and innovative teacher education programs and teaching subjects. Based on the final report, an open call was made in Financial Year (FY) 2021, in which applications from 14 universities were received, and four were adopted, including Tokyo Gakugei University, the University of Fukui, Osaka Kyoiku University, and Hyogo University of Teacher Education, since March 2022 (MEXT, n.d.b).

This section presents the case studies of two of the four universities: Hyogo University of Teacher Education and the University of Fukui. The case studies of these two universities provide an overall picture of teacher education programs being prepared at flagship teacher education universities and the specific content of key subjects.

In June 2023, the authors visited two flagship universities – the Hyogo University of Teacher Education and the University of Fukui – using snowball sampling. The authors interviewed three university employees who were the leading figures in teacher education courses in ICT at these two universities to examine their initiatives and experiences in establishing and implementing such courses. The following two sections introduce some of the accounts the authors obtained from these employees, together with the program materials that we gained from our visits.

Agile Subject Development and Build-up Programs at Hyogo University of Teacher Education

Hyogo University of Teacher Education was established in 1978 based on a philosophy and principles different from those of conventional universities. As of 1 May 2022, there were 1,451 students, including 668 in the Faculty of School Education, 607 in the Graduate School of School Education (381 in the Master's Degree Program and 226 in the Professional Degree Program), and 176 in the Joint Graduate School (PhD Program) of the Science School of Education. The total number of full-time teachers was 131. Hyogo University of Teacher Education was designated as a flagship university for teacher training under the theme 'Teacher-Training Program for Developing Autonomous Learners', and on 1 April 2022, the Center of Teacher Education Program for Transformation (C-TEX) was established as the core organisation for this project. On 8 April, STEAM Labs were established at the university and at university-attached primary and junior high schools, with the cooperation and support of private companies.

In FY2024, new subjects related to the use of technology, including the digital learning environment and information use, theories of primary school programming education materials, information morality and security education, and educational data science, are scheduled to be established.

The authors visited the Director and Deputy Director of the C-TEX Centre at the university and obtained contemporaneous explanatory material. According to the material (Moriyama, 2023, p. 2), the image of teachers the university is aiming for is 'human resources who can improve, enhance, and create the quality of education using digital technology'. In particular, the university hopes to produce teachers who can conduct: Level 1, digital education human resources set by the Hyogo University of Teacher Education, which uses digital technology in some aspects of teaching and school work; Level 2, which uses a learning management system (LMS) to support schoolwork; and Level 3, which takes learners' learning logs and makes use of them. Level 4 involves creating new value using digital technology, which students aim to achieve while studying as in-service teachers after employment.

A distinctive feature of a university is its 'agile approach' to subject development (Moriyama, 2023, p. 4). This is not a waterfall approach in which individual subjects are developed after the entire teacher education curriculum has been organised, but a method in which the entire curriculum is developed by repeatedly planning, designing, implementing, and testing, beginning with the main subjects once the approximate direction, objectives, and goals have been established. This allowed for the optimisation of matching the objectives and goals of the subjects with the needs of the students while listening to their voices.

Furthermore, the stacked design, as shown in Figure 4.1, described in the university curriculum reform is noteworthy (Moriyama, 2023, p. 5). This reform consists of the following three steps: enhancement of AI and data science subjects (Step 1), ICT utilisation and informatics education subjects (Step 2), and establishment of new STEAM education subjects (Step 3).

In Step 1 (AI and Educational Data Science), the subject structure is based on an understanding of statistics and machine learning and aims at learning analysis, evidence-based educational improvement, and individual optimisation through statistical analysis software and LMS. AI and data science, a common subject and educational data science, teaching subject fall under Step 1 (Moriyama, 2023, pp. 5–6).

The systematisation of ICT use and informatics education subjects in Step 2 consists of an overview of educational informatisation (understanding the significance and theory of ICT use, promotion of learning guidance and school work by effectively using the significance of ICT use, and teaching methods for developing students' information literacy, including morals in pupils), individual theories of the digital learning environment and information (ICT lesson utilisation using the GIGA environment and practical methods for information-oriented lessons), theory of primary school programming education materials (research and practical methods for primary school programming education materials), and information morality and security education (research and practical methods for information morality and security education materials at primary schools) (Moriyama, 2023, pp. 6–7).

Step 3 involved the establishment of a new STEAM education subject consisting of two courses: an introduction to STEAM education and a STEAM education exercise. STEAM education is sometimes implemented on a trial basis in undergraduate liberal arts seminars. For example, microplastics are widely used in lunchboxes in Japan's unique lunchbox culture; however, the problem of bamboo overgrowth also occurs. Therefore, a bamboo lunchbox was developed in the course. In collaboration with the municipality of Kasai City in Hyogo Prefecture, where the university is located, the university is also working with fifth-year primary school students on a period of integrated study called Designing the City of the Future (Moriyama, 2023, pp. 8–9).

52 Takayoshi Maki et al.

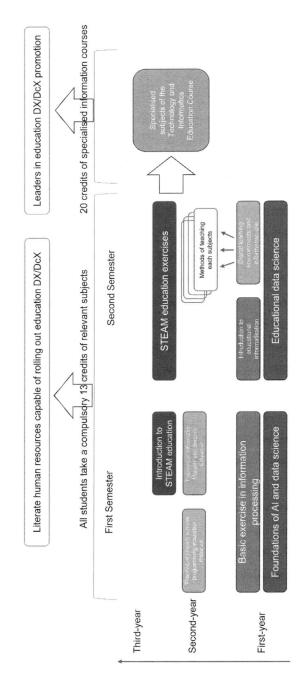

Figure 4.1 Digital Human Resource Development at Hyogo University of Teacher Education (Plan)

Introduction to ICT-Based Education at University of Fukui

The University of Fukui was founded in 1949 as a new national university with two faculties – arts and sciences and engineering – based on the Normal School and Technical College. Currently, the university has four faculties: education, engineering, medicine, and international and regional studies. As of 1 May 2022, there were 3,978 undergraduate students, 964 postgraduate students, and 2,176 teaching staff, of whom 612 were teachers. The number of teaching staff is higher because approximately 1,100 administrative and other staff members work at the Faculty of Medicine.

Under the theme of 'cultivating teachers', practical skills to support 'independent, interactive, and deep learning', the University of Fukui is working on curriculum organisation and network building with a long-term development cycle of practice, reflection, and reconstruction at its core. One perspective of the overall design is to support and extend the reflective project-learning cycle through the full use of ICT and DX in the development of GIGA schools. The specific subjects to be developed for this connection are scheduled to launch in 2024.

When the authors visited the university, we spoke with a professor, the teacher educator in charge of ICT-based education at the university's General Teaching Development Division. The professor specialises in class-design engineering and is involved in research on using avatars in classrooms and measuring the effectiveness of classes. As shown in Figure 4.2, his subject, introduction to ICT-based education, is positioned as an introductory subject aimed at students' conceptual understanding of the future of education and ICT utilisation. The subject envisaged that students would be able to teach using ICT in years two to four.

The outline of ICT education states: 'To understand the characteristics and significance of ICT use in school education, to learn about methods of learning and teaching through experience of ICT use, and to acquire the basic knowledge and skills for using ICT in education'. The objectives were to: (1) understand the significance of using ICT in education (including learning guidance and schoolwork) and how it should be used; (2) acquire basic teaching methods for learning to use ICT and plan and implement lessons to use it effectively; and (3) deepen the understanding of information use skills (including information morality) and acquire basic teaching methods to help children and students acquire these skills. As shown in Table 4.1, the 15 lessons were largely composed of three

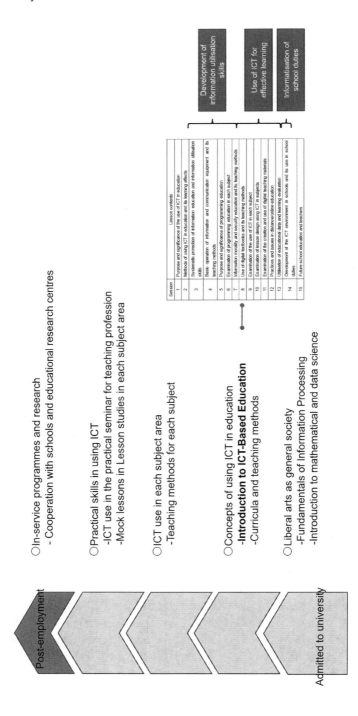

Figure 4.2 Positioning of Introduction to ICT-Based Education

Preparation of Future Teachers Teaching with Technology **55**

Table 4.1 Course Content of Introduction to ICT-Based Education

Session	Lesson Contents
1	Purpose and significance of the use of ICT in education
2	Methods of using ICT in education and its learning effects
3	Systematic promotion of information education and information utilisation skills
4	Basic operation of information and communication equipment and its teaching methods
5	Purpose and significance of programming education
6	Examination of programming education in each subject
7	Information morality and security education and its teaching methods
8	Use of digital textbooks and its teaching methods
9	Examination of the use of ICT in each subject
10	Examination of lesson design using ICT in subjects
11	Examination of the creation and use of digital teaching materials
12	Practices and issues in distance / online education
13	Utilisation of educational data and learning evaluation
14	Development of the ICT environment in schools and its use in school duties
15	Future school education and teachers

Note: Author's translation of syllabus prepared by Professor Kobayashi (Kobayashi, 2023b).

pillars: the development of information utilisation skills, use of ICT for effective learning, and informatisation of school duties.

The results indicated that 98% of the students were satisfied with the course. Even though it was a compulsory class, they thought it was difficult, and they acquired the ability to use ICT. Moreover, it was good that they were able to get misty-eyed by questioning the meaning of school, teachers, and ICT (Kobayashi, 2023a, p. 3). This could be called a redefinition of learning.

The professor is currently working to encourage students to consider changes in the classroom through ICT usage. To introduce the actual task, the students exchanged opinions on what could be performed with one device per student using Jamboard, followed by a mutual review of the pros and cons of ICT using Google spreadsheets and Slido (an application), and sharing the role of teachers in 2050. The results were then published on the website for mutual review, and students were given a confirmatory test using MS-Forms (Kobayashi, 2023a, p. 3). On that day, the professor asked his students to imagine the year 2050 and think about what they would value as teachers.

Conclusion

This chapter assesses the situation of ICT-integrated teacher education in the early stages of its implementation by examining flagship teacher education universities in Japan from two perspectives: the role of ICT courses in the overall teacher education curriculum and the aims of ICT courses.

First, it became evident that ICT courses in the entire pre-service teacher education curriculum are not just a single course, as in the case of the Hyogo University of Teacher Education; for example, several subjects are prepared in a three-step stacked format. Another ICT course was arranged before and after the ICT course at the University of Fukui, Japan. Thus, ICT subjects in pre-service teacher education programs in Japan are positioned within the overall curriculum, which is consistent with the findings of previous studies. Second, the University of Fukui case indicated that the introduction to ICT-based education courses included the purpose of questioning the meaning of school and teachers by moving away from a technical and instrumental perspective of ICT and utilising ICT. This is consistent with the findings of previous studies. From these two perspectives, Japanese pre-service teacher education programs, that incorporate ICT, address key points identified in previous studies. However, flagship pre-service teacher education universities only began in 2022, and future research is required, such as on how graduates are developing ICT-enhanced teaching in schools.

References

Central Council for Education, Ministry of Education, Culture, Sports, Science and Technology (MEXT). (2021). *Reiwa no nihongatagakkoukyouiku no kouchiku wo mezashite: Subete no kodomo tachi no kanou sei wo hikidasu, kobetsusaitekinamanabi to kyoudoutekinamanabi no jitsugen (toushin) (chu kyoushin dai 228 gou)* [*Towards the construction of "Japanese-style school education in Reiwa era": Realisation of individual, optimal and collaborative learning that draws out the potential of all children*] (Report, Central Council for Education No. 228).

Retrieved August 2, 2023, from https://www.mext.go.jp/content/20210126-mxt_syoto02-000012321_2-4.pdf

Education Revitalization Executive Council. (2019, May 17). *Eleventh recommendation: Innovation in education in response to technological progress and the reform of upper secondary schools for a new era.* Retrieved October 20, 2023, from https://www.mext.go.jp/component/b_menu/shingi/giji/__icsFiles/afieldfile/2019/08/30/1420732_009.pdf

Imai, M. (2010). *Kaizen: Nihon kigyo ga kokusaikyoso de seikoushita keiei nouhau* [*Kaizen: The key to Japan's competitive success*] (M. Imai, Trans.). McGraw-Hill/Irwin. (Original work published 1986)

Iwabuchi, K., Hodama, K., Onishi, Y., Miyazaki, S., Nakae, S., & Suzuki, K. H. (2021). Covid-19 and education on the front lines in Japan: What caused learning disparities and how did the government and schools take initiative? *Primary and Secondary Education During Covid-19*, 125–151. https://doi.org/10.1007/978-3-030-81500-4_5

Japan Institute of Country-ology and Engineering. (n.d.). *Kokudo woshiru/Igaito shiranai nihon no kokudo* [*Knowing the land/Surprisingly little is known about Japan's land*]. Retrieved August 2, 2023, from https://www.jice.or.jp/knowledge/japan/commentary01

Japan International Cooperation Agency. (2004). *The history of Japan's educational development: What implications can be drawn for developing countries today.* Retrieved August 2, 2023, from https://openjicareport.jica.go.jp/pdf/11778784.pdf

Kaneko, K. (Ed.). (2022). *Saishin no kyoiku kaikaku 2022–2023* [*Latest education reforms 2022–2023*]. Kyouikukaihatsu Kenkyusyo.

Kay, R. H. (2006). Evaluating strategies used to incorporate technology into preservice education: A review of the literature. *Journal of Research on Technology in Education, 38*(4), 383–408.

Kitazawa, T., & Akahori, K. (2020). Kyoinyousei ni okeru STEM/STEAM kyouiku no tenbou [Prospects of STEM/STEAM education in teacher training]. *Japan Journal of Educational Technology, 44*(3), 297–304. https://doi.org/10.15077/jjet.45004

Kobayashi, K. (2023a). *ICT katsuyou kyouiku gairon deno torikumi* [*Approaches in the introduction to using ICT in education*]. PowerPoint Slides.

Kobayashi, K. (2023b). *ICT katsuyou kyouiku gairon* [*Introduction to using ICT in education*]. Course Syllabus.

Ministry of Education, Culture, Sports, Science and Technology (MEXT). (2020a). *Basic act on education.* Retrieved August 2, 2023, from https://www.mext.go.jp/en/policy/education/lawandplan/title01/detail01/1373798.htm

Ministry of Education, Culture, Sports, Science and Technology (MEXT). (2020b). *Society 5.0 jidai ni taioushita kyoinyousei wo sendousuru kyoinyousei furaggushippu daigaku no arikata nit suite* [*The flagship university for teacher education leading the way in teacher education in the society 5.0 era*] (Final Report). Retrieved August 2, 2023, from https://www.mext.go.jp/b_menu/shingi/chukyo/chukyo3/082/sonota/1421812_00001.htm

Ministry of Education, Culture, Sports, Science and Technology (MEXT). (2021). *Kyou ikusyokuinmenkyohousekoukisokutou no ichibu wo kaisei suru syourei no sekou touni tsuite (Tsuuchi)* [*Enforcement of the ministerial regulations partially amending the regulations for enforcement of the education personnel licensing act (Notification)*]. Retrieved August 2, 2023, from https://www.mext.go.jp/b_menu/hakusho/nc/mext_00030.html

Ministry of Education, Culture, Sports, Science and Technology (MEXT). (2022). *"Reiwa no nihongata gakkoukyouiku" wo ninau kyoshi no yousei, saiyou, Kenshu no arikata nit suite: "Aratana kyoushi no manabi no sugata" no jitsugen to tayouna senmonsei wo yuusuru sitsu no takai kyousyokuin shudan no keisei* [*The education, recruitment and development of teachers who will lead "Japanese-style school education in Reiwa era": The realisation of a "new form of teacher learning" and the formation of a high-quality group of teachers and staff with diverse expertise*] (Report, Central Council for Education No. 240). Retrieved August 2, 2023, from https://www.mext.go.jp/b_menu/shingi/chukyo/chukyo3/079/sonota/1412985_00004.htm

Ministry of Education, Culture, Sports, Science and Technology (MEXT). (2023). *On the next basic plan for the promotion of education* (Report, Central Council for Education No. 241). Retrieved August 2, 2023, from https://www.mext.go.jp/b_menu/shingi/chukyo/chukyo0/toushin/1412985_00005.htm

Ministry of Education, Culture, Sports, Science and Technology (MEXT). (n.d.a). *Improvement of academic abilities (courses of study)*. Retrieved August 2, 2023, from https://www.mext.go.jp/en/policy/education/elsec/title02/detail02/1373859.htm

Ministry of Education, Culture, Sports, Science and Technology (MEXT). (n.d.b). *Kyoinyousei furaggushippu daigaku towa* [*What is a teacher education flagship university?*]. Retrieved August 2, 2023, from https://www.mext.go.jp/a_menu/koutou/houjin/mext_01646.html

Moriyama, J. (2023). *Hyogo kyouiku daigaku niokeru ICT katsuyou ni kakaru kyouin yousei* [*Teacher preparation for the use of ICT at the Hyogo University of Teacher Education*]. PowerPoint Slides.

National Institute for Educational Policy (NIER). (2019). *OECD seitono gakushu toutatsudo cyousa 2018 nen chousa (PISA 2018) no pointo* [*OECD Pupil achievement survey 2018 (PISA 2018) key points*]. Retrieved August 2, 2023, from https://www.nier.go.jp/kokusai/pisa/pdf/2018/01_point.pdf

Ogura, M., Sato, K., Muramatsu, H., & Morishita, T. (2021). Kyouinyouseikatei ni okeru GIGA sukuru kousou ni taiou shita gakusei wo taishou toshita kyouin no ICT katsuyou shidouryoku no ikusei wo mezashita kokoromi [An attempt to develop teachers' ICT application teaching skills for students in teacher training programs in response to the GIGA school initiative]. *Research Report of JSET Conferences, 4,* 1–8. https://doi.org/10.15077/jsetstudy.2021.4_1

Shimoda, A. (2023). Tai ni okeru kousen kyouiku moderu no tenkai: Pairotto kou deno 5 nen me no torikumi [Transferring KOSEN education to Thailand: Case study of two technical colleges]. *The Bulletin of National Institute of Technology, Hiroshima College, 45,* 99–106. https://doi.org/10.32221/hiroshimashosenkiyo.45.0_99

Sugimura, M. (2019). "Houhou toshiteno hikaku" no shiten kara mita nihongata kyouiku no kaigai tenkai [Discussion of projects on overseas dissemination of Japanese-style education models through analysis with comparative education as a methodology]. *The Japanese Journal of Educational Research, 86*(4), 524–536. https://doi.org/10.11555/kyoiku.86.4_524

Tondeur, J., Roblin, N. P., Van Braak, J., Fisser, P., & Voogt, J. (2013). Technological pedagogical content knowledge in teacher education: In search of a new curriculum. *Educational Studies, 39*(2), 239–243.

Tondeur, J., Van Braak, J., Sang, G., Voogt, J., Fisser, P., & Ottenbreit-Leftwich, A. (2012). Preparing pre-service teachers to integrate technology in education: A synthesis of qualitative evidence. *Computers & Education, 59*(1), 134–144.

Watsuji, T. (1961). *A climate: A philosophical study.* Printing Bureau, Japanese Government.

Narratives of Teacher Educators on the Integration of Information and Communication Technologies to Prepare Pre-service Teachers in Specific Subjects

5

Thuthukile Jita and Alice Dhliwayo

Introduction

Various authors have argued that expert practitioners for teacher education programmes are in favour of a subject-specific approach, with the argument that information and communication technology (ICT) applications differ according to the subject being taught (Dewa & Ndlovu, 2022; Graham et al., 2020; Kopcha, 2010; König et al., 2022). Previous studies have not explored the experiences of teacher educators with the use of ICTs in teaching specific subjects. There has been an upsurge of research on technology-integration skills in pre-service teachers (PSTs), especially as informed by the technological pedagogical content knowledge (TPACK) framework (Baran et al., 2019; Jita & Sintema, 2022; Naaz & Kumari, 2021; Tiba & Condy, 2021). This is a resultant reaction to scholars' belief that teacher education is a dynamic factor that significantly impacts the holistic development of the learners in primary and secondary schools because

DOI: 10.4324/9781003406631-5

PSTs graduate from universities to teach in those schools (Graham et al., 2020; Naaz & Kumari, 2021; Tiba & Condy, 2021).

Information and Communication Technology in Teacher Education

ICTs have become fundamental to teaching and learning since COVID-19. Some scholars see them as requisite to teacher qualifications, as well as being a part of learners' exposure during teaching and learning processes (Gülbahar, 2008; Naaz & Kumari, 2021). It can be argued that ICT has become the world, and if education is preparing today's learners for active participation in the world, then ICT must occupy a central role in that preparation. It is logical to look to schools and teacher educators for ICT literacy for the nation (Gülbahar, 2008).

In South Africa, there is growing participation in professional learning for teacher educators as they engage in the training of PSTs. The key driver for this need is the increasing demand of technology use in the classroom, in general. Yet, the same technology is conspicuously absent from the generality of South African public classrooms (Chisango & Marongwe, 2021). During apartheid, education was stratified along racial lines and Black schools lacked in almost everything, including infrastructure and educational equipment or tools. Post-apartheid, the South African government implemented unsegregated education (Dlamini, 2022). However, vast disparities still exist in terms of ICT integration for primary and secondary education, even in cases where ICT tools are available (Chisango & Marongwe, 2021).

Research has indicated unequal access to opportunities in teacher training for efficacy in ICTs for teaching and learning as one of the major factors militating against the deprivation of 21st-century technology skills for learners and improved motivation for classroom practice (Jita & Sintema, 2022; Torres & Giddie, 2020). This has shifted attention to universities, with the need to produce teachers who are digitally literate and would need no immediate supplementary ICT-integration training upon joining the field (Dewa & Ndlovu, 2022). Studies on ICT in public schools in South Africa are fraught with discourse articulating resource shortages and poor teacher efficacy (Dlamini, 2022; Graham et al., 2020; Torres & Giddie, 2020). Furthermore, those from universities indicate unequal opportunities to learn for PSTs (Dewa & Ndlovu, 2022; Jita & Sintema, 2022; Tiba & Condy, 2021).

Literature suggests that there are teachers who still view ICT integration as a waste of time and stick to traditional methods due to lack of exposure of what ICT does for the classroom (Chisango & Marongwe, 2021; Kolobe & Mihai, 2021; Mhlanga, 2021). By impacting the university classroom, the chances are higher of improving the efficacy of in-service teachers when they are joined by well-trained new teachers and of breaking the vicious cycle of nonintegration in public schools (Adu & Zondo, 2023).

However, much less is known about how teacher educators locally and internationally across various university disciplines experience the use of a range of ICTs to teach their different disciplines. This chapter therefore sheds light from the narratives of a selected group of teacher educators on how they experience the use of a range of ICTs and applications to teach in several subject areas. The study is suggestive of a differentiated approach to providing support for university lecturers (and students) who are integrating ICTs in their teaching and learning.

Community of Practice Framework

Jean Lave and Etienne Wenger pioneered the idea of a community of practice (CoP) in 1991 (Brown, n.d.). They defined the CoP as a collection of people who share the same interests towards achieving the same goals. The workplace is the obvious context for CoPs. However, in the present global village, CoPs are also lived and experienced online, on educational platforms or on social media platforms (Aljuwaiber, 2016).

Principles of Community of Practice

A CoP has three crucial characteristics: the domain, the community and the practice (Wanger-Trayner & Wanger-Trayner, 2015). The domain entails the identity of members as defined by their shared interests and competences around the domain. Teacher educators share competences in PST training in their areas of specialization (Brown, n.d.). In a CoP, teacher educators discuss pedagogy and curricula and carry out collaborated research towards the production of the same PSTs in the same faculty but in different subject areas. The CoP is where practitioners share tools, stories, experiences, methodologies and expertise (MacDonald, 2008).

Besides these characteristics, a CoP has guiding principles, which include sharing best practices and consistent quality feedback (Brown, n.d.). Best practices are shared through a collaborative reflection on the practice, active engagement with individual learning, and learning from members' skills, insights and views (Aljuwaiber, 2016). As members engage in collaborated activities, it is expected that feedback on data or findings be precise and of good quality through knowledge of theory and practice of the profession.

Sub-Saharan Africa is inundated with a growing need for interventions that work for the classroom, and the teacher factor is cited as the most important in the realization of a 21st-century-compliant education for the region (Graham et al., 2020). It is imperative for higher education to equip PSTs with the skills to enable implementation of integrated education at the grassroots level (Nowfeek & Mahrool, 2021). The CoP answers the demand by providing hands-on processes backed by theory in such a way that results are continuously applicable for the classroom in which they are developed as workable and sustainable solutions. At the same time, PSTs are exposed to what works and why it works, with ease of transferability for their teaching practice classrooms.

Methodology

The Community of Practice Case Study

A group of ten teacher educators in one university was purposively selected to create a CoP with the objective to develop each other professionally and model the use of ICTs in their teaching and learning. These educators taught a range of modules for PSTs in the areas of natural sciences, technology, accounting, mathematics, geography, life skills, agriculture and languages, across levels from Grade R to Grade 12. The participants would meet on a regular basis to discuss the challenges and opportunities of incorporating ICTs into their various modules and share a variety of applications and tools they can use to improve their scholarship and profession.

We obtained ethical clearance from the institution and subsequently explained to the participants the purpose of the study. After they willingly agreed to take part, we advised them that they were free to withdraw at any stage of the study without any need for providing an explanation. We also ensured participants' confidentiality throughout the whole process of the study.

Data Collection and Analysis

For the CoP, participants would meet regularly to share experiences with the different applications they used in their teaching and learning activities in various subject areas. During these meetings, participants discussed and taught each other how to use particular apps for integration, and in the process, they would develop their professionalism and efficacy with technology. Scholars have long lamented the gap between research and practice (Albion et al., 2015; Bereiter, 2013). The CoP helps to bridge that gap, as participants will be practising what they learn in the research process. The participants of this study also used the CoP as a sounding board, where they learnt new applications and tested their own efficacy on colleagues before going on to model them for their PSTs in actual teaching and learning sessions.

We employed a semi-structured interview protocol as our main data collection tool because of its ability to provide rich verbal and non-verbal material to answer the main questions of the study (Adeoye-Olatunde & Olenik, 2021). The interviews were protocol driven, where the same protocol was used consistently for each interview. This ensured support to the participants in clarifying and unpacking their narratives by responding with deepening enquiries to their answers, which guaranteed trustworthiness and validity (Dolczewski, 2022). We then used the thematic approach to data analysis, paying close attention to human-generated meanings to own experiences from the participants.

Findings and Discussions

The aim of the chapter was to provide lessons from the narratives of a selected group of teacher educators on the integration of ICTs for subject areas of specialization for teaching and learning in one university in South Africa. Participants presented varying experiences with differing applications on various technological tools in divergent subject areas. The data were categorized into four main themes based on the participants' various narratives. The themes are subsequently discussed.

Teacher Educators' Choices of ICT Tools

The global COVID-19 pandemic has provided impetus to higher education institutions (HEIs) to increase remote and hybrid learning through a variety of tools and applications. The site selected for this study had policies and ICT infrastructures in place for digitalization purposes, such as learning management systems (Blackboard), high-speed internet connectivity around the campus and designated ICT courses in different programmes. Participants indicated using a variety of tools together with Blackboard and laptops provided by the university for enhanced ICT integration. Participants favoured the use of laptops and mobile devices as accompaniment to Blackboard and smartboards. P1 explained this choice for her teaching practice module on integrating ICT as an improvement to both hybrid and remote learning:

> I use the tablet for teaching. I am able to quickly log in while I say to the students they must log in on Blackboard, but I use the tablet for . . . displaying the PowerPoint. Even if they ask questions, I could quickly search on the tablet. . . . I am able to move around the rows while carrying it; unlike when I have to go back to the laptop and review where the platform is, I'm walking with the platform, which is the tablet.

Orlando and Attard (2016) argued in their study that early-career teachers using different mobile devices experience complications. P1 refuted this argument by demonstrating that the use of mobile devices such as tablets allows mobility, which enhances engagement in the classroom. P2, an accounting lecturer, used both the tablet and the smartphone as mobile devices for quick assessments through games and online quizzes:

> Having a mobile tool is handy . . . you move around with it and upload your slides and show one at a time while you explain to your students; and at the end of each concept, we play an assessment game and I get to know who needs help where. So, it assists with prompt individualised feedback.

P1 and P2's responses align with Barnwell's (2016) assertion that mobile devices are ideal for individualised learning, and they support learning on the go. However, P5 preferred using the laptop in the lecture hall

66 Thuthukile Jita and Alice Dhliwayo

and allowed students to use their devices, which would mostly be smartphones. She explained that the laptop is a familiar tool and that it helps her to confidently deliver lessons with a lot more efficacy:

> I use the laptop with my literature for Foundation Phase pre-service teachers, for PowerPoint; and as for mobiles, I don't use them in class for teaching, but I have academic groups with them. I use the WhatsApp for prompt feedback and for some discussions that need action while they are not in the classroom.

This finding aligns with Nowfeek and Mahrool (2021), who asserted that when teachers are equipped with pedagogical skills in ICT use, they use them often and effectively for practice with students. Hence, what teacher educators choose to use with their students is that which they are comfortable with and which can help them to effectively deliver their lessons.

Teacher Educators' Choice of ICT Apps

P5 was very excited about the CoP in relation to applications available to use for lessons with PSTs:

> Look how many apps I learnt to use with my class. I used the tablet for digital stories. The tablet has all I need for that, the music, pictures, the videos for multimodal stories. And now I will try to add apps I learnt from colleagues for my students to increase variety as they work on their digital stories on their own devices.

This process of learning offers modelling for PSTs on how they would in turn integrate ICT for their own classes when they join the world of work (Naaz & Kumari, 2021). TE found that when PSTs are exposed to learning with ICT, it is a precursor to their pedagogical practice and useful for their future careers. P5 went on to explain that with the confidence she has gained through the CoP, she will encourage her PSTs to produce digital storybooks to enter periodical competitions where such are selected for use in schools. In addition, she will encourage them to produce their own digital apparatus for future use.

P2 explained that he used videos on mobile devices for personalized learning:

Integration of Information and Communication Technologies **67**

> While I am on laptop, my students are on mobiles the way I used them with Grade 12 students when I was a teacher out there, because I want them to use them in turn when they go out to do actual teaching. I would download videos, both of topics I have taught and those ahead, so they can self-regulate as they learn. I love games for assessment where they use their mobiles.

This finding resonates with literature indicating that digital natives learn better and more effectively when learning is personalized and when mobile devices or digital tools are part of the learning process (Barnwell, 2016).

P1 explained that she used a variety of applications, especially on the laptop and other ICT tools:

> I use the tablet for E-portfolio with my honours class. I use also PowerPoint; everybody is using it, but how do you use the PowerPoint? I use so many interactive activities; I give them groupwork, for example, and then I say they must use any device for presentation in micro teaching. Some tools are well known, like Word doc; then we use pdf, but when they submit E-portfolio, I need them to group all that material that they have in form of a pdf, it will look to them like a WOW!, they are the ones who created it, then put it in a website.

Letting PSTs work on any format to prepare the Eportfolio and for micro teaching helps students to develop various digital competences that are requisite for lesson presentations later in their professional practice.

Furthermore, P3, who taught natural sciences for the Foundation Phase, said:

> I use the laptop, but now I will try the tablet after the CoP if it aligns well with my pedagogical practice. I use videos to model different ways of teaching in my module. . . . I draw up videos where teachers are teaching, so that we can discuss pedagogy, how the teacher is engaging with learners, and I will ask questions on all the elements of classroom management in the video.

The generality of studies from South African universities on PSTs' experiences with ICT during teaching practice have indicated predictors of non-implementation of ICT when they graduate to serve as in-service teachers (Dewa & Ndlovu, 2022; Jita & Sintema, 2022; Mahlo & Waghid, 2023). This is a result of a variety of reasons, which includes a dearth of exposure to ICT-integrated teaching and learning, among other reasons (Dewa & Ndlovu, 2022; Momani & Jamous, 2017; Tiba & Condy, 2021). This is why we used the CoP to model mobile technologies in a design-based programme.

P4 explained that she engages her PSTs a lot in her engineering and technology modules and uses a variety of tools and apps, where she experiments a lot and shares in the CoP. Resources used by her include TikTok, WhatsApp, videos and games such as Kahoot! and Make It True.

> I encourage my students to use their smartphones. When I ask a question and they don't answer, I tell them to take out their phones and find out the answer. I want to employ with my students this semester the Make It True app . . . where they make a situation true using binary codes and logic games. . . . It's a creative way of making students engage, enjoy and learn at the same time.

These varied activities taking place tend to expose PSTs to what actually works for pedagogy. These are positive in-situ interventions aided by CoP, which are sorely needed to develop a culture of ICT integration for pedagogy (MacDonald, 2008). The approach is in line with literature, which posits that an equipped teacher is a catalyst towards transformative education in the Fourth Industrial Revolution (4IR) (Aljuwaiber, 2016; Meyer et al., 2019; Nowfeek & Mahrool, 2021). With CoP, educators are afforded concurrent development with their students.

Challenges Faced by Teacher Educators with ICT Integration

Teacher education in the 4IR has become the most important link to transformation in education, and higher education is faced with the most critical challenge of developing approaches to teaching and learning that are 21st-century compliant (Fengliang, 2020). According to Hornsby and Osman (2014), South Africa has to cope with the exponential growth of student numbers in HEIs. This has resulted in large classes and a concern for quality, which extensive use of technology can dispel. However, while universities are providing infrastructure to meet these challenges, teacher educators, who are a key factor in this matrix, need to be fully prepared to

Integration of Information and Communication Technologies **69**

realize success. This need for training was echoed as the biggest challenge by P5:

> I definitely know my content, but to fully integrate it is a challenge. It would be nice if we could have training in using these devices more effectively to integrate content.

P3 also lamented lack of skills:

> I was only trained in the use of Blackboard. . . . If I can be skilful enough to design with technology my lessons, . . . I can only use with confidence the videos and WhatsApp, which are basic really.

However, all the participants agreed that the need for mobile devices such as tablets for students was very important.

> Maybe if it can be financed for students to get tablets . . . they need to handle them and all actively participate. At the moment, we work with their phones and in the lecture halls there are no computers, so it becomes a challenge for equal opportunities to learn for the PSTs. We can have them fixed in the lecture halls and used during lectures for security so they can use them when they meet them in schools.
>
> (P2)

P5 reiterated by saying that, "It will be nice if all my students had a tablet. Not all have phones, and many times their phones have connectivity problems."

The non-abundance of ICT infrastructure is a limiting factor to ICT-integrated education in HEIs. Student phones, which they use as mobiles for learning, have some challenges even when they are on campus. P4 alluded to students failing to mark the digital register using their phones due to a variety of reasons. These include unavailability, phone disk space, and connectivity, even though they are within the range of university Wi-Fi (Keshnee, 2017).

> The challenge is modelling those tools and apps, because some do not have these mobiles and if they have, they are the ones which cannot have WhatsApp or other apps on them. When they go to schools with ICT tools, they can't use them. We want intensive training for our students to build skills in them.
>
> (P4)

70 Thuthukile Jita and Alice Dhliwayo

The adoption of mobile devices on campus and off campus by both teacher educators and PSTs for teaching their subjects will then require establishment of policies to assist users in both schools and HEIs to support teaching and learning processes and lead to digital transformation, where ICT tools such as WhatsApp will be user friendly. This case study further proposes an innovative strategy that a higher education institution, one research site and a single program at a time, can undertake to successfully address the challenges of using ICT.

Community of Practice and Teacher Educators' Professional Growth

The CoP was intentionally made small to encourage participants to open up and learn from each other for professional growth and to model their areas of specialization on the same group of PSTs, going on to build possibilities for culture-building within the teaching practice (Pyrko et al., 2017). The process targets the use of ICT in schools, which has become a nagging problem for the South African context (Dlamini, 2022). The central role of the CoP was to bridge knowledge gaps in ICT integration among participating teacher educators in a safe environment (Baran et al., 2019; Gülbahar, 2008). In this regard, P2 shared:

> The biggest benefit is sharing the experiences of colleagues. In the recent workshop, I was fascinated by the projects colleagues were doing. We also get to share our best practices.

P3 was very enthusiastic about the CoP and what it was doing to her scholarship: "It's a safe space to learn, knowing you are not judged. The collaboration of scholarly papers on pedagogy, and the room to further engage with colleagues even after the workshop, are all helping a lot." P4 also echoed how the community was growing her profession: "I wish we could have a country of practice. . . . I liked the critical views from colleagues. It's a chance to step back and reflect and also collaborate papers with colleagues." P5 also expressed her sentiments concerning this: "Next meeting I'm going to show my app for digital stories which I am trying out; if I crack it on colleagues, I will then take it to my class."

Bringing a group of teacher educators as a platform for sharing knowledge and emerging practices with one another had the effect of exciting participants and making them look forward to upcoming sessions. These sessions, through a CoP, further promote digitalization through learning with others and develop support structures for colleagues before taking their ideas to class. Therefore, a statement from P4 suggested that the CoP will keep spiralling, and hopefully the "digital divide" will become narrower and narrower in the institution where the CoP is practised.

Conclusion

Research has shown that modelling of ICT integration for PSTs has the greatest impact on transformational education in pedagogical practice. This chapter set out to provide narratives of teacher educators' experiences of ICT integration for a variety of curricular areas through a CoP. Consistent from the findings were the different approaches and needs of different participating teacher educators as they integrated ICT into their different subject areas. There was also proof of the sufficiency of a CoP in providing teacher educators with a safe space to learn and grow professionally in a way to enhance their ICT-integration skills for both content transmission and modelling for PSTs (Nowfeek & Mahrool, 2021). The CoP also created a safe space for scholarship in reflecting on their practice and on the challenges related to this practice for both educators and PSTs. Pyrko et al. (2017) argued that members of a CoP are practitioners who share experiences, stories, tools, methodologies and expertise. In the present environment of dynamic and emerging technologies, the CoP provides stability and productive growth to practice. In light of the findings, it is important for HEIs to direct funding towards acquiring mobile ICT tools, such as tablets for lecture halls. This will provide PSTs with the opportunity to handle ICT and to learn how to integrate it in subject areas for greater efficacy. It will also teach them how to use it in the future world of work. Barnwell (2016) portrayed the 21st century as a digital-driven society where learning should be anytime and anywhere. The present ICT infrastructures in HEIs of computer labs and libraries fall short of this mobility, hence the call by participants for tablet-equipped lecture halls instead. The participants' narratives also indicate a need for differentiated approaches to address educators' needs in ICT integration with PSTs.

Limitations and Recommendations

The study relied on qualitative data alone from a small sample in one university, which places some limitations for generalization. The nature of the study made researcher bias a high-risk factor due to the phenomenological nature of the whole process. We suggest that future research may include large populations from varied faculties and a mixed-method approach, which would allow for triangulations. Further research can be carried out to ascertain the level of impact such studies have on PSTs during teaching practice.

References

Adeoye-Olatunde, O. A., & Olenik, N. L. (2021). Research and scholarly methods: Semi-structured interviews. *Journal of the American College of Clinical Pharmacy*, 4(10), 1358–1367. https://doi.org/10.1002/jac5.1441

Adu, E. O., & Zondo, S. S. (2023). Perceptions of educators on ICT integration into the teaching and learning of economics. *EUREKA: Social and Humanities*, 1, 61–71. https://doi.org/10.21303/2504-5571.2023.002530

Albion, P. R., Tondeur, J., Forkosh-Baruch, A., & Peeraer, J. (2015). Teachers' professional development for ICT integration: Towards a reciprocal relationship between research and practice. *Education and Information Technologies*, 20(4), 655–673. https://doi.org/10.1007/s10639-015-9401-9

Aljuwaiber, A. (2016). Communities of practice as an initiative for knowledge sharing in business organizations: A literature review. *Journal of Knowledge Management*, 20(4), 731–748. https://doi.org/10.1108/JKM-12-2015-0494

Baran, E., Bilici, S. C., Sari, A. A., & Tondeur, J. (2019). Investigating the impact of teacher education strategies on preservice teachers' TPACK. *British Journal of Educational Technology*, 50(1), 357–370. https://doi.org/10.1111/bjet.12565

Bereiter, C. (2013). Principled practical knowledge: Not a bridge but a ladder. *Journal of the Learning Sciences*, 23(1), 4–17. https://doi.org/10.1080/10508406.2013.812533

Barnwell, P. (2016, April 27). Do smart phones help or hurt children? *The Atlantic*. https://www.theatlantic.com/education/archive/2016/04/do-smartphones-have-a-place-in-the-classroom/480231/

Brown, N. (n.d.). What are communities of practice? *Dr Nicole Brown*. https://www.nicole-brown.co.uk/communities-of-practice/

Chisango, G., & Marongwe, N. (2021). The digital divide at three disadvantaged secondary schools in Gauteng, South Africa. *Journal of Education*, 82, 149–169. http://dx.doi.org/10.17159/2520-9868/i82a09

Dewa, A., & Ndlovu, N. S. (2022). Use of information and communication technologies in mathematics education lecturers: Implications for preservice teachers. *The Journal for Transdisciplinary Research in Southern Africa*, 18(1), a1165. https://doi.org/10.4102/td.v18i1.1165

Dlamini, R. (2022). Factors constraining teacher integration of ICT in Gauteng schools. *Independent Journal of Teaching and Learning*, 17(2), 19–37 http://www.scielo.org.za/pdf/ijtl/v17n2/02.pdf

Dolczewski, M. (2022). Semi-structured interview for self-esteem regulation research. *Acta Psychologica*, 228, 103642. https://doi.org/10.1016/j.actpsy.2022.103642

Fengliang, L. (2020). Ellen Hazelkorn, Hamish Coates, and Alexander C. McCormick (ed): Research handbook on quality, performance and accountability in higher education. *Higher Education*, 79(5), 939–940.

Graham, M. A., Gerrit, S., & Kapp, R. (2020). Teacher practice and integration of ICT: Why aror aren't South African teachers using ICTs in their classrooms. *International Journal of Instruction*, 13(2), 749–766. https://doi.org/10.29333/iji.2020.13251a

Gülbahar, Y. (2008). ICT usage in higher education: A case study on pre-service teachers and instructors. *The Turkish Online Journal of Educational Technology*, 7(1), 32–37. https://files.eric.ed.gov/fulltext/EJ1102897.pdf

Hornsby, D. J., & Osman, R. (2014). Massification in higher education: Large classes and student learning. *Higher Education*, 67, 711–719. https://doi.org/10.1007/s10734-014-9733-1

Jita, T., & Sintema, E. J. (2022). Exploring classroom use of ICT among pre-service science teachers in selected SADC countries. *African Journal of Research in Mathematics, Science and Technology Education*, 26(3), 218–236. 1https://doi.org/10.1080/18117295.2022.2139105

Keshnee, P. (2017). A snapshot survey of ICT integration in South African schools. *South African Computer Journal*, 29(2), 36–65. https://dx.doi.org/10.18489/sacj.v29i2.463

Kolobe, L., & Mihai, M. (2021). The integration of technology in supporting progressed learners in English first additional language comprehension. *Perspectives in Education*, 39(2), 303–323. https://doi.org/10.18820/2519593X/pie.v39.i2.21

König, J., Heine, S., Jäger-Biela, D., & Rothland, M. (2022). ICT integration in teachers' lesson plans: A scoping review of empirical studies. *European Journal of Teacher Education*, 1–29. https://doi.org/10.1080/02619768.2022.2138323

Kopcha, T. J. (2010). A systems-based approach to technology integration using mentoring and communities of practice. *Educational Technology Research and Development*, 58(2), 175–190. https://doi.org/10.1007/s11423-008-9095-4

MacDonald, R. J. (2008). Professional development for information communication technology integration: Identifying and supporting a community of practice through design-based research. *Journal of Research on Technology in Education, 40*(4), 429445. https://files.eric.ed.gov/fulltext/EJ826085.pdf

Mahlo, L., & Waghid, D. Z. (2023). Exploring information and communication technology integration among teachers in township public primary schools. *South African Journal of Education, 43*(1), 1–11. https://files.eric.ed.gov/fulltext/EJ1392039.pdf

Meyer, E. T., Shankar, K., Willis, M., Sharma, S., & Sawyer, S. (2019). The social informatics of knowledge. *Journal of the Association for Information Science and Technology, 70*, 307–312. https://doi.org/10.1002/asi.24205

Mhlanga, D. (2021). The Fourth Industrial Revolution and COVID-19 pandemic in South Africa: The opportunities and challenges of introducing blended learning in education. *Journal of African Education, 2*(2), 15–42. https://doi.org/10.31920/2633-2930/2021/v2n2a1

Momani, A. M., & Jamous, M. (2017). The evolution of technology acceptance theories. *International Journal of Contemporary Computer Research, 1*(1), 51–58.

Naaz, I., & Kumari, P. (2021). ICT for pre-service and in-service teachers: Implications and challenges. In S. Solanki, A. Raj, & V. Rastogi (Eds.), *Teacher education generation next: Perspectives, opportunities and challenges* (pp. 160–169). Universal Academic Books Publishers & Distributors.

Nowfeek, M. R. M., & Mahrool, F. (2021). The contribution of integrated ICT in teaching and learning practice: Teachers' perspective. *International Journal of Multidisciplinary Research Review, 8*(5), 78–89. https://doi.org/10.22192/ijamr.2021.08.05.004

Orlando, J., & Attard, C. (2016). Digital natives come of age: The reality of today's early career teachers using mobile devices to teach mathematics. *Mathematics Education Research Journal, 28*, 107–121. https://doi.org/10.1007/s13394-015-0159-6

Pyrko, I., Dörfler, V., & Eden, C. (2017). Thinking together: What makes communities of practice work? *Human Relations, 70*(4), 389–409. https://doi.org/10.1177/0018726716661040

Tiba, C., & Condy, L. J. (2021). Identifying factors influencing pre-service teacher readiness to use technology during professional practice. *International Journal of Information and Communication Technology Education, 17*(2), 149–161. https://doi.org/10.4018/IJICTE.20210401.oa2

Torres, K. M., & Giddie, L. (2020). Educator perceptions and use of technology in South African schools. *Peabody Journal of Education, 95*(2), 117–126. https://doi.org/10.1080/0161956X.2020.1745611

Wanger-Trayner, E., & Wanger-Trayner, B. (2015, June). *Introduction to communities of practice: A brief overview of the concept and its uses.* https://www.wenger-trayner.com/introduction-to-communities-of-practice/

Girls and Computer Science   **6**

Professional Development and Teachers as Role Models

James Hughes and Agnes Chigona

Introduction

As this chapter's first author, let me share my positionality and some context with the reader. This study was part of my Postgraduate Certificate in Education (PGCE) studies. I worked in the field of technology for 25 years. While in the IT industry, I noticed that few women were taking up jobs in this industry. Hence, for my PGCE project, I decided to understand if the lack of female role models in IT is the reason why many girls are not pursuing Computer Science in school. Hence, the research being reported in this chapter is based on the project I did for my training to become a qualified teacher in Computer Science at school. The second author is a seasoned researcher and teacher educator and is here to mentor me in writing for publication.

Diversity is one of the key focuses of modern societies, and the push for equality has never been greater. This is not just being driven by any ideological positions but also has drivers within the business world. Clear links between the diversity of a company's workforce and improved financial performance are emerging (Dame Vivian Hunt, 2015), and this becomes of vital importance in education because diversity within the workplace hinges upon diversity within educational subject areas. According to de las Cuevas et al. (2022, p. 239), "the gender gap in STEM-related job

DOI: 10.4324/9781003406631-6

positions is a fact, and it is closely related to the low percentage of women studying STEM degrees". This is a problem in both the developed and developing countries.

As far back as 1994 in the USA, Margolis and Fisher were "working on the gender gap in computer science" (Margolis & Fisher, 2002, p. 13), and their work is just one amongst many investigations into this subject. As part of the outcome of their research, they highlight school as a crucial environment where the disparity between the sexes is entrenched early, and they see "a further increase in boy's confidence, status, and expertise in computing and a decline in the interest and confidence of girls" (Margolis & Fisher, 2002, p. 33). Battey et al. showed that "most gender equity professional development in STEM lacks essential elements to effectively promote and implement gender equity in the classroom".

Despite this issue being known about for at least 20 years, girls currently account for only 21.4% of those taking Computer Science at General Certificate of Secondary Education (GCSE) (Hope, 2021), so any proposed solutions have thus far had minimal impact, hence why this is a vital topic of importance to consider for those in education.

For those unaware, GCSEs are what pupils will leave secondary school within the UK, and 5 passes above grade C are a rough equivalent of a High School Diploma in the USA. The primary author of this chapter is a schoolteacher who took up his first teaching job in September 2023, where all the qualified Computer Science teaching staff were men and, his Year 10 (9th grade) GCSE Computer Science class consisted entirely of boys.

The first author has been an IT professional for 25 years, and hence is familiar with the issues around the low number of women involved in Science, Technology, Engineering and Maths (STEM) jobs and the attempts to make these occupations more diverse, with some trade unions setting targets to get 30% of women into these workplace roles within the next 5 years. Within computer science in particular in 2017, graduates entering IT roles in the UK were predominantly male, with only 19.1% being women (Prospect, 2017). According to Ryle-Hodges et al. (2022, p. 6), the existing digital skills gap in the industry is compounded by the gender imbalance.

Nonetheless, these statistics have serious long-term implications for the IT industry in the UK. Hence, this chapter focuses on gender inequality in the computing world and tries to answer the following question:

Is a lack of female role models for girls a key reason why they don't take Computer Science at GCSE?

The answer to this question could further inform what to include in teacher professional development (TPD), in particular those teaching Computer Science, considering that teachers are the first influence on pupils in school. Merayo and Ayuso (2023, p. 1493) have indicated that "active teaching environments may have a positive impact on their desire to study STEM and this impact may be greater for under-represented students" (1493). Therefore, in-service teachers should be exposed to more gender training to deal with gender imbalance in STEM subjects.

One feature that may be noticeable in this chapter is the distinction between "computer science" as a general field of interest and "Computer Science" as a specific GCSE subject. The capitalisation will indicate when the GCSE subject is being discussed rather than the former.

Background to the Problem

Although the focus of this chapter is specific to female role models, we have considered the nature of interaction with computers for men and women in general, the history of gender imbalance in computing and the evidence for women's aptitude for computer science.

It is interesting to note that the use of computers in general appears not to be subject to this gender imbalance, as Margolis and Fisher (2002, p. 2) assert that, going into the 21st century, "women are surfing the web in equal proportion to men, and women make up a majority of internet consumers". This is confirmed by the data recorded by the Office of National Statistics (ONS) for the UK (ONS, 2020), and yet despite being equal users of computers, the absence of women in tech fields is still evident today (Young et al., 2023). Statistics released within the past three years show that females make up 32% of workers in computing roles globally (World Economic Forum, 2021). Recently, Yates and Plagnol (2022, p. 3080) reported that

> there have been numerous attempts by the UK government, schools and the industry to improve the representation of women in STEM-related fields (science, technology, engineering and maths) more generally, but they have had limited success, particularly within the field of technology.

About a decade earlier, Misa confirmed the lack of women in computer science (Misa, 2011, p. 6), and stated that this is not "merely an academic problem" but symptomatic of industry; yet Misa refers to figures from the National Science Foundation (NSF) in the USA to confirm that this was not always the case and that in "the late 1980s, women constituted fully 38%" of the computing workforce and that the peak for women as undergraduate computing students was 37% (Misa, 2011, p. 4). Although this peak was not emulated in the UK, it does provide an opportunity for us to discuss later in this section what attracted women to the study of computing and work in the computing industry at that time and what has led to the decline. Misa declares that this striking upswing and downturn has never been seen in any other profession.

Although the UK did not experience this boom and bust of female involvement in the computing industry, as the 'boom' never happened, many women were involved in codebreaking during World War II, such as Mavis Batey and Margaret Rock, whose stories can be found in the chapter "Dilly's girls" in Smith's *The Debs of Bletchley Park* (Smith, 2015). This shows that there were ideal candidates for the computing revolution, and yet women appear to have been overlooked post-war. Hicks (2018) has put forward a compelling case that Britain, as declared in the title of her book, *Lost Its Edge in Computing*; this was as a result of discarding women technologists, and with it, the UK failed to become a global player in the modern computing world.

Despite this, there have always been talented and exceptional women involved in computing, even when tracing its origins back to times when women's position in society was even more unequal than it is today. Ada Lovelace was the architect of coding in the early 19th century, and Grace Hopper is "revered for her work, which led to the development of the programming language COBOL" in the middle of the 20th century (Arnold et al., 2021, p. 14). The primary author's experience with his alternative placement in a primary school in Llanelli, a town in South Wales, bears this out; those who gave the best solutions and showed the most aptitude for programming in the lessons he taught were all girls and yet, according to Arnold, it is clear that "women coders and IT professionals have been scarce since Lovelace became the first" (Arnold et al., 2021, p. 14). This makes the question all the more puzzling: why, given that girls outperform boys in Computer Science GCSE results (JCQ, 2021) and that history is littered with examples of female excellence in the subject, is Computer Science not popular with girls?

Again, with regards to attainment in such subjects, Yates and Plagnol (2022, p. 3080) show that girls and women are more than holding their own, outperforming their male counterparts both at school and university. Yet many of these mathematically adept women do not pursue careers in the most technical roles within the sector despite high salaries in these fields.

Nonetheless, the plight of Computer Science as an imbalanced subject is only highlighted by the progress in other subjects towards gender equality. While there are many "positive articles about how females have caught up in academia", according to Franklin (2022, p. 15), "this is not the case for computer science". Again, this raises the question that if other STEM subjects are becoming more gender-balanced, why not Computer Science?

It is clear from the evidence so far that it is not a lack of access to computers, nor a lack of talent or ability that prevents girls from taking Computer Science, and that it stands out against the huge progress being made in equality in other subject areas. We have touched on some historical aspects of women seemingly being frozen out of computing just as things were beginning to look promising, and now turn the attention to suggested reasons as to why the imbalance exists today. Possible explanations include gender stereotypes, computing stereotypes, lack of confidence;=, perceived difficulty of the subject. teaching methods, genuine differences between sexes and a lack of role models (Yates & Plagnol, 2022; Young et al., 2023).

Wagman and Parks (2021) believe that the gender imbalance in Computer Science is much about how life is socially constructed.

> Technologies, whether hardware or software, are socially shaped by gender power relations and cultural beliefs that influence the design, decision-technical content and use of such artefacts. Automated making systems employing algorithms thus pose the risk of reflecting and amplifying existing patterns of gender inequities.
>
> (Young et al., 2023, p. 5)

Nonetheless, many gender stereotypes are already present when children enter the earliest stages of education. Martin relates an example from her field notes in which a girl, Nina, aged 3, has already learnt that "she is a girl and that girls wear pink and play with pink toys" (Jackson et al., 2010). This bias becomes entrenched in the habits of the computing industry, where "the current designs of computer games appeal overwhelmingly to boys" due to the main designers being male (Margolis & Fisher, 2002, p. 43). There are even allegations that female game developers have been harassed and hounded, although conversely, according to Hepler, this has led to the creation of "a community of female game developers determined to see each other succeed" (Hepler, 2019, p. 9).

Despite the recent growth of the female game industry, there is evidence that there may be genuine differences in the sexes. Margolis found that the females to whom she talked saw themselves as people who scrutinise "the worth of each computing project in terms of what it is doing to change or help the world" (Margolis & Fisher, 2002, p. 53), but that the males seemed interested in computers without needing to see a context. Specifically, one female saw the creation of computer games as not "worth the energy or talent that it takes" (Margolis & Fisher, 2002, p. 53) and that computer science should make a more positive contribution to society.

As reported by Congor (2017) around the issue of a lack of equality in computing, certain traits were more commonly found in women, such as "openness directed towards feelings and aesthetics rather than ideas", and that generally, women have "a stronger interest in people rather than things, relative to men". This context was used to justify why a press for more equality in jobs was not only unnecessary but unfair, stating that "differences in distributions of traits between men and women may in part explain why we don't have 50% representation of women in tech and leadership. Discrimination to reach equal representation is unfair, divisive, and bad for business" (Congor, 2017). If there are genuine differences between men and women, are those differences hard-wired or are they socially constructed, and how far do they contribute to the question of girls' apparent lack of interest in Computer Science?

Teaching methods and teaching materials are seen to be crucial. According to Wang et al. (2023, p. 1), "textbooks use images, in addition to text, for delivering knowledge, thereby convey attitudes and values of students including those on gender bias". In many science textbooks, females are less represented as images for illustrations compared to males. These biases in the teaching and teaching materials affect in subtle ways the pupil's career choices, as well as their perception of science (Wang et al., 2023, p. 1). This means curriculum designers in STEM should be careful to not perpetuate gender biases in education. Luft et al. (2020,

p. 3) argue that "those who are responsible for designing educational initiatives need to be purposeful in their integration of STEM". The researchers stress the need to ensure that teacher educators who offer the professional learning of STEM teachers (both female and male) are well knowledgeable.

The focus of this research is female role models in Computer Science. It is clear from the history discussed that there are many examples, and more are becoming known through books such as Hepler's (Hepler, 2019), bringing autobiographies of industry examples, but the question is whether these role models are making an impact on girls as they go through school, and that was the crucial question to answer in my research.

Research Methodology

The approach to collecting the information for the chapter was to survey pupils with questionnaires. Two main questions were designed to establish who the pupil's main role model is, and if they have taken or are planning to take Computer Science. These closed questions were "amenable to statistical treatment and analysis" (Cohen et al., 2011, p. 382).

While the question regarding taking Computer Science is quite straightforward to implement in the questionnaire, one of the difficult decisions was whether to ask children who their 'role model' was in computing or whether to infer this from a different type of question. The technique used here was to ask the children to: "Name the first person who comes into your head when you hear the words computer science" to provide an instinctive reaction, rather than asking them who their role model was.

Additional questions included an awareness of any women involved in computer science who could potentially be role models, particularly relating to the Year 7 group, as they received interventions highlighting women involved with Computer Science, and also questions examining the pupil's reasons for taking, or not taking, computer science. The question about identifying a woman connected with computer science was a closed 'Yes' or 'No', and they were asked to confirm a name to prove that they understood and provided a suitable answer. The question about reasons for taking or not taking Computer Science at GCSE consisted of a multiple choice (select all that apply) initially, and then being asked to choose the primary reason as a single (most important) one.

To avoid "poor question design and wording" (Cohen et al., 2011, p. 261), the questionnaire was piloted on another group of children who were of a similar age to those taking part in the study. Piloting helped validate the questionnaire. The process helped to ensure the questions would capture the information the survey intended to measure.

The survey was administered to two groups of pupils. Those in Year 9 (8th Grade), who have made their choices as to what subjects they will be taking for GCSE, and those in Year 7 (6th Grade), who had some experience of Computer Studies and other science subjects and may or may not have had an idea of what they want to do in the future. This sample allowed the researcher to see if attitudes change as pupils progress through their schooling. However, it should be noted that the school and department where the study took place had the head of IT, a male identified as Mr X, a second male identified as Mr Y and a female identified as Ms Z. These three educators with pseudonyms were part of the research.

With the Year 9 group, the aim was to find out their choices and what influenced those choices. Brief discussions with each of the survey respondents were conducted as a follow-up to the questionnaire. The discussions lasted for 5 minutes on average. The aim was to explore why they (the respondents) made their choices in the survey.

With the Year 7 group, the aim was to get an idea of what they think about Computer Science as a potential GCSE subject, whether they know a woman connected with computer science and an indication of who might be a potential role model for them. After the first questionnaire with the Year 7 group, there were two intervention lessons with them and a subsequent questionnaire after each intervention. The first intervention was a cartoon video called 'Hidden Figures' that tells the story of four black women involved in NASA, whilst the second intervention was an interview with a female (Ms Z) connected with Computer Science. The same questionnaire was used to collect more data.

Regarding the sample size, in the Year 9 group, 16 of the 29 in the class returned consent forms, and in the Year 7 group, 16 of the 28 returned consent forms. One of the most frustrating aspects of this research was the number of pupils in both the Year 9 and Year 7 groups who were happy to have their answers used in the research but who failed to return the assent/consent forms. This denied the researcher access to a fuller set of data that might have yielded more information.

Microsoft Forms were used, and the form was sent to the pupil's Teams profile, which is something they were familiar with. This had the effect of preventing multiple responses by the same person, preventing "anyone determined to fix the results of the survey" (Denscombe, 2017, p. 27), which is essential in attempting to avoid any bias in the results. It also ensured that the researchers had their names from which to confirm whether they had consented for their data to appear and allowed the researchers to derive their sex, in consultation with their teacher.

One interesting point is that Ms Z had been at the school for some time and provided an opportunity for the researcher to see what the impact of having a female teacher, and therefore potentially a role model, has had on the take-up of computer science by girls in the school. The number of boys and girls taking computer science each year since she arrived provided some additional useful data to consider.

Ethical Considerations

Denscombe believes it is "hard to overstate the importance of research ethics in the context of contemporary social research" (Denscombe, 2017, p. 4) and discusses one of the key principles of research ethics being that no one should suffer harm as a result of taking part in the research. This study conforms to the guidelines of the university from the British Educational Research Association ([BERA], 2018). To protect participants and the school where the research took place, pseudonyms were used.

Having reviewed the guidelines and, agreeing that a "questionnaire will always be an intrusion into the life of the respondent" (Cohen et al., 2011, p. 377), consent to involve children in the study was obtained both from those responsible for the children and the children themselves. Consent from parents and/or guardians was obtained because the children are underage. The data collected from the children were also anonymised. Two consent forms were given out to all those taking part, and only those who signed the forms and did not withdraw their consent before the deadline were used in this study. All data was anonymised. Pupils were informed of "their rights to withdraw at any stage or not to complete particular items in the questionnaire" (Cohen et al., 2011, p. 377) and also given guarantees both of anonymity and that the research would not harm them, and lead to improvement in the provision of teaching for girls in computer science.

Results and Discussion

The results are presented in tables of data and graphs. It should be noted that of those who consented in Year 7, not everyone was present for all three lessons in which the questionnaires were completed, so there are 16 respondents for the first, 15 for the second and 14 for the third. This had a minimal impact on the dataset. The discussion on 'role model' is indicative of the responses to the question "Name the first person that comes to mind when you hear the words 'computer science'." The results are organised under the following themes:

- Computer Science Take-Up
- Role Models
- Other Patterns
- Women in Computing
- Grasp of Equality

Computer Science Take-Up

Although the increase is not uniform, when looking at the split of sexes taking computer science since Ms Z arrived at the school, there is a clear trend of an increase both in the literal number of girls taking the subject and the percentage of the classes being girls. While we cannot directly infer that Ms Z's arrival at the school has had an impact on the take-up of the subject by girls, it is certainly suggestive, especially when considering that my first Computer Science GCSE class in an all-male department consisted of no girls at all (see Figure 6.1).

When looking at the two research groups (see Figure 6.2), the data looks promising, with three out of seven girls (approximately 43%) in Year 9 taking Computer Science as a subject and suggesting a class comprising 37.5% girls, although this doesn't correlate with the actual overall year group data above, in which the take-up is 20% girls and 80% boys, suggesting those taking or planning to take computer science are more likely to respond to the research.

In Year 7 the percentage of girls indicating they were likely to take Computer Science remained constant through the interventions and, although the percentage of the class can be misleading, as seen with Year 9, the actual numbers are promising. If three girls in every Year 7 class took the subject at GCSE, that would represent a major increase, even on the improving yearly figures.

Girls and Computer Science   85

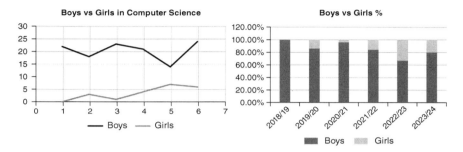

Figure 6.1 Girls vs Boys in Computer Science GCSE Class since 2018

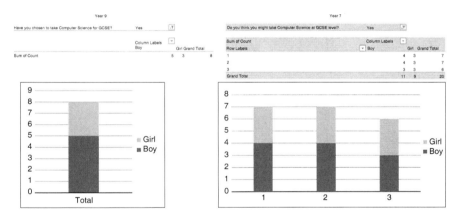

Figure 6.2 Girls Choosing Computer Science at GCSE

Role Models

It is clear from the data in Figure 6.3 for all group that the most popular role model is their current teacher, Mr X, which seems to indicate that he exerts quite an influence on both groups. The potential fear that pupils would name someone who was certainly not a role model was minimal, as only two pupils in Year 9 gave examples such as 'Robocop' and 'The scam phone calling person', and all the answers for Year 7 were sensible.

Figure 6.3 Pupils Choice of Role Models in Computer Science

Since two of the three girls who are taking Computer Science named Mr X and three of the four not taking the subject named Mr X, there appears to be no correlation between the choice of role model and whether a girl decides to take Computer Science.

Given that not a single woman was mentioned as a role model by anyone in Year 9, this may be a contributing factor to girls being reluctant to take up Computer Science. It may be argued that if there was a question asking the pupils to name a woman connected with computer science, they could have indicated as to whether they were even aware of potential female role models.

Of the Year 7 pupils, it should be noted that only one woman was mentioned as a role model, and this only after the final intervention, suggesting that implanting female role models will take considerable time and effort. Although it was initially surprising that Mr Y appeared as a role model for a few pupils, many of the class have registered with him in his computer room, which might explain this.

Other Patterns

Even though there was no correlation between the named role model and the choice of subjects, other interesting patterns emerged from the data. In all the multiple-choice answers to the question of why girls did not choose computer science, not one was a pointer towards a lack of a role model in Year 9, and the single main reason in Year 7 was unanimously a preference for other subjects (see Figure 6.4).

While there is not enough data to analyse this fully, it does tie in with ideas from the literature review that there are inherent differences in males and females that lead to different choices of subjects, although,

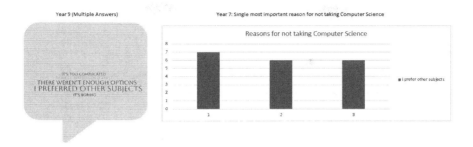

Figure 6.4 Preferences for Other Subjects

Year 9 - Asked individually

Sex	Have you chosen to take Computer Science for GCSE?	Comp Sci instead of Science
Girl	No	Yes
Girl	No	Maybe
Girl	No	No
Girl	No	Yes - Definitely

Year 7 - Asked in questionnaire

Sex	Girl
Do you think you might take Computer Science at GCSE level?	No
Questionnaire Number	2

If you could take Computer Science INSTEAD of Science would you?	Count
Maybe	4
Yes	2
Grand Total	6

Figure 6.5 Mandatory GCSE Science vs Computer Science

even if this is the case, we are not able to determine if this is down to conditioning through childhood or natural reasons.

Following the data obtained herein, researchers determined how far the preference for other subjects extended. Was Computer Science interesting, but simply further down the list of priorities for girls?

Having realised that some pupils simply aren't interested in being taught mandatory GCSE Science while covering a class for a month as a cover supervisor last year, the schoolteacher researcher was curious to find out if pupils might be interested in taking Computer Science instead. He framed an additional question for the Year 7 students in the second questionnaire and asked the Year 9 girls individually whether they would

Can you name a woman in the field of computer science?

Sex	(All) ▾		
Sum of Count	**Column Labels** ▾		
Row Lables ▾	**1**	**2**	**3**
No	13	7	1
Yes	3	8	13
Grand Total	**16**	**15**	**14**

Figure 6.6 Naming Women in Computer Science

have taken this option. The results were overwhelmingly positive in both groups, with one girl adding an emphatic 'definitely!' when asked.

Women in Computing

The additional data for Year 7 around naming women involved in computing was interesting, showing a move from only one girl being able to name a woman to only one girl being unable to name a woman by the end of the interventions (see Figure 6.6).

As to who these women were, when widening the list to include the boys' responses (with 'Unknown' substituted for a blank answer), Ms Z received one nomination and Ada Lovelace two in the first questionnaire. After the 'Hidden Figures' video, some of the characters from that story were added, and after the final intervention, Ms Z became the most popular, with a number recalling either characters from the video or characters that had been discussed with Ms Z as part of the lesson (see Figure 6.7).

Grasp of Equality

One final point to note is that all the data collected is against a clear backdrop of a grasp of the concept of equality amongst all pupils. Most of the class agreed that Computer Science is a subject for both boys and girls; only one girl named it as a 'boys subject', and she changed her mind by the second questionnaire (see Figure 6.8) As a result, the question was dropped for the final questionnaire to avoid questionnaire fatigue.

Girls and Computer Science 89

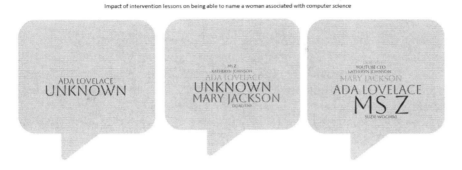

Figure 6.7 Impact of Intervention on Naming Women in Computer Science

Is Computer Science a subject for boys or girls or both?

Sum of Count Row Lables	Column Labels	
	1	2
Both	15	15
Boys	1	
Grand Total	**16**	**15**

Figure 6.8 Computer Science Subject Is for Both Boys and Girls

Conclusions and Recommendations for Educators

What is clear from the research is that the teacher is the most likely role model for pupils when it comes to computer science. This is strengthened by the evidence of improved take-up of Computer Science at GCSE by girls over time once a female teacher joined the department. In the absence of female staff, a vicious cycle is created, with a lack of girls taking Computer Science meaning there are likely to be fewer female teachers in the future.

With this finding, both the pre-service and in-service teacher education must equip both male and female teachers with knowledge and skills to deal with gender imbalance in STEM subjects.

The most disturbing fact was that only 3 of 16 pupils in a Year 7 class, more than two terms into a Computer Studies curriculum, could name a woman connected with computing. If pupils cannot even name a single woman connected with computing, then where will they find their role models? A commitment to teaching lessons on the role of women in computing might potentially influence more girls to see Computer Science as a viable subject.

Even though there is a preference for other subjects amongst girls amidst limited choices, those subjects may be preferred because of a lack of role models for girls to make them feel that the subject is one they would prefer over others. The option of taking Computer Science instead of mandatory Science is also one that could be explored to improve take-up.

Although the sample used in this research is small, there is enough information to make some recommendations. Teachers should ensure they use examples and situations to which girls can more easily relate when covering computing. They should ensure that girls get access to computing facilities without feeling intimidated by boys. There should be lessons that present positive female role models and the avoidance of gender stereotypes within the classroom. In other words, teaching methods and teaching materials should be used in a way that gender biases are not perpetuated (Wang et al., 2023), but rather girls are encouraged to take STEM subjects such as Computer Science. Therefore, teacher education, both pre-service and in-service, should ensure teachers are well-equipped to avoid gender stereotypes and use teaching methods and materials that encourage both boys and girls to pursue STEM careers.

References

Arnold, G., Dee, H., & Herman, C. (2021). *Women in tech: A practical guide to increasing gender diversity and inclusion.* BCS Learning & Development Limited. https://books.google.co.uk/books?id=3xpCzgEACAAJ

BERA. (2018). *Ethical guidelines for educational research* (4th ed.). https://www.bera.ac.uk/publication/ethical-guidelines-for-educational-research-2018

Cohen, L., Manion, L., & Morrison, K. (2011). *Research methods in education* (7th ed.). Routledge.

Congor, K. (2017). *Exclusive: Here's the full 10-page anti-diversity screed circulating internally at Google.* https://gizmodo.com/exclusive-heres-the-full-10-page-anti-diversity-screed-1797564320

Dame Vivian Hunt, D. L., & Prince, S. (2015). *Why diversity matters.* https://www.mckinsey.com/capabilities/people-and-organizational-performance/our-insights/why-diversity-matters

de las Cuevas, P., García-Arenas, M., & Rico, N. (2022). Why not STEM? A study case on the influence of gender factors on students' higher education choice. *Mathematics, 10*(2), 239.

Denscombe, M. (2017). *The good research guide: For small-scale social research projects* (6th ed.). Open University Press.

Franklin, D. (2022). *A practical guide to gender diversity for computer science faculty.* Springer International Publishing. https://books.google.co.uk/books?id=hYByEAAAQBAJ

Hepler, J. B. (2019). *Women in game development: Breaking the glass level-cap.* CRC Press LLC.

Hicks, M. (2018). *Programmed inequality: How Britain discarded women technologists and lost its edge in computing.* MIT Press. https://books.google.co.uk/books?id=ZA38DwAAQBAJ

Hope, L. (2021). *Why aren't more girls in the UK choosing to study computing and technology?* https://www.theguardian.com/careers/2021/jun/28/why-arent-more-girls-in-the-uk-choosing-to-study-computing-and-technology

Jackson, C., Renold, E., & Paechter, C. (2010). *Girls and Education 3–16: Continuing concerns, new agendas.* McGraw Hill, Open University Press.

JCQ. (2021). *Outcomes for key grades for the UK, England, Northern Ireland & and Wales, including UK age breakdowns.* https://www.jcq.org.uk/wp-content/uploads/2021/08/GCSE-Full-Course-Results-Summer-2021.pdf

Luft, J. A., Diamond, J. M., Zhang, C., & White, D. Y. (2020). Research on K-12 STEM professional development programs: An examination of program design and teacher knowledge and practice. In *The handbook of research on STEM education* (pp. 361–374). Routledge.

Margolis, J., & Fisher, A. (2002). *Unlocking the clubhouse: Women in computing.* MIT Press. https://books.google.co.uk/books?id=StwGQw45YoEC

Merayo, N., & Ayuso, A. (2023). Analysis of barriers, supports and gender gap in the choice of STEM studies in secondary education. *International Journal of Technology and Design Education, 33*(4), 1471–1498.

Misa, T. J. (2011). *Gender codes: Why women are leaving computing.* Wiley. https://books.google.co.uk/books?id=EjDYh_KHls8C

ONS. (2020). *Internet users dataset.* https://www.ons.gov.uk/businessindustryandtrade/itandinternetindustry/datasets/internetusers

Prospect. (2017). *Prospect supports women in STEM campaigns.* https://www.prospects.ac.uk/prospects-press-office/prospects-supports-women-in-stem-campaign

Ryle-Hodges, J., Krieger, M. & Chadeesingh, L. (2022). *Gender balance in computing: Options evenings and booklets.* https://static.teachcomputing.org/GBIC-Research-Report-Options-evenings-and-booklets.pdf?ref=blog.teachcomputing.org&_ga=2.245556993.468913736.1681212946-742715738.1680528321

Smith, M. (2015). *The Debs of Bletchley Park and other stories.* Aurum. https://books.google.co.uk/books?id=8rJDBgAAQBAJ

Wagman, K. B. & Parks, L. (2021). Beyond the command: Feminist STS research and critical issues for the design of social machines. *Proceedings of the ACM on Human-Computer Interaction, 5*(CSCW1), 101.

Wang, Y., Tlili, A., Hosny Saleh Metwally, A., Zhao, J., Li, Z., Shehata, B., & Huang, R. (2023). If images could speak: A social semiotics analysis of gender representation in science textbook images. *Journal of Curriculum Studies*, 1–18.

World Economic Forum. (2021). *2021 The global gender gap report.* https://www.weforum.org/reports/global-gender-gap-report2021%0Afile:///Users/natalienunes/Documents/AshridgeHULTBusinessSchool/ArticlesHULT/WEF_GGGR_2021.pdf

Yates, J., & Plagnol, A. C. (2022). Female computer science students: A qualitative exploration of women's experiences studying computer science at university in the UK. *Education and Information Technologies, 27*(3), 3079–3105.

Young, E., Wajcman, J., & Sprejer, L. (2023). Mind the gender gap: Inequalities in the emergent professions of artificial intelligence (AI) and data science. *New Technology, Work and Employment*, 1–24.

Pre-service Teachers' Pedagogical Awareness of Technology Integration in the Classroom 7

Chikondi Sepula and Clement Simuja

Introduction

Pre-service teachers often take content and methods courses, but these do not always focus enough on the overlap between these subjects when it comes to teaching with the aid of technology. As a result, a visible discrepancy exists between understanding what to teach and actively implementing technology in the teaching process (McGarr & Gallchóir, 2020; Billington, 2023). Billington's (2023) intervention study on pre-service teachers' development of technological pedagogical content knowledge via technology integration provides an interesting insight. This suggests that the teaching methods used by educators might differ from the way they learned the subject in their own student years. He further asserts that acquiring subject matter knowledge with the use of technology significantly deviates from learning to instruct using the same technology. To enhance proficiency in technology integration, various scholars emphasize exploring the pedagogical choices made by teachers and how technological integration should affect these decisions (Mishra & Koehler, 2008; Anderson & Putman, 2022). They advocate that pre-service teachers ought to nurture an evolved, comprehensive understanding of practical teaching with technology (Booker, 2017). Additionally, a comprehensive investigation into efficacious technology

DOI: 10.4324/9781003406631-7

integration necessitates recognition and acknowledgement of the present circumstances and obstructions hindering technological uptake in classrooms.

In response, South Africa's Department of Basic Education has instigated educational tech in public schools to supplement teacher resources. However, a sense of insufficiency and lack of confidence in technology integration persists (Kola, 2021). This may result from their pre-service training's limited demonstration of practical applications. Even though initial teacher programs are now incorporating technology, research demonstrates that many future teachers still feel ill-equipped and poorly supported in exploiting its benefits (Chigona & Chigona, 2013; Mabaso et al., 2023).

Existing literature indicates that most pre-service teachers struggle with constructivist ways of technology use in teaching (Kusaeri & Aditomo, 2019; Mabaso et al., 2023). Past studies such as that of Tanase and Dinsmore (2023) find that technology is underused in effective instructional approaches like student-centric education. This highlights a gap between expected and realized roles of pre-service teachers, questioning current teacher training programs' efficacy. Changes are required for better training in technology integration. A deeper comprehension of technology's role in education necessitates that both teacher educators and pre-service teachers display effective technological pedagogies.

This is vital to ensure pre-service teachers transcend traditional methods, shifting toward more innovative and interactive approaches. Regrettably, many pre-service teachers tend to mimic their own learning experiences, thereby neglecting the need for instructional evolution driven by technology (Mabaso et al., 2023). Consequently, this study aims to explore the encounters of pre-service teachers within the Computer Application and Technology (CAT) method course. Specifically, it delves into their practicum teaching experience to identify their pedagogical choices, implementation, and reflection associated with technology integration and how the pre-service teachers and we as researchers reflected on this phenomenon. The study is led by the research question: What are the lived experiences of pre-service teachers in the Computer Application and Technology methods course regarding their pedagogical awareness and understanding of technology integration during their practicum teaching experiences?

To answer the research question, the chapter first introduces the context for the study. Then it reviews a broad range of literature related to the research to achieve the objective matter. It also introduces a theoretical framework to drive the study. Following this, the research methodology, encompassing data collection and analysis, is thoroughly discussed. Results and discussions are subsequently explored in detail. Finally, the study concludes with a presentation of the study's conclusions and recommendations.

Research Context

The research was conducted at an Eastern Cape university in South Africa, involving four students from the Postgraduate Certificate in Education (PGCE) course. This course trains graduates from non-education majors aiming to teach two subjects. They specialize in one subject for grades 7–9, the Senior Phase, and another for grades 10–12, the Further Education and Training Phase. All four participants chose Computer Applications Technology as their second methods subject.

In 2020, our university's PGCE program introduced a technology-focused and constructivist teaching approach. Adopting a strategy to equip CAT student educators with necessary competencies for effective teaching, our approach was guided by Tunjera's (2019) finding that pre-service teacher training often lacks technological integration. We aimed to enhance technology integration within teacher training, which we believe, following the TPACK framework of Mishra and Koehler (2006), would provide teachers with more interrelated and profound knowledge, useful for their instructional practice.

Moreover, the study was built around the idea that research exploring how these pre-service teachers gain pedagogical awareness through teaching practice and insights gathered could enhance existing educational strategies and optimize the overall curriculum of our PGCE programme. This premise could also guide us to understand when and how our pre-service teachers incorporate technology into secondary CAT classrooms. Unlike others in educational technology, our research offers a unique approach, exploring these pedagogical decisions from a phenomenological perspective.

Overview of Literature

Teacher training programs play a pivotal role in integrating technology into teaching. They develop the educational philosophy of future teachers and knowledge to incorporate technology into their practices (Mishra & Koehler, 2006; Bueno et al., 2023). The successful incorporation of these skills into teacher education practice lies heavily on the teacher educators, necessitating their scrutiny to ensure coherence and modelling technological pedagogical content knowledge integration in the teacher education programme. By doing so, they will better prepare their trainee teachers by utilizing a constructivist teaching approach (Assadi & Hibi, 2020). Engaging in this level of experience allows pre-service teachers to start constructing their own knowledge while considering the advantages of successfully incorporating the technological pedagogical model into their classrooms.

Echoing Assadi and Hibi's (2020) advice, this can also encourage trainee teachers to experience the constructivist approach firsthand. This practice will likely be a significant part of their teaching in the future classroom. Nevertheless, additional efforts are required specifically for pre-service CAT teachers to bridge the gap between their technology knowledge and its application, particularly the incorporation of technology in their teaching practices. Therefore, both the understanding and the practical application of integrating technology remain a work in progress within the sphere of teacher preparation.

Even though specific studies about technology's influence on pre-service teachers' pedagogical choices are scanty, research indicates technology in classrooms can be beneficial. Kartal and Dilek (2021) observed its usage in an effective learning environment, while Chevalier et al. (2020) confirmed its role in cultivating scientific thinking, such as problem-solving.

Building on the idea of technology's positive influences, Kola (2021) argues that teachers with a good grasp of technology, content, and pedagogy, as defined by the TPACK framework (Mishra & Koehler, 2008), are better prepared to effectively use student-centered, technological tools. We concur with Kola's assertion that deep understanding of the reciprocal relationship among content, knowledge, and technology aids teachers in making knowledgeable decisions about the strategic use of technology. For instance, it helps in choosing suitable tools and creating efficient strategies. This knowledge notably boosts pedagogical awareness. Evidence strongly suggests that technology improves both student learning and teachers' pedagogical skills. Despite the benefits, more research is needed to explore how technology influences the pedagogical choices of CAT pre-service teachers, a currently understudied area.

Teacher training programs, such as the PGCE, profoundly influence pre-service teachers' ability to incorporate technology, based on our experience as teacher educators. Similarly, Booker (2017) noted a mismatch between pre-service teachers' education and classroom teaching, especially in technology integration. Booker observed that the pre-service teachers' technology integration significantly was influenced by the practices they encounter during their practical teaching in schools. Such experiences present an opportunity for linking theory and practice and cultivating their pedagogical thoughts in a technology-inclusive environment.

Furthermore, Booker (2017) highlights the need for reflective learning in teacher training, with a focus on technology integration. Apeanti's (2016) study aligns, citing the positive relationship between the positive predisposition towards technology integration among pre-service teachers and exposure to technology-enriched settings. This emphasizes a need for teacher training to mirror real classroom settings, bridging the gap between theoretical learning and practical application. This could foster effective technology integration in classrooms. Additionally, we argue that a learning experience alongside practical technology application during training can significantly enhance pre-service teachers' attitudes towards future classroom technology use.

Theoretical Framework

The TPACK theory, proposed by Mishra and Koehler (2006, 2008), integrates teachers' understanding of technology, their teaching methods, and particular subjects. This perspective is based on Shulman's (1986) concept that teachers need Pedagogical Content Knowledge. TPACK connotes how technology corresponds to subject knowledge and teaching methods through three main knowledge domains: Content Knowledge, Pedagogical Knowledge, and Technology Knowledge. Their interaction facilitates further comprehension in PCK, TK, PK, TCK, TPK, and TPCK, emphasizing the contextual dependencies of these areas and the singular inadequacy of any technology in every teaching situation.

This study rests on the premise that the integration of technology by pre-service teachers in their teaching-learning activities bolsters their pedagogies. The model of TPACK is intricately tied to context, entailing a unique set of internal and external influences (Harris & Hofer, 2014).

As such, it is crucial to acknowledge the context-dependent nature of this model. The current study employs TPACK as a framework for understanding pre-service teachers' pedagogical awareness and technology integration during their practicum teaching experiences.

Methodology

In this study, a phenomenological approach (Hallett, 1995), a specific type of qualitative research, was utilized. The essence of phenomenological research rests in the exploration of human experiences from the perspectives of those who live them (Creely, 2018). This method requires the researcher to venture into the internal realms of each participant's lived experiences to comprehend how they perceive a certain phenomenon (Creely, 2018). In this context, the study focused on engaging with four pre-service teachers, seeking to unearth their day-to-day experiences in the classroom following the integration of technology into their teaching practices. The method employed was transcendental phenomenology (Eddles-Hirsch, 2015), which provided an avenue to examine the facets of integrating technology into pedagogy through a qualitative case study approach. This method allowed for profound exploration and description of the participants' experiences, offering important insights into the dynamics between technology and teaching practices in the classroom setting.

This research used a case study (Merriam, 1988) approach to explore the teaching strategies and perspectives of pre-service CAT teachers during their practicum. Specifically, we focused on their use and incorporation of technology in teaching. The participants were purposefully chosen pre-service CAT teachers from a PGCE course at a South African university. The data collection process included semi-structured interviews, classroom observations, and focus group discussions. The second author meticulously observed two distinct lessons from each participating individual. The interviews and focus group discussions were audio-recorded.

Semi-structured interviews with open-ended questions were used for their versatility, enabling in-depth exploration of the subjects' perspectives and experiences. Email was used to share these questions in advance, allowing for comprehensive understanding and thoughtful responses. Post-practicum, a 90-minute focus group discussion provided a platform to discuss their teaching, learning, and research experiences guided by the first author. Participants joined voluntarily and were encouraged to share experiences without any pressure or deceit.

The study was approved by the Provincial Education Department and our university prioritized ethical practices. Participants voluntarily participated, with the freedom to withdraw at any time. Transparent communication, clear instructions, detailed informed consent, and rigorous adherence to ethical standards ensured participant understanding and rights.

In order to respect and fulfil the requests of the study's participants, their clan names were used. The individuals who took part in this study were identified as Maphanga, a female, Mabena, Mavuso, and Mbuyazi, all of whom are males. Utilizing clan names rather than pseudonyms was done not only to respect the culture and preferences of the participants but also to maintain anonymity. This approach aligns with ethical guidelines for conducting research at our institutions, which mandate the protection of subjects' identities unless explicitly permitted by them. Furthermore, using clan names in this study also reinforced their societal roles and statuses within the clan system, an aspect that was crucial in interpreting the findings more holistically.

Data Analysis

The research utilized a thematic analysis approach (Clarke et al., 2015) to identify, organize, analyze, and report patterns and themes within the collected data. This process encompasses distinct stages, including transcription, organization, coding, analysis, and interpretation. However, it was not linear but rather complex, iterative, and reflexive instead. For instance, the process of interpretation and analysis commenced during the interviews and focus group discussion as potential themes and codes started to emerge. The recorded interviews were transcribed using Microsoft Word software and analyzed with NVivo version 22 data analysis software, known for its versatility, robustness, and credibility. In accordance with the process of identifying, arranging, and interpreting codes, categories, and themes, as described by Creswell and Tashakkori (2007), the thematic analysis facilitated a comprehensive analysis of the gathered data. This also allowed the understanding of the concepts, classifications, and patterns evident in the data. Recurrent occurrences in the dataset as expressed by participants were used to generate codes. Through merging comparable codes, groupings and patterns were established and analyzed (Merriam, 1988), and relevant information was conveyed using verbatim quotes.

Findings from the Study

The findings of the study emerged from analysis of pre-service CAT teachers' pedagogical awareness, choices, implementation, and reflection associated with technology integration in their teaching methods. The main themes that emanated from the study were (a) the purposeful utilization of technology in classroom settings, variations in technology usage among selected pre-service teachers; (b) the significance of the experience of practicum teaching and pedagogical awareness and choices related to technology integration, and (c) researchers' perception of participants' technological pedagogical content knowledge.

Utilizing Technology Purposefully in Classroom Settings

Each of the participants was placed in a public school that had some technologies installed to support teaching and learning. The common technologies available in these schools were desktop computers, laptops, printers, Internet, tablets, projectors, computer laboratories, interactive whiteboards, and educational software, such as Microsoft Office, Google Suite, digital textbooks, and other learning applications. Two schools use Google Classroom, which allows for the uploading of course content and interaction between students and teachers.

The participants in this study all used technology in their teaching methods; however, significant variations were noticed in how each one implemented these technologies. For instance, Maphanga, Mbuyazi, and Mavuso all had access to technology in their respective schools, and noticeable differences were observed in their respective implementation and usage in their teaching methodologies. The three participants incorporated technology into their CAT classroom routine consistently. A notable expression from Mavuso was that:

Using different types of technology in my lessons helps a lot in improving the learning process. I use things like PowerPoint to provide presentations that are attractive and full of pictures. I also use phones, tablets, and internet resources to organize exciting activities, use different types of teaching materials, and expose students to so much more knowledge. Interestingly, when technology was employed, PowerPoint emerged as the preferred tool. Pre-service teachers utilized personal laptops, connected to school-provided projectors, to deliver detailed presentations featuring notes, diagrams, and videos. Regardless of this usage, observation of their lesson suggested an improved consistent adoption of technology-enhanced teaching methods in both lessons. Student-centered teaching was the dominant method observed, using online interactive activities, and gamification technologies such as Kahoot! were also intermittently incorporated into the lessons.

While both participants effectively incorporated YouTube videos into their teaching methodologies, the observational data revealed a nuanced divergence in the pedagogical roles they assigned to the video content. Mabena considered YouTube videos as a fundamental component of instruction. The videos served dual purposes to Mabane: they delivered core content and simultaneously supplemented content with real-world applications. His use of YouTube videos during the "Networks and Internet" lesson exemplifies this notion, where students were inspired to justify and articulate their insights on how visuals in the video selected best symbolized the concepts under study.

Conversely, Maphanga utilized YouTube videos to underpin and reinforce pre-existing textual content and prescribed images. The videos, in her approach, were complementary tools, fortifying concepts formerly presented. She observed that this method triggered elevated engagement levels among students as they attentively followed the videos. This could be attributed to the captivating power of visual aids and multimedia content in education, a fact corroborated by several education studies (Kimber & Wyatt-Smith, 2006; Kirkwood & Price, 2012).

This difference in perception highlights the potential flexibility and reflexive use of technology in CAT instructional practices. Maphanga commented during the focus group discussion:
When I make use of technology for my lessons, I always try to identify possible issues and make them clear for my personal understanding before I show it to my students. After the first lesson, I look at both the good and bad aspects, then I adjust small things in the future lessons. The comment shows that Maphanga's teaching strategies have a reflexive element that led to positive changes in how she teaches. Similarly, Mbuyazi showed a determined mindset in including technology tools in his teaching. He admitted he understood the students' responses about the different technology resources he chose to use. This feedback helped him decide if he should keep using a specific tool or look for other options to enhance the learning space.

In the context of his decision-making process about technology usage in the classroom, Mbuyazi described how he navigates. His reflection and decision-making process were guided by the responses and the needs of the students, showcasing the fluidity and adaptability of his teaching technique to the advantage of the learners. His approach not only validates student feedback but also promotes a more inclusive and responsive teaching environment.

The comment indicated a level of reflexivity to Maphanga's teaching that created positive changes in her instruction. Mbuyazi was also intentional about his approach to technology integration. He indicated that he was cognizant of the feedback from students about the various technologies he chose to integrate and whether he would continue using them or look for alternatives to enhance the learning experience. When explicitly asked about his procedural approach toward employing technology-based tools in the classroom, Mbuyazi expressed:

I think about the exact way I will apply it in my lessons, the right time and method to use it, how to make the students understand its use and role in the class, and also how to relate the technology to the objective of lessons, available soft content and to meet CAPS curriculum standard. Mbuyazi's comment aligns with the viewpoints of other participants, suggesting that he does not see technology integration as an independent element. Instead, he suggests it seamlessly becomes part of the structure of his instructional design and delivery.

Significance of Technology in Fostering Student Active and Engaged Learning Interest within the Classroom

The participants expressed a distinct understanding of the importance of engagement throughout the study. Each participant served as a crucial figure in fostering an effective learning environment for the students, particularly in the subject of CAT. The incorporation of technologies in pedagogical practices enhanced the students' ability to engage with and derive value from technologies. This was achieved by encouraging students to access, choose, establish, and interpret information independently. The adept integration of technologies addressed certain individual learning requirements, offering innovative solutions to a wide array of learning queries. In this context, Mavuso reflected on the supportive essence of technology for pre-service CAT teachers, referring specifically to his own experiences:

I find it better and simpler to use internet videos, like those on Youtube, to explain certain parts of my lessons. This is because CAT subject textbooks don't clearly explain some of the concepts. Besides, getting local materials for teaching is also quite expensive. In an attempt to captivate student interest at the commencement of a lesson, Maphanga employs videos, identifying them as technology capable of enriching lesson content. Maphanga's notion aligns with Mabena's perception, who regards these videos as instrumental in conveying subject matter and providing students with portrayals of real-life scenarios and situations. Moreover, Maphanga emphasizes the necessity for an educator to remain sensitive to and aware of the student's level of engagement with the class material and how the incorporation of technology can serve as a catalyst to amplify instructional engagement. Subsequently, during the interview, she expressed:

Students are the ones who use technology or take part in activities for learning. . . . They may understand the lesson, but if they don't find it enjoyable, it might not be as effective. Maphanga's adept use of technology seemed to foster continuous engagement among students, a fact that was particularly prominent during the observation of two lessons. Participants noted that the implementation of educational games such as Kahoot! not only hooked students' interest in the topic but also brought real-world examples into the CAT curriculum. The inclusion of multimedia elements, such as images, audio, and videos within Kahoot!, was reported to be highly effective in capturing learners' attention and sparking their interest to participate actively in lessons. However, the use of technology as a teaching aid is not without its drawbacks. According to Mbuyazi, there are risks of over-reliance on technologies, which could inadvertently dull students' critical thinking skills. This is particularly concerning for technical subjects, such as CAT, as students seem to develop a habit of learning using technological means rather than critically thinking and analyzing the core concepts. Furthermore, all participants acknowledged that any technical glitches disrupted the smooth flow of lessons and frustrated some learners.

Researchers' Perception of Participants' Technological, Pedagogical, and Content Knowledge

As participant observers, it was critical to examine the pedagogical consciousness of technology use from our viewpoint, contributing our unique perspectives to what was observed. It was noted that the pre-service teachers acknowledged an evolution in their understanding of technological pedagogical content knowledge throughout the study.

This evolution they attribute to their reflection on the application of technology in their instruction. However, it is essential to mention that the participants mainly utilized technology for a more traditional, direct instruction approach, not necessarily fostering the cooperative learning environments that could be more beneficial. The observed applications of technology within these CAT classrooms consisted predominantly of technology education-based games and video-based learning. This usage aligns closely with Mishra and Koehler's (2006) definition of technological knowledge.

The participants in this study acknowledged the advantages of employing technology in the delivery of content. However, they did not differentiate whether their intention to integrate technology was influenced by the ability to develop or become conscious of other important knowledge areas, as proposed by Mishra and Koehler's (2006) TPACK framework.

The interaction between content knowledge and technology integration emerged as a significant theme in our analysis. The teaching practicum served as a practical test of the pre-service teachers' content knowledge. It not only reflects how they apply their theoretical knowledge in a classroom setting, but it is also the first clear evaluation of their comprehension as they embark on the teaching journey. Moreover, all participants noted that certain aspects of their content knowledge required clearing up prior to teaching their lessons. This underscores the importance of reflective practices in continual learning. Interestingly, we also found a reciprocal relationship between content knowledge and technology integration. The participants did not only see their content knowledge influencing their use of technology in lessons, but they also found that the technology used reciprocally influenced their understanding and application of their content knowledge. Therefore, the relationship between technology integration and content knowledge in this study was not unidirectional but complex and multifaceted.

Maphanga and Mavuso articulated a critical aspect of their experience as they stated that they lack practical content knowledge in the CAT subject. Interestingly, they attributed this challenge to an overreliance on YouTube videos. It is worth mentioning that Mavuso reported that utilizing online resources as a supplement for additional content and becoming adept at Google Classroom, which is used at the school, reduced his study time for lesson preparation. This observation sheds significant light on the pedagogical implications of technology integration. All participants acknowledged the benefits of effectively merging technology in their teaching, underscoring the critical role of technological pedagogical content knowledge (TPCK), which was heavily influenced by their existing content knowledge.

Discussion and Conclusion

We aimed to understand how initial pedagogical awareness resulting from technology integration by pre-teachers' methods in a CAT practicum and how this phenomenon was experienced and interpreted by participants, including us.

This study's focus on pedagogical awareness aligns with the emphasis placed by Hofer and Harris (2010) on the crucial role teacher understanding plays in connecting curriculum-based learning goals to technology-specific tools. Hofer and Harris (2010) highlight the influence of specific technologies on teaching and learning processes. They advocate for an approach where teachers choose technologies based on the demands of learning activities. In this model, the emphasis is on the instructional needs of content-specific learning rather than on the inherent characteristics of the technologies. This way the technology is integrated into the learning process as opposed to being the focal point. Pedagogical awareness was employed in this research in a tactical manner. This allowed the researchers to investigate the ways in which the pre-service teachers made choices about the selection, use, and rationalization of technology in their CAT teaching strategies.

In this research, all of the participants were assigned to public secondary schools with technology resources available. This environment stimulated thoughtful self-inspection in the teacher trainees, encouraging them to examine their choices while using technology in a teaching setting. From this self-reflection, they were able to glean deeper insights into their methods, which led to more informed explanations, clarifications, and teaching suggestions. This reflective practice enhanced their pedagogical consciousness, providing insight into what components to integrate, how to do so, and why they made these specific choices for their CAT instruction. This aligns with Sari et al.'s (2021) assertion that within the realm of teaching with technology, reflective practice serves as an instrumental step in fostering a teacher's Technological Pedagogical Content Knowledge (TPACK). Not only does this practice inspire innovative problem-solving, but it also cultivates a deeper understanding of how technology can be integrated into teaching and learning (Hofer & Harris, 2010).

The growing comprehension of technologies integrated in teaching underscores the significance of nurturing technological pedagogical content knowledge understanding in pre-service teachers. As they were developing a better grasp on combining technological resources with pedagogy and content, they exhibited a more nuanced teaching approach. The participants' decisions regarding the selection of specific technologies to incorporate into their CAT lessons revealed significant insights into their pedagogical awareness. Essential platforms that participants engaged with included Kahoot!, YouTube videos, Google Classroom, PowerPoint presentations, and more. The use of these technologies offered participants the opportunity to gauge the effectiveness of each platform in delivering their instruction.

During the duration of the teaching practicum, the level of technology integration among the participants remained largely consistent. Nevertheless, it was only during the focus group discussion that they considerably improved in elucidating their rationale for certain technology choices and how they influenced teaching. This critical pedagogical understanding was particularly evident in the case of Mbuyazi, who was noteworthy within the focus group discussion. He expressed that the specific technology he used both augmented and hindered his lessons, contingent on the students' reception and technological comprehension. His commentary offered diverse viewpoints on technology. He suggested that the implemented technology not only enhanced his lesson but, at times, became the lesson itself. He utilized technology as a means to enhance his instruction. Mbuyazi and other participants' comments resonate with Santos and Castro's (2021) study suggesting that pre-service teachers' understanding and development of TPCK improve during their teaching internship. However, they found that more exposure and experience beyond the internships can further enhance their TPCK understanding.

Regrettably, the technology integration in the classroom in this study did not meet the hoped-for expectations of being centered around students and constructive learning methods. This aligns with the study by Shambare and Simuja (2022), which notes that in most schools in South Africa, technology usage for educational purposes remains limited primarily to basic tasks. Although every participant in the study provided chances for students to learn using and through technology, there is still room for improvement to encourage more meaningful learning experiences, as suggested by Tunjera and Chigona (2020). The various technological tools used in teaching not only defined what they taught but also how they integrated technology into their teaching methods.

From the study's findings, we recommended that pre-service teachers should be encouraged to cultivate their technological pedagogical content knowledge to enhance their understanding of effective technology integration in teaching. Furthermore, implementing student-centered technology strategies should be advisable, as they improve student engagement and enrich learning outcomes. Regular practice of reflective teaching can facilitate this proficiency development, providing pre-service teachers with the means to examine and refine their pedagogical understanding and technological usage. Therefore, it is pivotal that teacher education programs such as PGCE incorporate these elements to adequately prepare future educators for technology-rich learning environments.

References

Anderson, S. E., & Putman, R. S. (2022). Elementary special education teachers' thinking while planning and implementing technology-integrated lessons. *Education and Information Technologies*, 1–23.

Apeanti, W. O. (2016). Contributing factors to pre-service mathematics teachers' e-readiness for ICT integration. *International Journal of Research in Education and Science*, *2*(1), 223–238.

Assadi, N., & Hibi, W. (2020). Developing pre-service teachers' mathematics TPACK through an integrated pedagogical course. *Creative Education*, *11*(10), 1890.

Billington, B. (2023). *A case study: Exploring pre-service teachers' readiness for teaching in K-12 online learning environments while enrolled in a university-based teacher preparation program* [Doctoral dissertation, Drexel University].

Booker, S. (2017). *The evolution of pre-service teachers TPACK after completing an undergraduate technology integration course* [Doctoral dissertation, Kennesaw State University].

Bueno, R., Niess, M. L., Engin, R. A., Ballejo, C. C., & Lieban, D. (2023). Technological pedagogical content knowledge: Exploring new perspectives. *Australasian Journal of Educational Technology*, *39*(1), 88–105.

Chevalier, M., Giang, C., Piatti, A., & Mondada, F. (2020). Fostering computational thinking through educational robotics: A model for creative computational problem solving. *International Journal of STEM Education*, *7*(1), 1–18.

Chigona, A., & Chigona, W. (2013). South African pre-service teachers' teachers' under-preparedness to teach with information communication technologies. In *2013 second international conference on e-learning and e-technologies in education (ICEEE)* (pp. 239–243). IEEE.

Clarke, V., Braun, V., & Hayfield, N. (2015). Thematic analysis. *Qualitative Psychology: A Practical Guide to Research Methods, 3*, 222–248.

Creely, E. (2018). "Understanding things from within": A Husserlian phenomenological approach to doing educational research and inquiring about learning. *International Journal of Research & Method in Education, 41*(1), 104–122.

Creswell, J. W., & Tashakkori, A. (2007). Differing perspectives on mixed methods research. *Journal of Mixed Methods Research, 1*(4), 303–308.

Eddles-Hirsch, K. (2015). Phenomenology and educational research. *International Journal of Advanced Research, 3*(8).

Hallett, C. (1995). Understanding the phenomenological approach to research. *Nurse Researcher, 3*(2), 55–65.

Harris, J., & Hofer, M. (2014, March). The construct is in the eye of the beholder: School districts' appropriations and reconceptualizations of TPACK. In *Society for Information Technology & Teacher Education International Conference* (pp. 2519–2526). Association for the Advancement of Computing in Education (AACE).

Hofer, M., & Harris, J. (2010). Differentiating TPACK development: Using learning activity types with inservice and pre-service teachers. In *Society for information technology & teacher education international conference* (pp. 3857–3864). Association for the Advancement of Computing in Education (AACE).

Kartal, T., & Dilek, I. (2021). Pre-service science teachers' TPACK development in a technology-enhanced science teaching method course. *Journal of Education in Science Environment and Health, 7*(4), 339–353.

Kimber, K., & Wyatt-Smith, C. (2006). Using and creating knowledge with new technologies: A case for students-as-designers. *Learning, Media and Technology, 31*(1), 19–34.

Kirkwood, A., & Price, L. (2012). The influence upon design of differing conceptions of teaching and learning with technology. In *Informed design of educational technologies in higher education: Enhanced learning and teaching* (pp. 1–20). IGI Global.

Kola, M. (2021). Pre-service teachers' action research: Technology education lesson planning in a South African University. *Educational Action Research, 29*(1), 99–117.

Kusaeri, K., & Aditomo, A. (2019). Pedagogical beliefs about critical thinking among Indonesian mathematics pre-service teachers. *International Journal of Instruction, 12*(1), 573–590.

Mabaso, N., Tiba, C., Condy, J., & Meda, L. (2023). WhatsApp as an educational tool: Perspectives of pre-service teachers. *Technology, Pedagogy and Education, 32*(4), 521–536.

McGarr, O., & Ó Gallchóir, C. (2020). Exploring pre-service teachers' justifications for one-to-one technology use in schools: Implications for initial teacher education. *Technology, Pedagogy and Education, 29*(4), 477–490.

Merriam, S. B. (1988). *Case study research in education: A qualitative approach.* Jossey-Bass.

Mishra, P., & Koehler, M. J. (2006). Technological pedagogical content knowledge: A framework for teacher knowledge. *Teachers College Record, 108*(6), 1017–1054.

Mishra, P., & Koehler, M. J. (2008). *Introducing technological pedagogical content knowledge* (Vol. 1, p. 16). Annual Meeting of the American Educational Research Association.

Santos, J. M., & Castro, R. D. (2021). Technological pedagogical content knowledge (TPACK) in action: Application of learning in the classroom by pre-service teachers (PST). *Social Sciences & Humanities Open, 3*(1), 100110.

Sari, Y. R., Drajati, N. A., & So, H. J. (2021). Enhancing EFL teachers' technological pedagogical content knowledge (TPACK) competence through reflective practice. *TEFLIN Journal: A Publication on the Teaching & Learning of English, 32*(1).

Shambare, B., & Simuja, C. (2022). A critical review of teaching with virtual lab: A panacea to challenges of conducting practical experiments in science subjects beyond the COVID-19 pandemic in rural schools in South Africa. *Journal of Educational Technology Systems, 50*(3), 393–408.

Shulman, L. S. (1986). Those who understand: Knowledge growth in teaching. *Educational Researcher, 15*(2), 4–14.

Tanase, M., & Dinsmore, D. (2023). Mapping the interrelations between pre-service teachers' beliefs and knowledge of learning to their principles of effective instruction. *Journal of School and Educational Psychology, 3*(1), 1–21.

Tunjera, N. (2019). *Teacher educators' instructional strategies in preparing pre-service teachers to teach with digital technology in the 21st century* [Doctoral dissertation, Cape Peninsula University of Technology].

Tunjera, N., & Chigona, A. (2020). *Assisting teacher educators with constructive technology integration into curriculum delivery in the 21st century* (pp. 12–18). Conference of the South African Institute of Computer Scientists and Information Technologists. https://dl.acm.org/doi/10.1145/3410886.3410900

Exploration of Foundation Phase

8

Pre-service Teachers' Perspectives on Their Abilities to Integrate Technology in the Classroom

Clement Simuja

Introduction

The advancements in Information and Communication Technologies (ICT) has necessitated the incorporation of these technologies into education systems, leading to significant transformation in educational perspectives and delivery methods. In particular, teacher education programs in South Africa and other countries are shifting toward technology integration, which goes beyond just providing teachers with technical skills but makes them competent in deploying relevant technologies in actual classroom settings (Chigona & Chigona, 2013; Dewa & Ndlovu, 2022). Tiba and Condy (2021) point out a disparity between what pre-service teachers are taught and how they actually utilize technology in the classroom. This disparity is largely attributed to a lack of competence and readiness to use technology for teaching. Most pre-service teachers may understand the theoretical usage of technology but struggle to implement it effectively within a dynamic classroom environment. In South Africa, some studies indicate that pre-service teachers lacking technology experience feel unprepared to utilize technology effectively in the classrooms (Tiba & Cand, 2021; Pozas & Letzel, 2023). As a result, some

DOI: 10.4324/9781003406631-8

avoid using technology in teaching and learning, even when there is available technology infrastructure in schools (Tunjera, 2019). On top of this, each school has its unique suite of technologies, making it hard to ready teachers for every potential scenario. Considering these elements, Tunjerai (2019) proposes that teacher education should aim to foster a readiness in teacher trainees to blend technology into their teaching. Familiarizing them with various forms of technology and having hands-on practice can bolster this ability and confidence, thereby managing to integrate technology effectively (Dewa & Ndlovu, 2022).

To best prepare pre-service teachers, Piedade (2021) suggests that teacher educators need to support their students' technological abilities. I argue for a broader approach and suggest that it is important for teacher educators to delve into how their students envision using technology in their eventual teaching careers. This could potentially forecast how skillfully these future teachers will embed technology in their classrooms. Understanding pre-service teachers' abilities in utilizing educational technology is crucial given that the expectation for technology integration in teaching. Hence, this chapter focuses on a study exploring pre-service teachers' thoughts and feelings about their abilities to integrate technologies in teaching. The study thoroughly examined the existing methods used to encourage technology integration within the Bachelors of Education Foundation Phase (BEd FP) program. The primary aim was to pinpoint the chances provided to pre-service teachers to grasp the nuances of technology integration, intending to bolster the learning associated with the challenging task of seamlessly introducing technology into teaching.

Fostering Technology Integration in Teacher Training

The ability to use ICTs is seen as essential for both in-service and pre-service teachers who incorporate ICT into their teaching methods. Although experienced teachers may sometimes find it difficult to incorporate technology, this difficulty tends to be more evident for newly qualified teachers and pre-service teachers. These teachers, who are just entering the teaching profession, often find the integration of educational technologies into their classrooms to be a significant challenge (Tunjera, 2019; Tiba & Condy, 2021). On the other hand, experienced teachers might sometimes have high expectations of pre-service teachers' proficiency and comfort level with technology (Dewa & Ndlovu, 2022). Although many pre-service teachers are used to applying technology for private and social use (Liza & Andriyanti, 2020), their exposure to educational technologies remains limited. Moreover, they might not have considered incorporating personal technologies into teaching procedures (Tiba & Condy, 2021). Even if the expectations of their technological skills might be demanding, new teachers must be ready to embed technology into their teaching methods (Tunjera, 2019).

Recent studies report that technology is becoming an integral part of teaching and learning in primary and secondary education levels (Martins & Wangenheim, 2022; Pozas & Letzel, 2023). Particularly in developing countries such as South Africa, skills for integrating technology are gradually becoming essential for both in-service and pre-service teachers (Tiba & Condy, 2021). Kaufman (2014) explored the challenges faced by novice teachers and discovered that many felt unprepared for technology integration due to insufficient training during their pre-service programs. These results highlight the need for teacher educators to consider the importance of technology in classroom settings and instil the necessary training to pre-service teachers. Simply put, teacher educators need to demonstrate effective technology use in their courses to prepare pre-service teachers for modern classrooms.

Research has indicated that the experiences pre-service teachers have with teacher educators during their training significantly impact their ability to incorporate technology into their future teaching practice (Niyibizi, 2021). Williams et al. (2022) emphasize that teacher educators need to demonstrate the use of technology, as this plays a crucial role in equipping future teachers with technological pedagogical content knowledge. Echoing this sentiment, a recent study by Niyibizi (2021) focused on understanding the role and effectiveness of modelling as a teaching strategy, particularly in the field of teacher education, revealing that teacher educators often use modelling as a key teaching strategy. Some pre-service teachers in the study noted that these modelling courses enhanced their understanding of how to combine technology with teaching methods and subject knowledge. Some of these teachers were even motivated to learn more about possible technologies to use in teaching. However, I argue that the effectiveness of these training programs depends on whether the pre-service teachers receive practical training in both personal and classroom use of ICT tools. Specifically, they should be taught to develop diverse learning resources suitable for the integration of digital technology in teaching and learning.

A study by Chaaban and Moloney (2016) investigated the preparedness and ability of teacher educators to effectively use technology to

Exploration of Foundation Phase **113**

achieve learning outcomes based on constructivist principles. They discovered that some teacher educators may not possess the necessary skills to show pre-service teachers how to achieve learning outcomes based on constructivism through technology. It was noted in certain situations that these educators focused more on content rather than on understanding technology. A study by Williams et al. (2022) focused on the teacher educators' competency in integrating technology. The study results indicated that many teacher educators do not possess the technological pedagogical content knowledge to demonstrate how pre-service teachers can achieve learning outcomes based on technology. This lack of competence in effectively using technology for teaching among teacher educators potentially leaves pre-service teachers under-prepared, hindering their ability to effectively integrate technology into their future teaching practices.

Research Context

The research setting was the final year class of the BEd FP (Grades R–3) program at a university in South Africa's Eastern Cape province. The university offers this four-year degree to train pre-service teachers to teach grades R–3 learners and instil values to shape responsible citizens of South Africa. It aims to equip these pre-service teachers with the necessary pedagogical knowledge to cater to learners from different social backgrounds. In the fourth year, students undertake compulsory subjects including language, mathematics, life skills, art, linguistics, teaching practice, and education studies. They also have the option to select additional second language endorsements, such as Afrikaans and isiXhosa. However, the BEd FP curriculum at the selected university has no dedicated educational technology course in the fourth year; instead, they model and infuse technology throughout all method courses. This approach allows for a more explicit link between technology and pedagogy and gives context to specific method content areas.

The strategy of modelling and enhancing technology integration within methods courses over three years seems to be accepted by some teacher educators. This may be because the teacher educators stress the importance of integrating technology in pedagogical methods. Moreover, the pre-service teachers were provided with laptops as part of a university initiative. This initiative was designed to enable students to participate in teaching and learning during the pandemic years of 2020 and 2021. Given the modern cultural expectation for teachers to integrate technology, it is important to understand pre-service teachers' perception of their confidence in using educational technology. Pre-service teachers play a critical role in the success of technology integration in teacher education programmes and schools; thus, gauging their perception of educational technology is essential before implementing any initiative (Niyibizi, 2021). Previous research indicates that the way pre-service teachers view educational technology greatly impacts its adoption and use in their classrooms. Therefore, this study posits that successful technology integration in education requires a comprehensive understanding and reflection on pre-service teachers' perception of their ability to use and integrate technology.

Theoretical Framework

The study adopted the TPACK framework developed by Mishra and Koehler (2006). The TPACK framework expands upon Shulman's previous work (1986). This framework provides a useful mechanism for understanding the knowledge, skills, and dispositions teachers require for effective technology integration into classrooms (Mishra & Koehler, 2006). The TPACK framework describes the intricate links between the spheres of technological knowledge, pedagogical knowledge, and content knowledge for beneficial tech integration. TPACK suggests that effective technology incorporation into teaching practices should consider these three areas: content, pedagogy, and technology – interrelated and active components that shape teaching (Mishra & Koehler, 2008). When these forms of knowledge intersect, both in theory and practice, they form flexible knowledge, which is crucial for successful technology integration in teaching. The knowledge aspects that result from TPACK are presented in further detail in Table 8.1.

The TPACK framework was initially set up to assist educators in equipping teachers with the necessary knowledge for integrating technology into learning (Mishra & Koehler, 2006). A large portion of current research using TPACK focuses on the training of pre-service teachers (Hofer & Harris, 2012; Tondeur et al., 2020). Some scholars employ TPACK to illustrate the growth of technology integration (Niess, 2011; Saubern et al., 2020). In contrast, others use it as a structure to create learning spaces that emphasize technology integration (Mishra & Koehler, 2008). Considering that this research was conducted in a teacher training

Table 8.1 The Seven Constructs in the TPACK Framework (Chai et al., 2011, p. 1184)

The Constructs	Abbreviation	Definitions
Content Knowledge	CK	Knowledge of subject matter
Technological Knowledge	TK	Knowledge of various technologies
Pedagogical Knowledge	PK	Knowledge of the processes or methods of teaching
Technological Content Knowledge	TCK	Knowledge of subject matter representation with technology
Technological Pedagogical Knowledge	TPK	Knowledge of using technology to implement different teaching methods
Pedagogical Content Knowledge	PCK	Knowledge of teaching methods for different types of subject matter
Technological Pedagogical Content Knowledge	TPACK	Knowledge of using technology to implement teaching methods for different types of subject matter

setup, the TPACK model offers an explanation for how the technological insights of the selected pre-service teachers suggest their abilities to integrate technologies in early education classrooms.

Methodology

The primary aim of this study was to understand how pre-service teachers at the foundational level perceive their abilities to integrate technology in classroom settings. A qualitative case-study research design (Merriam, 1988) was employed in alignment with the interpretive paradigm. This approach was chosen with a view to gathering detailed data to inform the research objective. The interpretive-phenomenological paradigm provides a lens to interpret perspectives and meanings through the subjective viewpoints of the participants (Thorne, 2014). Purposive and convenience sampling were employed based on the assumption that selected participants had gained requisite knowledge in technology, pedagogy, and content after having been guided by their teacher educators, and that they possessed an insightful understanding of the use of technology in teaching and learning (Campbell et al., 2020). The sample included seven pre-service teachers in their final year of the BEd FP degree at a university located in Eastern Cape, South Africa. The participants consist of two males, four females, and one who identifies as neutral, with ages ranging from 22–25 years old, and allocated code of PST 1 to PST7. Semi-structured interviews and sharing circle discussions were used to collect data.

To fully understand the perceptions of the selected pre-service teacher, the author intentionally put aside own beliefs and experiences as a teacher educator and focused on the participants' viewpoints. This ties into the research method of phenomenology, which values the exploration of conscious awareness through analyzing the relationship between individuals and technology (Shambare et al., 2022).

Data Collection and Analysis

Semi-structured interviews and sharing circle discussions were the primary methods of data collection. Merriam (1988) describes a semi-structured interview as a dynamic interaction among two or more people, giving rise to contextual results using open-ended questions. Sharing circles are a specific type of focus group practice rooted in indigenous perspectives where data is gathered through group dialogues (Lavallée, 2009; Rocke, 2015). In African settings and among indigenous communities, particularly in the Eastern Cape province where this study took place, individuals regularly form a circle, often around a fire, for discussions. Additionally, teachers frequently gather in a circle during breaks for conversations. In research, sharing circles serve to gather and share knowledge by drawing out people's experiences, thoughts, and viewpoints. The size of a sharing circle can range between three to twelve persons (Lavallée, 2009). For this study, seven participants were deliberately chosen to engage in one sharing circle. The sharing circle was facilitated by the author, who initiated discussions based on open-ended questions related to the research objectives. This approach allowed for a co-creative process where participants were free to share their experiences, thoughts, and viewpoints, thus enriching the data collected.

The author ensured the validity of the study by reviewing relevant literature and creating an initial semi-structured interview and sharing circle guide. These materials were refined using the insights of a subject matter expert. All seven purposively selected BEd FP pre-service teachers participated in semi-structured interviews, receiving the interview questions via email ahead of the interview. These interviews were conducted in person, with rigorous ethical safeguards in place and a duration of 30 minutes, and were audio-recorded for transcription. The one-on-one format of the interviews helped maintain the independence of the pre-service teachers' responses, preventing any influence from others' viewpoints. To create a comfortable environment and a balanced power dynamic, the author made it clear to the participants that he sought to understand their experiences ahead of the interviews. Furthermore, the author and the participants agreed on a mutually convenient time for the interviews and sharing circle.

The author utilized a thematic analysis technique for understanding patterns and themes in the collected data. This technique involved several stages, such as transcription, organization, coding, analysis, and interpretation. The process was not straightforward but complex and ongoing. The interviews conducted were transcribed in written text using Microsoft Word and analyzed with NVivo software, known for its reliable data analysis capabilities. This process aligns with the method highlighted by Peel (2020), allowing for a thorough study of the data collected. This paved the way for understanding various themes and categories in the data. The recurring instances in the data were marked as codes and similar codes were grouped together to establish categories and themes which were then interpreted (Peel, 2020).

Findings from the Study

Sense of Confidence to Effectively Integrate Technology in Teaching

The majority of the pre-service teachers (PSTs) involved in this study expressed a high level of confidence in their ability to use technology in a teaching context. Their perceptions were explored in order to gain insights into their first-hand perspectives on integrating technology in the classroom. Upon posing the question, "How sure are you in incorporating technology into your teaching methods?" it was observed that five out of the seven participants expressed a high degree of confidence. Interestingly, PST 3 and PST 5, respectively, provided further insights during their respective interviews:

I feel quite confident about integrating technology into my teaching methods. I see countless opportunities it offers. For example, I can utilize digital tools to create a more interactive and engaging atmosphere for

118 Clement Simuja

my students."I feel moderate confident about my capabilities in terms of integrating technology into my future classroom. Considering my experiences and knowledge, I have no doubt I can harness the potentials of technology to foster learning. The pre-service teachers conveyed a robust belief in their abilities, as demonstrated by their examples of potential applications of technology in their classrooms. The participant PST5, however, admitted to being in the process of building confidence for technology integration. A sense of moderate confidence was observed from three participants. PST6 was unique in expressing a keenness to expand her technological knowledge for teaching, as she felt less confident about it. Her desire to learn more was evidenced by her examples and reflective pauses during the sharing circle discussions:

For instance, I want to learn about innovative ways to incorporate technology in math activities, and language arts lessons. I believe this knowledge would help me design engaging and interactive lessons that truly enhance foundational phase learners learning. When asked how she could improve her ability to incorporate technology in her teachings, PST6 expressed a desire for more opportunities to learn from fellow pre-service teachers who use some technologies. Her comments align with the views of other pre-service teachers, demonstrating a growing confidence gained from participating in courses that demand teamwork using technology. They commented that certain assessments provided them with the chance to cooperate with peers in exploring technologies suitable for the foundation phase of their forthcoming teaching career. This rise in self-assuredness was common among six participants. Some voiced their confident readiness to use technology in teaching. Others regarded themselves as diligent learners, capable of acquiring the necessary skills to successfully integrate technological tools in teaching.

Pre-service Teachers Are Heavily Expected to Successfully Integrate Technology in Teaching

The pre-service teachers involved in this research expressed confidence in their ability to integrate technology in teaching. That said, they still felt a certain pressure to align with the perception of being digital natives due to their generation. Notably, five of them admitted to the presence of this stress, often attributed to their age. While some accepted this as a given, others questioned it. A few participants shared their viewpoint that their technology competence likely surpasses that of teacher educators and experienced in-service teachers. This, they believed, is due to their age and prior experiences. During the sharing circle discussion, PST7 commented: "most of my friends here and back home are good at using technologies". The perspective of PST7 was that he grew up in an urban environment and attended technology-rich private schools, and his unique educational experiences had inherently equipped him to integrate technology in teaching. This viewpoint was also corroborated by other participants, such as PST5, who validated the sentiments expressed by PST 7 on the issue:

I think we are really good with technology these days. Since I use my phone and laptop for most of my time . . . I am really at ease with utilizing technologies. During the sharing circle, some participants highlighted that they developed a strong dependency on the technologies they frequently used. This led to the perception among students that their technological competence had increased significantly. This was largely due to the university issuing laptops amidst the COVID-19 pandemic and the subsequent shift to online learning during academic years 2020 and 2021. This stance is common among pre-service teachers who view themselves as part of a technologically adept generation. Furthermore, they attribute their ability to perceive teaching using technology to their experience with technology throughout their lives.

Three student teachers acknowledged the pressure to integrate technology excellently into their methods, viewing it as a challenge rather than a deterrent. For example, PST3 shared during an interview that her early education spent in a rural, resource-limited school consisted mostly of traditional teaching tools like chalkboards and chalk. This led to limited exposure to technology integration during her formative educational years. She further expressed her worry that her language course tutor and peers expected her to possess technology skills and knowledge. Despite encountering such obstacles, PST3 understood that she was under pressure. However, she was determined to continuously strive to maintain her growth and prominence in learning the use of technology and technology integration in teaching.

The study found similar comments from other participants about their own learning experiences, indicating that their perceptions of technology integration might differ from those of their lecturers. In this instance, PST4 details his reflections regarding the technological pedagogical expertise of his Arts professor, simultaneously comparing it to his own. He expressed a strong aspiration to continue learning in order to prevent

120 Clement Simuja

the perceived deficiency common among many pre-service teachers. PST4 commented:

> I have noticed that our lecturers' way of using technology does not always match with what I know about using technology in teaching. This makes me question my own growing technology-teaching skills. . . . It also makes me think about how I will be able to use these tools and strategies more effectively in my own future classes.

PST4, similar to others, voiced worries due to the pressure to excel in any teaching environment, regardless of the technological resources present.

The majority of the participants revealed a sense of anticipation to incorporate technology into their teaching methods. Some, drawing from their experience and familiarity with technology from an early age, felt confident in their ability to do so. However, two participants felt uneasy as they believed they were inadequate in meeting these expectations. All participants acknowledged the importance of staying updated with technology integration to fulfil these demands effectively.

Possession of Technological Pedagogical Content Knowledge (TPACK) as a Crucial Competency

The pre-service teachers in this research emphasized the importance of technology knowledge to meet expectations for classroom integration. They stressed that knowing how the available technologies work is key. However, they also pointed out that simply having technology knowledge is not sufficient for effective technology integration. Apart from technology knowledge, they suggested that knowledge of how technology can be used pedagogically to enhance content delivery is equally essential. The discussions during the sharing circle affirm this perspective. When the participants were asked, "What supports your abilities and confidence in using technology for teaching?", their responses indicated that understanding and experiencing the technologies used in BEd FP teaching methods courses and content delivery significantly influences their integration of technology in education. PST5 expressed:

> In my Arts teaching method class we have learned a lot about different technologies. This has made me feel more at ease. I have

gotten better at using these tools and I found it easier to use them in my teaching during practice at Nombulelo high school.

In the same vein, PST2 reiterated similar sentiments, outlining:

throughout my everyday life as a BEd FP student, I believe myself to be proficient in utilizing the technology I need.

The comments from PST5 and PST2 offer a broad perspective on preservice teachers' understanding and confidence in employing technology in their everyday lives. The comparison of their ordinary technology use with its application in a classroom setting could differ significantly. For instance, while PST5 and PST2 regularly use technology for communication or entertainment in their personal life, they struggle to effectively apply it in a teaching context. However, confidence in teaching with technology can vary. PST4, as an example, described her confidence as moderate and recognized that her teaching practicum at a private school significantly helped her understand how to apply technology in teaching contexts. Specifically, her mentor teacher showed her how to integrate various technologies into life skills and isiXhosa instruction. These experiences aided her in drawing a connection between her technological knowledge and her pedagogical choices for teaching life skills and isiXhosa to early-grade learners.

Some participants discussed the relevance of combining technology and teaching methods, even if they did not identify themselves as highly skilled technology users. One particular participant, PST5, who is comfortable yet not expert with technology, recounts her experience with assisting a Grade-3 learner in English vocabulary and history subjects during teaching practicum. Her account was as follows:

The experience during the TP really opened my eyes. Many students came to ask me how to use different apps and software on their tablets.

Clearly, PST5 took pride in assisting learners in innovative technology use, built on her pre-existing technology skills. Even though she was confident about her everyday technology abilities, teaching practicum allowed her hands-on practice, enhancing her confidence in integrating technology within teaching.

122 Clement Simuja

Some participants revealed their understanding that despite their satisfactory base of technology knowledge, they recognize the necessity for continuous learning. Three participants, PST1, PST3, and PST4, highlighted the importance of ongoing technology learning, both during their pre-service teaching phase and into their future professional careers. PST4 and PST3, respectively, particularly shared thoughts about the need for continued learning regarding technology:

> us as teachers we should keep up with developments in technology. It is not about using the latest technology, but the most effective one. If a better technology is available, we should use it.
> I enjoy learning about new technology, engaging with it, and figuring how it works. However, with technology continually being developed, it becomes challenging to keep pace.

In this study, the pre-service teachers recognized the importance of continually updating their knowledge of technology due to its ever-evolving nature. Even though they have not joined the professional teaching community yet, they see ongoing technological learning as vital for their future careers. Collectively, they acknowledge the significance of technological pedagogical content knowledge for the successful integration of technology. Even though their understanding of technology varied, they understood its benefits in teaching. They realized the link between knowing about technology, teaching methods, and content knowledge. Reassuringly, even those who lacked confidence showed eagerness to learn more about technology, enabling them to incorporate it effectively into their future teaching practices.

Discussion

The study was designed with the objective of gaining insights into the perspectives of pre-service teachers about their abilities to integrate technology in their teaching methods. The findings reveal that these teachers were generally confident about teaching with technology. The pre-service teachers also felt an underlying pressure or expectation to be competent in teaching with technology, which pushed them to enhance their skills. Among the participants, five out of seven expressed facing this pressure. This pressure was largely self-imposed, however, and some participants felt it stemmed from their role within society in an era intertwined with technology. They believed that experienced teachers, learners in schools, and teacher educators (lecturers) held high expectations of them regarding technology proficiency. Several study respondents shared their teaching practicum experience about times when more experienced teachers expected them to help with technology-focused activities in the classroom. The responses to these expectations were mixed. Some participants were worried that their skills with technology might not be enough, whereas others used these expectations as motivation to improve their capability to meet these expectations.

Pre-service teachers' comments during the sharing circle discussions were about how technological, pedagogical, and subject matter knowledge contributes to incorporating technology in teaching. They understand that it is important, but pedagogical knowledge forms the root of this understanding. They recognize that being knowledgeable about technology is vital for its effective integration. They also state that pedagogical and content knowledge are crucial components in incorporating technology. A study by Mustafa (2016) correlates these views, stating that linking first-hand comprehension of technology with a grasp of pedagogy and content significantly impacts readiness for technology-mediated teaching. Participants noted that certain assessments and learning tasks in the BEd FP programme contribute to their mastery of pedagogical and content knowledge. These are the foundations necessary for them to efficiently blend technology in learning contexts.

Successful technological teaching experiences bolster efficacy for technology integration, as noted by Saubern et al. (2020). This idea is at the heart of the TPACK framework, which advocates for the merge of technological knowledge and pedagogical expertise in a certain subject context as an important tactic to understand effective technology integration. According to Mishra and Koehler (2008), this blend is pivotal in understanding the successful application of technology. Importantly, if self-assessment of technology integration capabilities aligns with the TPACK approach, it emphasizes the necessity for pre-service teachers to engage in practical experience with technology. To enhance their learning curve, these teachers should have a rich spectrum of opportunities to master various technology tools (Tiba & Condy, 2021).

Conclusion and Implications of the Study

The study concludes that most pre-service teachers in this study express substantial confidence in integrating technology into their teaching methods. Their firm belief in their own capabilities was supported by examples of how they planned to use technology in their own future teaching and classrooms. These pre-service teachers could see the potential benefits of using technology to create an engaging learning environment for their students. Some participants showed moderate confidence and an eagerness to further build their technological pedagogical content knowledge and skills. Nevertheless, some still felt they were in the process of building confidence, indicating a need for practical experience beyond theoretical understanding. The study reinforces the importance of practical experience with technology, alongside theoretical knowledge, to boost pre-service teachers' confidence and ability for future technology integration. It suggests that engaging teachers in a range of opportunities to grasp various technology tools can enhance their learning in technology integration. The alignment of pre-service teachers' self-assessment of technology integration capabilities with the TPACK framework underlines the crucial role of applied, hands-on experience.

The study underscores the important role of both theoretical knowledge and practical experience in building confidence and ability in pre-service teachers for future technology integration in the classroom. It also suggests that understanding pre-service teachers' self-perceptions and readiness to utilize technology can guide teacher educators in providing tailored, effective technology training, thus facilitating a smooth transition into modern, technology-infused teaching environments.

References

Campbell, S., Greenwood, M., Prior, S., Shearer, T., Walkem, K., Young, S., Bywaters D., & Walker, K. (2020). Purposive sampling: Complex or simple? Research case examples. *Journal of Research in Nursing*, *25*(8), 652–661.

Chaaban, Y., & Moloney, R. (2016). Educating pre-service teachers in technology use: A study of provision at Lebanese universities. *International Journal of Education*, *8*(2), 14–31.

Chai, C. S., Koh, J. H. L., Tsai, C. C., & Tan, L. L. W. (2011). Modeling primary school pre-service teachers' technological pedagogical content knowledge (TPACK) for meaningful learning with information and communication technology (ICT). *Computers & Education*, *57*(1), 1184–1193.

Chigona, A., & Chigona, W. (2013). South African pre-service teachers' teachers' under-preparedness to teach with information communication technologies.

In *2013 second international conference on e-learning and e-technologies in education (ICEEE)* (pp. 239–243). IEEE.

Dewa, A., & Ndlovu, N. S. (2022). Use of information and communication technologies in mathematics education lecturers: Implications for pre-service teachers. *Journal for Transdisciplinary Research in Southern Africa, 18*(1), 1–8.

Hofer, M., & Harris, J. (2012). TPACK research with inservice teachers: Where's the TCK? In *Society for information technology & teacher education international conference* (pp. 4704–4709). Association for the Advancement of Computing in Education (AACE).

Kaufman, K. (2014). Information communication technology: Challenges & some prospects from pre-service education to the classroom. *Mid-Atlantic Education Review, 2*(1).

Lavallée, L. F. (2009). Practical application of an Indigenous research framework and two qualitative Indigenous research methods: Sharing circles and Anishnaabe symbol-based reflection. *International Journal of Qualitative Methods, 8*(1), 21–40.

Liza, K., & Andriyanti, E. (2020). Digital literacy scale of English pre-service teachers and their perceived readiness toward the application of digital technologies. *Journal of Education and Learning (EduLearn), 14*(1), 74–79.

Martins, R. M., & Gresse Von Wangenheim, C. (2022). Findings on teaching machine learning in high school: A ten-year systematic literature review. *Informatics in Education, 22*(3).

Merriam, S. B. (1988). *Case study research in education: A qualitative approach.* Jossey-Bass.

Mishra, P., & Koehler, M. J. (2006). Technological pedagogical content knowledge: A framework for teacher knowledge. *Teachers College Record, 108*(6), 1017–1054.

Mishra, P., & Koehler, M. J. (2008). *Introducing technological pedagogical content knowledge* (Vol. 1, p. 16). Annual Meeting of the American Educational Research Association. https://www.scirp.org/reference/referencespapers?referenceid=1565931

Mustafa, M. E. I. (2016). The impact of experiencing 5E learning cycle on developing science teachers' technological pedagogical content knowledge (TPACK). *Universal Journal of Educational Research, 4*(10), 2244–2267.

Niess, M. L. (2011). Investigating TPACK: Knowledge growth in teaching with technology. *Journal of Educational Computing Research, 44*(3), 299–317.

Niyibizi, E. (2021). Modelling in teacher education: Beliefs of teacher educators in Rwanda. *African Journal of Teacher Education, 10*(1), 87–105.

Peel, K. L. (2020). A beginner's guide to applied educational research using thematic analysis. *Practical Assessment, Research, and Evaluation, 25*(1), 2.

Piedade, J. M. N. (2021). Pre-service and in-service teachers' interest, knowledge, and self-confidence in using educational robotics in learning activities. *Educação & Formação*, *6*(1).

Pozas, M., & Letzel, V. (2023). "Do you think you have what it takes?" Exploring predictors of pre-service teachers' prospective ICT Use. *Technology, Knowledge and Learning*, *28*(2), 823–841.

Rocke, C. (2015). The use of humor to help bridge cultural divides: An exploration of a workplace cultural awareness workshop. *Social Work with Groups*, *38*(2), 152–169.

Saubern, R., Henderson, M., Heinrich, E., & Redmond, P. (2020). TPACK-time to reboot? *Australasian Journal of Educational Technology*, *36*(3), 1–9.

Shambare, B., & Simuja, C. (2022). A critical review of teaching with virtual lab: A panacea to challenges of conducting practical experiments in science subjects beyond the COVID-19 pandemic in rural schools in South Africa. *Journal of Educational Technology Systems*, *50*(3), 393–408.

Shulman, L. S. (1986). Those who understand: Knowledge growth in teaching. *Educational Researcher*, *15*(2), 4–14.

Thorne, S. (2014). Applied interpretive approaches. In *The Oxford handbook of qualitative research* (Vol. 10). Oxford University Press.

Tiba, C., & Condy, J. (2021). Newly qualified teachers' integration of technology during curriculum delivery. *International Journal of Education and Practice*, *9*(2), 297–309.

Tondeur, J., Scherer, R., Siddiq, F., & Baran, E. (2020). Enhancing pre-service teachers' technological pedagogical content knowledge (TPACK): A mixed-method study. *Educational Technology Research and Development*, *68*, 319–343.

Tunjera, N. (2019). *Teacher educators' instructional strategies in preparing pre-service teachers to teach with digital technology in the 21st century* [Doctoral dissertation, Cape Peninsula University of Technology].

Williams, T., Sayed, Y., & Singh, M. (2022). The experiences of teacher educators managing teaching and learning during times of crises at one initial teacher education provider in South Africa. *Perspectives in Education*, *40*(2), 69–83.

Research-Based Teacher Preparation for Technology-Enhanced Education in Malawi

A Case Study

Foster Gondwe

Introduction

Globally, the problem of teacher knowledge as a barrier to teachers' use of technology prompts the question of how instructional technology is approached in teacher education programmes (Baran et al., 2019; Tondeur et al., 2018, 2012; Enochsson & Rizza, 2009; Kay, 2006). This chapter contributes a Malawian perspective to the growing body of knowledge about teacher preparation for technology-enhanced teaching and learning. Despite the prominence of instructional technology in Malawi, teachers' use of instructional technology is behind expectation, partly because teachers and student teachers have often reported to be under-prepared. Pre-service teachers in the country lack practical experiences of using technology, which limits student teachers' development of the required skills and knowledge for integrating technology. This is further compounded by the limited scope of the instructional technology modules in terms of content, lack of necessary teaching and learning resources such as computers, reliable internet, and other technologies.

DOI: 10.4324/9781003406631-9

A paradigm shift in pedagogy is required to engage pre-service teachers in more practical and authentic learning experiences.

Meanwhile, the literature suggests that research-based teacher education is one of the most effective strategies for preparing pre-service teachers in their future use of technology, as it can fill the gap between theory and practice in teacher education programmes (Tondeur et al., 2012). This chapter draws upon the case of the University of Malawi (UNIMA), one of the public teacher education institutions in Malawi, to illustrate a research-based approach to preparing teachers for technology-enhanced education. In this chapter, I present an example of Scholarship of Teaching and Learning (SoTL) practice that I implemented in an Instructional Technology course in the 2022–2023 academic year.

Context of the Study

This case study is bound within a four-year Bachelor of Education (B.Ed.) programme at UNIMA, which prepares secondary school teachers. Student teachers specialize in any of the following subject areas: Biology, Physics, Mathematics, Chemistry, Computer Science, History, Geography, Theology and Religious Studies, Languages (English, French or African Languages and Linguistics), and Social Studies. The student teachers undergo coursework (education foundations and teaching methodology courses) for four academic years and teaching practice for one term (which lasts for a minimum of three months). Graduates are expected to display characteristics that are relevant to improving the quality of secondary education in Malawi. For instance, graduates with a B.Ed. specializing in Biology are expected to display the following characteristics: knowledge and understanding; application and practice; generic cognitive skills; communication, ICT, and numeric skills; autonomy, accountability, and working with others (Chancellor College, 2016).

At UNIMA, institutional structures facilitating the use of instructional technology have emerged in line with specific functions that technology is expected to serve. For instance, the E-Learning centre has been focusing on using digital media for online instruction, while the ICT centre and ICT committee coordinate the use of ICT for general purposes, including teaching, research, and administration. The ICT centre was established in 2008 with the mandate to provide and support centralized ICT services to staff, students, and surrounding communities. The ICT policy provides the vision for ICT integration, which includes guiding "students, staff, faculty and research affiliates in their use of ICT systems in teaching, learning, research, consultancies and outreach in order to maximize benefits, capitalize on opportunities and gain a competitive advantage as a world-class ICT driven University" (University of Malawi, 2016, p. 7). The ICT centre offers technology training for students and faculty, resolves technical hiccups such as networks, and runs the day-to-day management of the University's information technology infrastructure.

In the B.Ed. programme, instructional technology is featured in multiple ways, which also certainly influences teacher educators' and student teachers' understanding of instructional technology (Tondeur et al., 2012; Kay, 2006). The B.Ed. specializing in Computer Studies is one of the strategies for incorporating instructional technology into the teacher education programme at UNIMA. Student teachers enrolled in this programme are expected to develop technical skills, such as setting up software solutions to support teaching and learning (Chancellor College, 2016). However, not all student teachers specialize in Computer Studies.

Another strategy, which is the focus of this case study, is a separate module called Instruction, Media and Technology. This 2-credit elective module introduces "basic principles of teaching and learning and to equip prospective teachers with skills of selecting, modifying, producing, designing, and utilising media for instructional purposes in order to make the teaching/learning process effective, efficient and humane" (Chancellor College Faculty of Education, n.d., p. 1). The module covers topics such as teaching and learning using locally available resources, systematic planning in the teaching/learning process, hands-on experience with the electronic equipment commonly used in the classroom, and design and production of instructional media. Student teachers also undergo micro teaching experience to practice using various instructional technologies. One of the core textbooks for the course is *Instructional technology and media for learning* by Smaldino et al. (Prentice Hall, 2005)

Problem Statement

Gondwe (2021) interviewed student teachers to understand their experiences with the Instructional Technology module offered at UNIMA. While acknowledging to have gone through the module, the interview data suggested student teachers' dissatisfaction with the fact that the module appeared once in the teacher education programme. The student teachers recommended the introduction of instructional technology in all courses:

> That technology course should not only just come once in 4 years. . . . What we learn in instructional technology should appear in all courses in education . . . like we have language teaching methods . . . for example, English. . . . There are many technologies that we can use to teach a language . . . but when we are learning how to teach language, they don't use instructional technology.
> (interview extract, as cited in Gondwe, 2021)

The above interview extract suggests that the students experienced problems with the curriculum and curricular organization, which they thought requires improvement. Gondwe's (2020) study also reported that the module was not preparing student teachers with the required skills and knowledge for integrating technology. This is because of its limited scope in terms of content, a situation that seems to be worsened by lack of necessary teaching and learning resources such as computers, reliable internet, and other technologies. Since I started teaching the course, my interaction with the student teachers has shown that the instructional technology module is more theoretical, which suggested the need to engage them in more practical and authentic learning experiences. Research-based teacher education is one of the effective strategies for preparing pre-service teachers in their future use of technology. As presented in the next section, research evidence and research activities by teacher educators can fill the gap between theory and practice in teacher education programmes.

Theoretical Perspective: Research-Based Teacher Education

Research-based teacher education is one of the reform efforts in teacher education around the world (Kosnik et al., 2016). Kosnik et al. (2016) suggest that research-based teacher education entails that teacher educators and education institutions should base their practice on research, as well as conduct research for accountability purposes. Infusing research into teacher education is important because learning to teach is challenging for student teachers and teachers who are relegated as receivers rather than contributors to knowledge creation. The literature shows that helping teacher candidates to frame themselves as researchers is crucial to their professional learning and innovation, and bridging the gap between the theory and practice of teaching (Munthe & Rogne, 2015; Puustinen et al., 2018). However, in the literature, there is no universally agreed-upon definition of research-based teacher education, as the meaning varies from programme to programme, and sometimes the concept is used interchangeably with inquiry-oriented or research-informed teacher education (Jakhelln et al., 2021).

Building upon the above-highlighted conceptualization of research-based teacher education and its rationale, in this case study I present a reflection on a research-based approach to teaching an Instructional Technology course for third-year B.Ed. students at UNIMA. The reflection is presented through the lens of SoTL as an example of research-based teacher education. There are several ways of understanding SoTL, and researchers in the field respect such diversity (Trigwell, 2013). However, SoTL models that reflect different conceptualizations of SoTL have several components in common, such as an understanding that scholarship of teaching is "about making transparent, for public scrutiny, how learning has been made possible" (Trigwell & Shale, 2004, p. 525). Moreover, Trigwell (2013) reports that researchers undertake SoTL for several purposes, such as to improve their knowledge of teaching or to enhance students' experience of learning.

Considering that SoTL models have several components in common, and that the diversity in conceptualizing SoTL is also accepted in the field, in this case study I adapted a model proposed by Trigwell et al. (2000). The Trigwell et al. (2000) model was based on an empirical study of academics' approaches to SoTL, and its relevance to this case study lies in its activity-oriented focus of SoTL. The following SoTL activities proposed by Trigwell et al. (2000) and partly reflected in another SoTL model by Trigwell and Shale (2004) were deemed appropriate to guide my reflection:

- Engaging with the scholarly contributions of others, including the literature of teaching and learning of a general nature, and particularly that in the discipline of information technology and teacher education.
- The focus of a reflection on my own teaching practice of preparing teachers for technology-enhanced education and the learning of student teachers within the context of technology and teacher education.

- The quality of my communication and dissemination of aspects of practice and theoretical ideas about teaching and learning in general, and teaching and learning within technology and teacher education.
- My conception of teaching and learning: whether the focus is on student teachers' learning and teaching or mainly on teaching.

In Malawi, the National Council for Higher Education (2015) recommends higher education institutions to ensure a strong link between research and teaching. However, in practice, it is not clear how faculty connect research to their teaching. Therefore, considering the need to keep making sense of conceptions and strategies of research-based teacher education (Afdal & Spernes, 2018), in this chapter I illustrate how teacher education programmes in Malawi and similar contexts can implement research-based teacher education. My point of departure is Afdal and Spernes' (2018) observation that implementing research-based teacher education requires complex decisions at curricular and pedagogical levels, including the context of a teacher education programme.

The SoTL Case Study

Guided by Trigwell et al.'s (2000) model of SoTL, I engaged the literature on how student teachers learn about using technology (e.g., Baran et al., 2019; Parish & Sadera, 2019; Uerz et al., 2018; Tondeur et al., 2018, 2012; Enochsson & Rizza, 2009; Kay, 2006). The cited literatures synthesize what matters in the preparation of pre-service teachers for technology-enhanced education. Based on the literature, I planned an assessment task that involved students in an authentic experience of selecting, evaluating, and utilizing instructional technology appropriate for an identified instructional problem. The following sections present the implementation process and outcomes of the authentic assessment tasks I implemented.

Component 1: Instructional Problem Analysis

I put the student teachers in groups of six, and asked them to consult experienced teachers of the subject (s) that they were specializing in. According to Kay (2006), partnership with teachers in schools is one of the strategies for preparing pre-service teachers for technology integration.

In this case study, the students' interaction with the experienced teachers focused on understanding topics that the practicing teachers found difficult to teach and why the topics were difficult to teach. From the topics shared by the practicing teachers, the students were supposed to choose one topic for their group project. I instructed them to clarify the problem that the experienced teachers faced when teaching the topics. To support their clarification of an instructional problem, I provided some guiding questions: Could the instructional problem be resolved by proper instruction design? What content-specific technology/media can help to resolve the instructional problem? In the groups, the student teachers analyzed instructional problems faced by practicing teachers. The group discussions took place mainly on WhatsApp and occasionally face-to-face. Holding group discussions on WhatsApp was meant to give the students an experience of utilizing social media for learning.

The expected learning outcome of this activity is for the students to develop the ability to identify and analyze an instructional problem/opportunity in the real-world context. I also expected that the students would develop the ability to identify and reflect on instructional and non-instructional solutions for the identified problems. Grading of this component focused on demonstration of thorough problem analysis. Outcomes showed that the students were able to identify instructional problems experienced by practicing teachers. For example, one group reported that "Secondary school students fail to visualise the structure of an atom" while another group reported "Lack of practical resources in schools makes it difficult to teach and learn scientific investigation".

Component 2: Reflective Question

While participating in the group discussions, each student was asked to create a question to guide their participation in the group project activities. I provided them with examples of such questions: "How do I teach Silent Trade using role play?" or "How do I develop Form 4 students' mental models in the rate of reaction?" Answers to these individual questions were expected to be reported during the end-of-semester examination. Expecting them to create a question whose answers were to be reported during an end-of-semester examination was meant to achieve two purposes: (1) to support inquiry-based learning and reflective practice and (2) to incentivize participation in group discussion. I had learnt that non-participation is one of the challenges of group work. Even where students attend group discussion meetings, attendance itself does not mean participation for learning.

I informed the students that grading this component would be based on the quality of the question, especially questions that demonstrate curiosity. A question was supposed to be one that could be answered based on the student's participation in group discussions, and likely to yield an essay response. As a result, the questions that the students created suggest that the expected learning outcome was achieved. For example, one student created a question, "How can I teach data types in object-oriented programming using code combat games?" while another student focused on "How can I teach the topic of cyclone and anticyclone using audio visual technology?" However, although many students created relevant questions, most of them had challenges reporting coherent answers. I also found it difficult to grade the essay using a rubric. Instead, the grade was based on a holistic impression of the essays. From this experience, I learnt the difficulties associated with grading authentic assessment tasks.

Component 3: Instruction Design

Based on the instructional problem analysis, I asked the students to design an instruction. I provided them with the following as examples of framing their instructional design projects: "Development of Creative Writing Ability of Form Three Students Using Google Forms" or "The Effectiveness of Computer Simulations for Improving Form 2 Students' Conceptual Understanding of Light". The instruction design process adapted the ASSURE Model of instruction design (Smaldino et al., 2005), as shown in Table 9.1.

I also instructed the students to read Chapter 3 of the course textbook (Smaldino et al., 2005).

From this activity, I expected the students to develop the ability to select appropriate instructional media and methods, as well as apply the ASSURE model. Among other criteria, grading for this component focused on demonstration of thorough problem analysis, accuracy, relevance of the expected content, and alignment of media with methods.

The outcomes suggested that some students developed the expected abilities. The students framed their instructional design projects following the example I gave them. For example, one group identified their project as "Addressing Challenges Associated with Teaching and Learning of Scientific Investigation Using Motion Media, TALULAR and Resource Persons". In terms of problem analysis, another group reported that

Technology-Enhanced Education in Malawi **135**

Table 9.1 Instruction Design Template

Stage	Description/Explanation	Justification
1 Analyze the learners	What learner information will be useful to achieve your instruction objective? (Identify one category of information)	Why is this information useful? (State one reason)
2 State objectives	What objectives do you intend to achieve? (State two objectives)	What makes the objectives achievable? (State two reasons)
3 Select methods	What methods do you intend to use? (Propose two methods)	Why are these methods appropriate? (State two reasons)
4 Select media/ material	What materials will you use (propose two: one digital and one non-digital technology)?	Why are the materials appropriate? (State two reasons)
5 Require learner participation	How will you ensure learner participation? (Propose one strategy)	Why is your proposed strategy appropriate for learner participation? (State one reason)
6 Evaluation	How will you evaluate the instruction? (State one method) What information will you collect? (Identify one category of information)	Why is the evaluation method appropriate? (State one reason) Why is the information you intend to collect necessary? (State one reason)

Notes: the adapted ASSURE Model does not include "Utilize technology, media & materials" because this aspect was a separate assignment.

"Programming Fundamentals" was a difficult topic to teach because it is more abstract and hence lacks clarity and has no pre-requisite knowledge. As part of learner analysis (Table 9.1), the group suggested that they would consider the learning environment. Although their instructional objective to "Solve real-life problems using programming" was not clear, they selected video and charts as instructional materials. They argued that a video would be suitable because "a student can replay the video so many times to get the concepts done if he or she is facing challenges".

Component 4: Selecting Instructional Media

Based on stage 4 of the instruction design process, I asked the students to select or design instructional media (digital or non-digital) appropriate for the instructional problem identified through their interaction with experienced teachers. The activity involved designing a multimedia presentation in line with the following guidelines:

- Explain how the technology works (four key features)
- Justify why the technology is appropriate for resolving the instructional problem identified in part A of the project (three reasons)
- Suggest some guidelines for the appropriate use of the selected technology (three suggestions)

Designing a multimedia PowerPoint was aimed at involving the students in practicing educational media production. Another aspect of instructional media production was that I instructed them to record a 10-minute video of the group members presenting the PowerPoint. Involving them in presentations and video-recording provided them an opportunity to practice utilization of instructional media. They were provided with the following as suggestions for outlining the multimedia PowerPoint:

- Slide 1: instruction design project title
- Slide 2: introduce the group members
- Slide 3: introduce the instructional problem
- Slide 4: introduce the technology and explain how the technology works
- Slide 5: why the technology is appropriate
- Slide 6: some guidelines for appropriate use of the technology

I allowed them to prepare more than six slides, provided they did not exceed 15 slides. I also instructed them to understand the concept of multimedia and read Chapters 4 (Visual Principles) and 12 (Video) of Smaldino et al. (2005). This was meant to help them apply their learning from reading.

The targeted learning areas for this activity included enhancing visual literacy, which is the ability to create visual messages, and developing oral and written presentation skills. Grading focused on clarity, accuracy, and complete coverage of the expected content, as well as quality of the presentation designs.

In line with Smaldino et al. (2005), most presentations were multimedia as they combined pictures, videos, and text; responded to the goals of visual design, including reducing effort to interpret the visuals, as well as contrasting figures with background. Some presentations also included interactive features that would increase active engagement with the audience to focus attention on the most important aspects of the message (e.g., highlighting or animations). Similarly, through the videos some students demonstrated the ability to communicate visually, including important elements such as legibility and audibility (Smaldino et al., 2005). These outcomes suggest the potential of learning instructional media through media production.

Discussion and Conclusion

The problem addressed in this study is that the instructional technology module at UNIMA has been more theoretical, suggesting the need to engage student teachers in more authentic learning experiences. Considering that research-based teacher education can help teacher educators and student teachers link between theory and practice in teacher education programmes, in this chapter I illustrate an approach to teaching about teaching and learning to teach with technology that is informed by inquiry and evidence (both one's own and that of others). The chapter is based on thinking backwards about my teaching approach of an instructional technology. Trigwell et al.'s (2000) model of SoTL helped me make sense of how my pedagogy of teacher education reflects research-based teacher education.

For starters, as I developed assessment tasks, I relied on the scholarly contributions of others, including the literature on teaching and learning in general, and in the discipline of instructional technology in particular. Among others, I attempted to model pedagogy by providing students with explicit examples and guidelines of how to perform a task. This seems to have enhanced communication of practical and theoretical ideas about teaching and learning technology and teacher education.

Another aspect of SoTL is that I reflected on my own practice of preparing teachers for technology-enhanced education and student teachers' learning about technology. For instance, based on my interaction with student teachers and fellow teacher educators, I realized that the student teachers' learning about using technology fell short of authentic experiences. Furthermore, according to Trigwell et al. (2000), SoTL also becomes visible in the educator's conception of teaching and learning: whether the focus is on student teachers' learning and teaching or mainly on teaching. With my conception of teaching and learning being more student-centred, I attempted to design learning tasks that were authentic, prompting the students to solve real-world instructional problems. I also found it helpful to consider the limitations of the context of UNIMA within which the student teachers were learning about using technology. This included issues of access to technology and the class size. For example, considering that the students had no access to proper cameras, I allowed them to use their mobile phones to record their presentations.

Based on these considerations, the key question is: in what sense, and how, is the gap between theory and practice bridged in this chapter? On the one hand, learning by doing/practising helped students to experience the actual use of technology rather than understanding it in abstract terms. On the other hand, as a teacher I also connected theory (what I knew about instructional technology in the literature) and the results of translating this knowledge into practice. Accordingly, this case study reflects some of the purposes of SoTL; i.e., to improve one's knowledge of teaching and to improve students' learning experience (Trigewell, 2013).

To help me gauge the influence of my teaching approach and continue reflecting on it, at the end of the module I asked the students to evaluate the course in terms of content, methods, and intention to transfer their learning, etc. The course evaluation form included the following items: What was your expectation from the course? Did the course meet your expectation? What is the most important thing that you have learnt from this course? What would you recommend to be changed in terms of teaching methods? What would you recommend to be changed in terms of content? What would you recommend to be changed in terms of the classroom? What would you recommend to be changed in terms of assessment? What didn't you like in this course? What aspects of this course do you intend to apply in your work?

Self-reported responses to these questions provided insights into students' learning, some of which can be linked to the assessment tasks presented in this chapter. The following are examples of students' responses to the question of the most important thing they learnt from the course: "I have learnt how to use media technology to enhance learning. I have also learnt very important part of TPACK and ASSURE model for the first time"; "I need to employ different methods and different technology to meet the objectives and goals of education"; "How to differentiate instruction technology from instruction design as well as instruction media because initially I thought it was the same thing"; "the use of instruction design model like ASSURE and ADDIE will benefit me beyond teaching field. now am able to think outside the box such that soon after my graduation, I will employ these skills to establish my multimedia company"; "How to design instructions and instruction media to produce effective learning. Using different techniques for effective learning considering that learners have different learning styles".

The students also reported their intention to transfer their learning from this course. Some of the responses included, "How to identify, design, use and evaluate instructions, media and technology to improve teaching and learning"; "Selection of instructional media and proper design of instructional and how to evaluate instruction"; and "The use of locally available materials and the various steps to take before using the instruction media".

Moving forward, the SoTL case study reported in this chapter illustrates the potential of research-based teacher education in improving student teachers' learning experience and one's knowledge of teaching. The SoTL approach in question, mainly characterized by active experimentation and reflection on one's personal teaching experience, can be tried in other contexts to confirm its effectiveness, including the following aspects: (1) teacher educators' modelling of pedagogy by providing students with explicit examples and guidelines of how to perform a task; (2) considering continuous assessment that involves students to create reflective questions, which can then be linked to summative assessments; and (3) the SoTL example suggests the potential of learning instructional media through media production, especially in contexts where student teachers' learning about using technology falls short of authentic experiences.

References

Afdal, H. W., & Spernes, K. (2018). Designing and redesigning research-based teacher education. *Teaching and Teacher Education, 74*, 215–228. https://doi.org/10.1016/j.tate.2018.05.011

Baran, E., Canbazoglu Bilici, S., Albayrak Sari, A., & Tondeur, J. (2019). Investigating the impact of teacher education strategies on preservice teachers' TPACK. *British Journal of Educational Technology, 50*(1), 357–370. https://doi.org/10.1111/bjet.12565

Chancellor College. (2016). *Proposal for bachelor of education biological sciences.* Chancellor College.

Chancellor College Faculty of Education. (n.d.). *Instruction, media and technology course outline*. Chancellor College Faculty of Education.

Enochsson, A., & Rizza, C. (2009). ICT in initial teacher training: Research review. *Education, 38*(38), 1–41. https://doi.org/10.1787/220502872611

Gondwe, F. (2020). ICT integration into teacher education: Teacher educators' experiences of policy at two teacher education institutions in Malawi. *Journal of International Development Studies, 1*(29), 117–128. https://doi.org/10.32204/jids.29.1_117

Gondwe, F. (2021). A case study on teacher educators' technology professional development based on student teachers' perspectives in Malawi. *Journal of Interactive Media in Education, 2021*(1).

Jakhelln, R., Eklund, G., Aspfors, J., Bjørndal, K., & Stølen, G. (2021). Newly qualified teachers' understandings of research-based teacher education practices- two cases from Finland and Norway. *Scandinavian Journal of Educational Research, 65*(1), 123–139. https://doi.org/10.1080/00313831.2019.1659402

Kay, R. H. (2006). Evaluating strategies used to incorporate technology into pre-service education: A review of the literature. *Journal of Research on Technology in Education, 4*(38), 385–410. https://files.eric.ed.gov/fulltext/EJ768720.pdf

Kosnik, C., Beck, C., & Goodwin, L. (2016). Reform efforts in teacher education. In J. Loughran & M. L. Hamilton (Eds.), *Handbook on teacher education* (pp. 207–224). Springer Academic Publishers.

Munthe, E., & Rogne, M. (2015). Research based teacher education. *Teaching and Teacher Education, 46*, 17–24. https://doi.org/10.1016/j.tate.2014.10.006

National Council for Higher Education. (2015). *Minimum standards for higher education institutions in Malawi*. https://nche.ac.mw/downloads/NCHE%20MINIMUM%20STANDARDS.pdfNa

Parrish, A. H., & Sadera, W. A. (2019). A review of faculty development models that build teacher educators' technology competencies. *Journal of Technology and Teacher Education, 27*(4), 437–464. https://www.learntechlib.org/p/208226/

Puustinen, M., Säntti, J., Koski, A., & Tammi, T. (2018). Teaching: A practical or research-based profession? Teacher candidates' approaches to research-based teacher education. *Teaching and Teacher Education, 74*, 170–179. https://doi.org/10.1016/j.tate.2018.05.004

Smaldino, S., Russell, J., Heinich, R., & Molenda, M. (2005). *Instructional technology and media form learning*. Prentice Hall.

Tondeur, J., Aesaert, K., Prestridge, S., & Consuegra, E. (2018). A multilevel analysis of what matters in the training of pre-service teacher's ICT competencies. *Computers and Education, 122*, 32–42. https://doi.org/10.1016/j.compedu.2018.03.002

Tondeur, J., Van Braak, J., Sang, G., Voogt, J., Fisser, P., & Ottenbreit-Leftwich, A. (2012). Preparing pre-service teachers to integrate technology in education: A synthesis of qualitative evidence. *Computers and Education, 59*(1), 134–144. https://doi.org/10.1016/j.compedu.2011.10.009

Trigwell, K. (2013). Evidence of the impact of scholarship of teaching and learning purposes. *Teaching and Learning Inquiry, 1*(1), 95–105. https://doi.org/10.2979/teachlearninqu.1.1.95

Trigwell, K., Martin, E., Benjamin, J., & Prosser, M. (2000). Scholarship of teaching: A model. *Higher Education Research & Development, 19*(2), 155–168.

Trigwell, K., & Shale, S. (2004). Student learning and the scholarship of university teaching. *Studies in Higher Education, 29*(4), 523–536. https://doi.org/10.1080/0307507042000236407

Uerz, D., Volman, M., & Kral, M. (2018). Teacher educators' competences in fostering student teachers' proficiency in teaching and learning with technology: An overview of relevant research literature. *Teaching and Teacher Education, 70*, 12–23. https://doi.org/10.1016/j.tate.2017.11.005

University of Malawi. (2016). *University of Malawi ICT policy*. University of Malawi.

Barriers to Self-Directed Learning for Student Teachers Learning within Asynchronous Online Environments During Coronavirus-19 Lockdown   **10**

Lungi Sosibo

Introduction and Background

The Coronavirus-19 (COVID-19) pandemic and its concomitant lockdown caused unprecedented disruptions in higher education institutions (HEIs) globally, as most of them had to close. Consequently, online teaching and learning (OTL) was adopted as the primary approach to complete the academic curriculum during the COVID pandemic (Bozkurt & Sharma, 2020; Hodges et al., 2020). Because the adoption of OTL was unplanned and rapid (Li & Lalani, 2020), challenges related to the lack of technical and practical skills to use ICT among teaching staff (Tunjera & Chigona, 2022; Crawford et al., 2020; Hodges et al., 2020) and lack of access to reliable ICT resources and the Internet for some students (Li & Lalani, 2020) began to emerge.

The switch to OTL placed a heavy burden on students to become self-directed (SD) learners. This switch meant that students, regardless

DOI: 10.4324/9781003406631-10

of whether they were taught via synchronous or asynchronous OTL methods, had to have high levels of self-directed learning (SDL) skills. However, I argue that SDL was more vital for students who learned via asynchronous than synchronous methods, as, unlike the latter, the former had no social interaction with their lecturers and peers during the COVID-19 lockdown. Unfortunately, SDL is generally associated with adult education, as it is not essential for traditional students (Mahlaba, 2020). Morris (2021) contends that SDL competence can help students adapt to volatile and rapidly changing conditions where face-to-face teaching and learning may not be possible.

This study investigated student teachers' barriers to SDL within an asynchronous OTL environment during the COVID-19 lockdown. The research question was: *Seeing that during the COVID-19 lockdown, you were taught primarily via asynchronous OTL methods without social interaction with lecturers to interpret information and knowledge for you, what barriers did you encounter with regulating your learning?* The meaning of asynchronous methods is explained in the literature review.

Context of the Study

This study was conducted online with 150 second-year students enrolled in a selected undergraduate teacher education programme (TEP) at the Faculty of Education at a South African university. This faculty offers a variety of undergraduate and postgraduate TEPs. Although ordinarily some courses are taught through a hybrid approach, in most courses, only contact teaching was used before the COVID-19 lockdown, despite the university's insistence on the former. To ensure curriculum coverage during the COVID-19 lockdown, the university and the Faculty of Education provided OTL capacity-development workshops for both lecturers and students.

Most of the participants came from low socioeconomic backgrounds and lived in impoverished Black and Coloured townships, squatter camps and rural areas. Since the university campus, student residences and computer laboratories were closed during the hard lockdown, these students did not have access to digital resources and data to access Wi-Fi. Consequently, they were compelled to learn via asynchronous and multi-modal OTL methods, which limited them to only accessing printed notes and recorded learning materials sent to them via WhatsApp and email messages or posted on Blackboard for them to access at their convenience.

Due to these circumstances, they were obliged to tap largely into their SDL skills.

Literature Review

Conceptual Definition of Synchronous and Asynchronous Online Teaching and Learning

Synchronous OTL is live, real-time and interactive. Students and instructors engage with the learning content in the same online learning space at the same scheduled time, with social interaction between the instructor, students and peers (Singh et al., 2021; Martin et al., 2020). Students log in and learn online via various interactive learning management systems (LMSs), such as Moodle, Blackboard, Zoom, MS Teams, Google Meet, eClass chat and video conferencing (Shahabadi & Uplane, 2015; Hrastinski, 2008), which also allow them to receive immediate feedback (Hung, 2021) and to ask or answer questions in real-time (Hrastinski, 2008).

Asynchronous OTL is not live or real-time: students and instructors cannot be online at the same time and in the same location (Singh et al., 2021; Hrastinski, 2008). Martin et al. (2020, p. 2) define *asynchronous online learning* as "A course where most of the content is delivered online and students can participate in the online course from anywhere and anytime." In this approach, there is no real-time online interaction or face-to-face meetings of students with their peers and lecturers. Students log in to an e-learning environment via, for example, Blackboard, email, WhatsApp text and voice notes, or cell phone text messages at any time and download documents (electronic or voice/recorded) or send messages to instructors or peers via these platforms. Discussion boards/forums can be used for students to interact with the course content, instructor and peers (Angelo State University, 2022). Loncar et al. (2014, as cited in Moosa, 2022) assert that asynchronous online discussion forums (AODFs) create social environments for students to interact as a community and to engage in a critical discussion of topics in a collaborative manner. The social isolation in asynchronous OTL environments caused by a lack of interaction with instructors and peers (Paulson, 2022; Hrastinski, 2008) suggests that students require a high level of SDL skills. Consequently, this study involved only those students who learned predominantly via asynchronous OTL methods.

The Synergy between Social Constructivism, Self-Directed Learning and Online Teaching and Learning

Some authors have emphasised a synergy between constructivism, SDL and OTL (van der Westhuizen, 2020; Reid-Martinez & Grooms, 2018; Secore, 2017). Unlike in traditional classrooms where instructors teach students so that they understand the content they are learning, in a constructivist, SDL and OTL classroom, the teaching-learning process is learner-centred. Students engage actively in the construction and co-construction of knowledge and ideas using their experiences, with the instructor facilitating, guiding and scaffolding student learning (Knowles, 1978; Vygotsky, 1978). Accordingly, Robinson and Persky (2020, p. 5) maintain that "faculty members shift from being the 'sage on the stage' where learning hinges on the instructor to either a 'guide on the side' or, ideally, an authentic co-learner" who facilitates learning. The task for instructors is not to teach students how to learn, but to co-construct meanings with them (constructivism) and provide them with opportunities to explore and try things out independently (SDL). OTL plays an important role in facilitating this process.

Theoretical Framework

Knowles' (1978) SDL underpinned this study. SDL involves a learning environment in which students make decisions about the knowledge, skills and information in which they want to become proficient (Knowles, 1978). According to Knowles (1978) and Morris (2019), students take the initiative to identify their learning needs, formulate goals, identify materials and resources they (will) need for effective learning to occur, implement learning strategies, manage and regulate learning, and monitor and evaluate learning outcomes.

When students self-direct, they take responsibility for the decisions they make about how they use information meaningfully to advance their learning (Brandt, 2020). Francis (2017) advocates that SD learners have the autonomy to choose what, why, how and where of their learning. When learners become autonomous, they can work independently or collaboratively with others, thus proving that knowledge is individual and social. Working collaboratively with others assumes social interaction with others, which is a critical factor in SDL and constructivism.

146 Lungi Sosibo

Jossberger et al. (2010) and Morris (2019) maintain that SD learners adapt easily to changing social and contextual situations, such as the COVID-19 pandemic. Alghamdi (2021) perceives adaptation as a skill that can help students direct their learning without an instructor telling them what to do, a fact echoed by Jossberger et al. (2010) and Morris (2019). Pink (2009) emphasizes motivation, or a drive to achieve set goals, while Brockett and Hiemstra (1991) stress personal responsibility as a factor affecting SDL. As alluded to earlier, OTL methods employed during the COVID-19 lockdown assumed that students must self-direct, self-regulate and take control of their learning, more so for students in asynchronous than in synchronous environments, as argued earlier.

Methodology

The qualitative case study design helped to uncover participants' perspectives on their barriers to SDL in the context of asynchronous OTL environments during the COVID-19 lockdown. Denzin and Lincoln (2018) state that qualitative research involves studying individuals in their natural settings and attempting to make sense of or interpret phenomena in terms of the meanings people bring to them. Pham (2018) argues that interpretive and phenomenological paradigms provide an in-depth understanding and interpretation of the lived experiences of the participants. Accordingly, I used interpretive-phenomenological inquiry (Frechette et al., 2020; Smith & Eatough, 2006) to uncover participants' interpretations of their lived experiences of self-directing their online learning in asynchronous environments and the barriers they encountered.

A sample of 150 second-year undergraduate students selected from a TEP offered in a Faculty of Education was used for this study. The criterion that students who used synchronous OTL more than 75% of the time were not eligible for this study was clearly stated in the letter appended to the data-collection questionnaire sent to the students. As such, the sampling procedure was purposive (Creswell & Plano Clark, 2011), as I believed that participants who learned via asynchronous OTL methods were knowledgeable enough to provide rich data about barriers to SDL in asynchronous OTL environments. A detailed explanation of synchronous and asynchronous OTL was attached to the questionnaire.

Data were collected through open-ended questionnaires sent via email and Google platform to students in March 2021, a year after the outbreak of COVID-19 in South Africa. Due to the lack of access to digital resources for the targeted participants, the questionnaire was limited to only five questions that the researcher believed they could answer quickly. For flexibility purposes, students were advised to send responses by any means convenient to them, including email and Google platform, or they could write them down and send them back by WhatsApp text. After a month, 18 (12%) responses were received. Due to the low response rate, I sent a second set of questionnaires to the same group of students, requesting those who had already responded to ignore it. At the end of May, the final deadline given to the participants, 26 (17%) responses were received. Including the previous responses, the response rate was 44 (29%). This response rate was low but understandable, considering that data collection was during the peak of the COVID-19 pandemic and that some students still struggled with accessing digital resources, as well as that results would not be generalisable to other contexts. Data were analysed through colour-coding, followed by labelling, organising, grouping and categorisation of data into emergent themes using multi-perspective analysis (Hoepfl, 1997).

To observe ethical considerations, the questionnaire contained a detailed explanation of the study, followed by assurance that participants would not suffer harm or receive financial compensation. The voluntariness of participation was explained. Consent forms were included in the questionnaire for participants to sign and return together with responses. Confidentiality and anonymity were explained. To conceal their identities, participants were requested to use aliases or pseudonyms aligned with their gender and real names, meaning that the pseudonyms had to be in the same language as their real names. Granted, this information did not help much in establishing the racial identity of participants in cases where pseudonyms were in English, but it helped with identifying the contributions of males and females. Participants were further informed that data would be stored in the external drive accessible only to the researcher and be destroyed after three years. The data-collection instrument was validated by an established researcher at the university.

Results

Data analysis yielded three themes presented in the following section.

Students' Personality Traits

It appears that factors such as the tendency to procrastinate, poor time management, lack of focus and lack of control affected participants adversely from self-directing their learning in asynchronous environments. For example, Janet, a mother and working student, experienced learning via asynchronous OTL during the COVID-19 lockdown as an opportunity and a distraction, pointing out that:

> Whereas learning via asynchronous OTL gives me the freedom to attend to my triple role as mother, student and employee, I often either ignore or postpone doing my assignments, leading to me falling behind on my schoolwork. It's bad not to have someone pushing you from behind, like your lecturer, family or friends.

Joseph expressed his inability to manage time, stating that:

> Without a fixed timetable as in normal classrooms, I often delay getting to do my work. My friend developed his schedule to guide his learning. Perhaps this is what I must do to control my learning as well.

Lungelo, on the other hand, raised a concern about his lack of focus and about his siblings being another distraction that caused him to lose control of his learning in asynchronous environments. He explained that:

> The convenience of learning asynchronously is destroying my future goals. Instead of concentrating on my classwork, I find myself joining conversations with my siblings or watching scary COVID news on TV. If not, I browse through the internet aimlessly or go to Facebook. Sometimes my mind wanders, and this affects me academically.

Other participants' explanations portrayed them as lacking self-dependence and autonomy to learn on their own (learner-centred) without being told by an instructor what to learn and when to do so (teacher-centred). This dependency appeared to hinder their SDL, as expressed by Clarence:

> COVID-19 has made it almost impossible for me to grasp the content without the help of my lecturers. I learn better with a teacher in front of me and with peer support in instances where I don't understand.

Martin's account echoed Clarence's sentiments when he expressed that:

> During lockdown, those of us without digital resources and Wi-Fi have been learning via notes sent via WhatsApp, email and text messages. This simply does not work for me because I am not good at teaching myself.

These participants' characteristics are such that they have no personal responsibility to control and regulate their learning (Brockett & Hiemstra, 1991). They also appear to lack SDL skills in setting, implementing and regulating their learning objectives (Morris, 2019; Knowles, 1978). Roberson et al. (2021) emphasise planning, organising and self-control skills for SDL, while Platt et al. (2014) highlight monitoring and regulating one's learning pace, self-discipline, self-responsibility and time management. Paulson (2022, p. 3) claims that:

> Asynchronous courses require students to have control over when and how they engage with course content and manage their time. This autonomy requires students to monitor and adjust their behaviour during the asynchronous course.

Some participants' attributes contrast with those advocated by Paulson (2022), that SD learners can use basic study skills, manage their time effectively and set their learning pace and clear goals. SDL posits that learners are responsible administrators of their learning process (Knowles, 1978), a trait that these participants appear to lack. Garrison's (1997) SDL model proposes integrating self-management, self-monitoring and self-motivation. From these participants' accounts, it is evident that although asynchronous teaching methods gave them the autonomy to access learning whenever and wherever they wanted, the disadvantage was that those who lacked SDL skills ignored their learning responsibilities.

Lack of a Sense of Community

Other students bemoaned the fact that asynchronous OTL deprived them of a sense of community, as they were unable to network, interact or share ideas with their lecturers and peers. Jongisa mentioned that isolation in asynchronous OTL environments shattered his dream of successfully carrying out his learning project, describing this method as a lonely learning journey that stifles active student engagement. Groupwork allowed us to connect, share ideas and make diverse interpretations of content.

Similarly, Phatheka mourned the loss of cooperative learning and support from peers, stating that:

Learning through asynchronous multimodal methods has robbed us of the opportunity to work and grow together as a [learning] community. Different perspectives in groups helped us to create our meanings of the content, which helped us when we prepared for the assessments.

As is commonly the case with asynchronous OTL, students predominantly work in isolation, especially if lecturers solely rely on this teaching method, as was seemingly the case for these participants who lacked resources.

Poor Online Course Design and Implementation Skills of Lecturers

Some participants reported a lack of structure in the class tasks and information overload. They associated these challenges with lecturers' poor online pedagogical skills to design courses effectively and to teach asynchronously using multimodal approaches. Caleb expressed that:

Some lecturers simply send WhatsApp voice notes or dump learning materials on Blackboard or email without proper instructions. This makes it difficult for us to understand or interpret the content and tasks given without the lecturer's input.

Popo concurred with Caleb, lamenting that:

Some lecturers give poor instructions or no instructions at all. As a result, we perform poorly because we must figure it all out on our own without proper guidance.

Caleb and Popo's concerns echo Ghafri's (2013) observation of a project on asynchronous online course design in which instructors failed to provide students with a clear syllabus or instructions on how to perform their tasks. Ghafri (2013) associated this with the lack of basic principles of self-directed online course design by instructors. Testimonies revealed that lack of structure hindered SDL.

Dave, on the other hand, criticised one of his lecturers for giving them group work within the context of asynchronous OTL, reporting that:

> Lecturer X simply sent us a task by email and told us to do it in groups. The fact that some of us learn via asynchronous multimodal methods should have signalled to her that we cannot connect asynchronously.

Groupwork provides students with a constructivist learning environment that helps them to make their interpretations of the content or to self-direct their learning. The inability to network or connect with peers via asynchronous OTL methods might have hindered their SDL. In their study of synchronous and asynchronous teaching and learning, Fabriz et al. (2021) reported that students in synchronous learning environments reported to have more peer-centred activities than did those in asynchronous contexts. These findings shed light on the complexity of group work in asynchronous OTL environments, especially in the context of the COVID-19 lockdown when universities were shut down, thus completely preventing those students without access to ICT resources from interacting with peers and lecturers.

Elaine was concerned with information overload, which she described as:

> In less than two months we were given an overwhelming amount of content on Blackboard to study and difficult assignments to complete. Six assignments were to be completed over two weeks.

Hrastinski (2008) suggests that synchronous meetings can assist with the discussion of complex issues and may serve as support for students. Unfortunately, within asynchronous OTL environments during COVID-19 lockdown and social distancing, such meetings were impossible. Giving students work in small chunks makes it easier for them to process information in any learning environment, thereby enhancing their SDL.

Jomo highlighted poor communication and feedback from lecturers, stating that:

> Some lecturers ignore our emails and calls when we need feedback. This compromises our learning, especially because we solely rely on

this feedback, as it plays a big role in shaping our understanding of content. We simply do not get this from some lecturers.

Feedback is an important aspect of teaching and learning. It shows whether students have grasped the content they have learned or whether the instructor should reteach content that students have not understood. Regarding students who learn via asynchronous OTL, feedback is one of the few forms of communication/interaction with the instructor and should therefore be provided timeously.

Discussion

This study investigated student teachers' barriers to SDL in the context of an asynchronous OTL environment during the COVID-19 lockdown. Results revealed that they encountered barriers related to various factors. Poor course design and implementation reflect asynchronous OTL environments that inhibited students' SDL. Even with asynchronous methods, students still need a structure that facilitates learning (Keirns, 1999). Paulson (2022) asserts that when teaching asynchronously, students' learning should be constructivist. Learning should be scaffolded by providing supportive learning environments that include guidance, information sharing, explanations, clarification and support (Vygotsky, 1978). Such a socio-constructivist environment is likely to enhance student SDL even in asynchronous OTL environments where there is minimal social interaction.

For Bates (2019, p. 167), a well-designed online course includes "clear learning objectives, carefully structured content, controlled workloads for faculty and students, integrated media, relevant student activities, and assessments strongly tied to desired learning outcomes." Unfortunately, participants' accounts revealed that some of these elements were lacking. In the context of OTL, Parchoma et al. (2019, p. 13) stress the importance of "designing conditions under which learners have a better chance to learn," which, it appears, were not integrated into this asynchronous OTL environment. Therefore, the importance for lecturers to acquire skills in designing and developing asynchronous online courses from a constructivist and SDL perspective cannot be overemphasised. To address this knowledge gap, Ghafri (2013) designed a project to equip e-learning instructors with strategies to design effective asynchronous SDL online courses. Equally vital is to equip lecturers with new digital pedagogies to integrate technological, pedagogical and content knowledge (TPACK) (Koehler et al., 2013).

Some participants mentioned poor communication and feedback mechanisms as what created barriers to SDL for them. Providing feedback to all students is critical. Steele and Holbeck (2018, p. 1) confirm this assertion, arguing that "Effective feedback is a necessary and important part of the learning experience regardless of the learning modality." Feedback is critical in both synchronous and asynchronous OTL environments, but even more so in the latter, where social interaction is sometimes virtually absent.

For other participants, SDL barriers appeared to be intrinsic and emanated from their varying personality traits, which confirms Alghamdi's (2021) assumption that SDL has a personal dimension and Brockett and Hiemstra's (1991) that SDL is both a personality characteristic (learner self-direction) and an instructional method (self-directed learning). The following personal attributes serve as SDL enablers: self-reliance, self-confidence, self-motivation, passion, self-discipline and self-mastery (Nash, 2021; Alsancak & Ozdemir, 2018); reflection, self-determination, motivation, resilience, and positive learning behaviours and skills (Singaram et al., 2022); and students' attitudes, values, beliefs and abilities Guglielmino (1977). This implies that SD learners possess personal attributes that non-SD learners lack, suggesting that not all students can self-direct their learning. The implication is that SDL is imperative in TEPs and that they (TEPs) should incorporate these personal attributes in preparing student teachers to be SD learners.

Some participants highlighted the absence of a sense of community in asynchronous OTL environments as a barrier to SDL. Like social constructivism, SDL is a collaborative and social-interactive process (Simons, 2000) in which students share ideas and co-construct knowledge. An online community of learning (CoL) might have strengthened students' SDL during the COVID-19 lockdown. Similarly, supplementing asynchronous with synchronous OTL methods can break isolation because, according to Hrastinski (2008, p. 52), "Synchronous sessions help e-learners feel like participants rather than isolates." But, as we know, lack of access to resources and social distancing prevented this from happening. Perhaps lecturers should have created optimal opportunities for student-lecturer-peer collaborations via AODFs (Angelo State University, 2022; Loncar et al., 2014 as cited in Moosa, 2022) alluded to earlier.

Contrary to Dave, who seemed to believe that group work in asynchronous OTL environments was impossible, some studies show that collaborative learning is possible in asynchronous OTL environments (Coker & Harris-Marion, 2021; Or-Bach & van Amelsvoort, 2013; Ellis & Hafner, 2008). Chau et al. (2021) report that studies on SDL with technology (SDLT) indicate that collaborative learning can improve students' SDL. Nonetheless, Ellis and Hafner (2008) highlight the difficulty of creating collaborative environments in asynchronous OTL environments, which seems to support Dave's concern. The organising role of the lecturer is critical in creating such collaborative asynchronous OTL environments.

Conclusion

It can be concluded that the COVID-19 lockdown was supposed to have provided students with an invaluable opportunity to acquire or practice SDL in challenging asynchronous OTL environments. Based on the arguments raised earlier, one can assume that SDL was more imperative for students taught via asynchronous than synchronous OTL methods. The results provide answers that demonstrate barriers for students to self-direct their learning in asynchronous OTL environments during the COVID-19 lockdown. Some barriers were intrinsic and related to their traits (e.g., procrastination, lack of motivation and adaptation, lack of focus, poor time management), while others were extrinsic (e.g., lecturers' poor course design skills, lack of a sense of community). I contend that if SDL had been integrated into the teacher education curriculum before the outbreak of the COVID-19 pandemic and its concomitant lockdown, self-directing their learning would have been seamless for student teachers. Similarly, if lecturers had adopted OTL as a normal teaching strategy before the outbreak of the COVID-19 pandemic, then they would have been able to design effective OTL courses with a clear structure for students to effectively self-direct their learning in synchronous and asynchronous OTL environments. A lot of work still needs to be done to equip lecturers with constructivist OTL skills and to integrate SDL into the teacher education curriculum, regardless of the teaching mode (traditional/online).

The results of this study cannot be generalised to other contexts. It would be beneficial to replicate this study in other contexts using a larger sample of students from different disciplines and universities. It would be equally important to investigate whether gender affected SDL among students learning in the same environments. Similarly, quantitative studies should be conducted to compare data obtained through qualitative methods.

References

Alghamdi, A. (2021). COVID-19 mandated self-directed distance learning: Experiences of Saudi female postgraduate students. *Journal of University Teaching & Learning Practice*, *18*(3), 1–20. https://doi.org/10.53761/1.18.3.14.

Alsancak, S. D., & Ozdemir, S. (2018). The effect of a flipped classroom model on academic achievement, self-directed learning readiness, motivation and retention. *Malaysian Online Journal of Educational Technology*, *6*(1), 76–91.

Angelo State University. (2022). *Online learning tools: Asynchronous communication tools*. https://www.angelo.edu/faculty-and-staff/instructional-design/onlineteaching/section_31.php

Bates, A. W. T. (2019). *Teaching in a digital age* (2nd ed.). Tony Bates Associates Ltd. https://pressbooks.bccampus.ca/teachinginadigitalagev2/

Bozkurt, A., & Sharma, R. C. (2020). Emergency remote teaching in a time of global crisis due to the Coronavirus pandemic. *Asian Journal of Distance Education*, *15*(1), I–VI. https://doi.org/10.5281/zenodo.3778083

Brandt, W. C. (2020). *Measuring student success skills: A review of the literature on self-directed learning*. National Center for the Improvement of Educational Assessment.

Brockett, R. G., & Hiemstra, R. (1991). *Self-direction in adult learning: Perspectives on theory, research and practice*. Routledge. https://doi.org/10.4324/9780429457319

Chau, K. Y., Law, K. M. Y., & Tang, Y. M. (2021). Impact of self-directed learning and educational technology readiness on synchronous e-learning. *Journal of Organizational and End User Computing*, *33*(6), 1–20. https://doi.org/10.4018/JOEUC.20211101.oa26

Coker, D., & Harris-Marion, T. (2021). Transforming asynchronous learning spaces. *Faculty Focus*. https://www.facultyfocus.com/articles/online-education/online-course-delivery-and-instruction/transforming-asynchronous-learning-spaces/

Crawford, J., Butler-Henderson, K. B., Rudolph, J., Malkawi, B., Glowatz, M., Burton, R., Magni, P. A., & Lam, S. (2020). COVID-19: 20 countries' higher education intra-period digital pedagogy responses. *Journal of Applied Learning and Teaching*, *3*(1), 1–20. https://doi.org/10.37074/jalt.2020.3.1.7

Creswell, J. W., & Plano Clark, V. L. (2011). *Designing and conducting mixed method research* (2nd ed.). Sage.

Denzin, N. K., & Lincoln, Y. S. (Eds.). (2018). *The Sage handbook of qualitative research* (5th ed.). Sage.

Ellis, T. J., & Hafner, W. (2008). Building a framework to support project-based collaborative learning experiences in an asynchronous learning network.

Interdisciplinary Journal of e-Learning and Learning Objects, 4, 167–190. https://doi.org/10.28945/373

Fabriz, S., Mendzheritskaya, J., & Stehle, S. (2021). Impact of synchronous and asynchronous settings of online teaching and learning in higher education on students' learning experience during COVID-19. *Frontiers in Psychology, 12*, 1–16. https://doi.org/10.3389/fpsyg.2021.733554

Francis, H. (2017). *The role of technology in self-directed learning: A literature review.* ACS Center for Inspiring Minds. https://www.academia.edu/35278698/The_role_of_technology_in_selfdirected_learning_A_literature_review

Frechette, J., Bitzas, V., Aubry, M., Kilpatrick, K., & Lavoie-Tremblay, M. (2020). Capturing lived experience: Methodological considerations for interpretive phenomenological inquiry. *International Journal of Qualitative Methods, 19*, 1–12. https://doi.org/10.1177/1609406920907254

Garrison, D. R. (1997). Self-directed learning: Toward a comprehensive model. *Adult Education Quarterly, 48*(1), 18–33. https://doi.org/10.1177/074171369704800103

Ghafri, T. K. A. (2013). Self-directed learning in asynchronous courses: Strategies for effective design and development. *Procedia – Social and Behavioral Sciences, 103*, 807–817. https://doi.org/10.1016/j.sbspro.2013.10.402

Guglielmino, L. M. (1977). *Development of the self-directed learning readiness scale* [Doctoral dissertation, University of Georgia]. Dissertation Abstracts International, 38, 6467A. https://www.proquest.com/openview/b153e58b2 4f8b15d04daab0a9d89d965/1.pdf?pq-origsite=gscholar&cbl=18750&diss=y

Hodges, C. B., Moore, S., Lockee, B. B., Trust, T., & Bond, M. A. (2020). The difference between emergency remote teaching and online learning. *EDUCASE Review.* https://er.educause.edu/articles/2020/3/the-difference-between-emergency-remote-teaching-and-online-learning

Hoepfl, M. C. (1997). Choosing qualitative research: A primer for technology education researchers. *Journal of Technology Education, 9*(1), 1–17.

Hrastinski, S. (2008). Asynchronous and synchronous e-learning. *EDUCAUSE Quarterly, 4*, 51–55.

Hung, L. T. (2021). How does online formative feedback impact student's motivation and self-directed learning skills during the COVID-19 pandemic? *Journal of Educational and Social Research, 11*(5), 11–20. https://doi.org/10.36941/jesr-2021-0101

Jossberger, H., Brand-Gruwel, S., Boshuizen, H., & van de Wiel, M. (2010). The challenge of self-directed and self-regulated learning in vocational education: A theoretical analysis and synthesis of requirements. *Journal of Vocational Education & Training, 62*(4), 415–440. https://doi.org/10.1080/13636820.20 10.523479

Keirns, J. L. (1999). *Designs for self-instruction: Principles, processes, and issues in developing self-directed learning.* Allyn & Bacon.

Knowles, M. S. (1978). Andragogy: Adult learning theory in perspective. *Community College Review, 5*(3), 9–20. https://doi.org/10.1177/009155217800500302

Koehler, M. J., Mishra, P., & Cain, W. (2013). What is technological pedagogical content knowledge (TPACK)? *Journal of Education, 193*(3), 13–19.

Li, C., & Lalani, F. (2020). *The COVID-19 pandemic has changed education forever. This is how.* World Economic Forum. https://www.weforum.org/agenda/2020/04/coronavirus-education-global-covid19-online-digital-learning/

Loncar, M., Neil, E. B., & Gi-Zen, L. (2014). Towards the refinement of forum and asynchronous online discussion in educational contexts worldwide: Trends and investigative approaches within a dominant research paradigm. *Computers & Education, 73*, 93–110. https://doi.org/10.1016/j.compedu.2013.12.007.

Mahlaba, S. C. (2020). Reasons why self-directed learning is important in South Africa during the Covid-19 pandemic. *South African Journal of Higher Education, 34*(6), 120–136. https://doi.org/10.20853/34-6-4192

Martin, F., Polly, D., & Ritzhaupt, A. (2020). Bichronous online learning: Blending asynchronous and synchronous online learning. *EDUCAUSE Review.* https://er.educause.edu/articles/2020/9/bichronous-online-learning-blending-asynchronous-and-synchronous-online-learning

Moosa, R. (2022). Mediating epistemological access through asynchronous online discussion forums during the COVID-19 pandemic: Implications for re-imagining online collaborative self-directed peer engagement and learning. *South African Journal of Higher Education, 36*(4), 117–136. https://doi.org/10.20853/36-4-5177

Morris, T. H. (2019). Self-directed learning: A fundamental competence in a rapidly changing world. *International Review of Education, 65*, 633–653. https://doi.org/10.1007/s11159-019-09793-2.

Morris, T. H. (2021). Meeting educational challenges of pre- and post-COVID-19 conditions through self-directed learning: Considering the contextual quality of educational experience necessary. *On the Horizon, 29*(2), 52–61. https://doi.org/10.1108/OTH-01-2021-0031

Nash, C. (2021). Medical professionals require curriculum support to overcome their reluctance to embrace self-directed learning in response to COVID-19. *Proceedings, the 3rd International Electronic Conference on Environmental Research and Public Health, Medical Sciences Forum, 4*(1), 1–6. https://doi.org/10.3390/ECERPH-3-08986

Or-Bach, R., & van Amelsvoort, M. (2013). Supporting asynchronous collaborative learning: Students' perspective. *International Journal of Online Pedagogy and Course Design, 3*(4), 1–15. https://doi.org/10.4018/ijopcd.2013100101

Parchoma, G., Koole, M., Morrison, D., Nelson, D., & Dreaver-Charles, K. (2019). Designing for learning in the yellow house: A comparison of instructional and learning design origins and practices. *Higher Education Research & Development, 39*(5), 1–16. https://doi.org/10.1080/07294360.2019.1704693

Paulson, E. (2022). *Student self-directedness in asynchronous learning.* https://tlconestoga.ca/student-self-directedness-in-asynchronous-learning/

Pham, L. T. M. (2018). *Qualitative approach to research: A review of advantages and disadvantages of three paradigms: Positivism, interpretivism and critical inquiry.* University of Adelaide. https://doi.org/10.13140/RG.2.2.13995.54569

Pink, D. H. (2009). *Drive: The surprising truth about what motivates us.* Riverhead Books.

Platt, C. A., Raile, A. N. W., & Yu, N. (2014). Virtually the same? Student perceptions of the equivalence of online classes vs. face-to-face classes. *MERLOT Journal of Online Learning and Teaching, 10*(3), 489–494.

Reid-Martinez, K., & Grooms, L. D. (2018). Online learning is propelled by constructivism. In *Encyclopedia of information science and technology* (Vol. IV, pp. 2588–2598). IGI Global. https://doi.org/10.4018/978-1-5225-2255-3.ch226

Roberson, D. N., Jr., Zach, S., Choresh, N., & Rosenthal, I. (2021). Self-directed learning: A longstanding tool for uncertain times. *Creative Education, 12*, 1011–1026. https://doi.org/10.4236/ce.2021.125074

Robinson, J. D., & Persky, A. M. (2020). Developing self-directed learners. *American Journal of Pharmaceutical Education, 84*(3), 292–296. https://doi.org/10.5688/ajpe847512

Secore, S. (2017). Social constructivism in online learning: Andragogical influence and the effectual educator. *E-Mentor, 3*(70), 4–9. https://doi.org/10.15219/em70.1300

Shahabadi, M. M., & Uplane, M. M. (2015). Synchronous and asynchronous e-learning styles and academic performance of e-learners. *Procedia: Social and Behavioral Sciences, 176*, 129–138. https://doi.org/10.1016/j.sbspro.2015.01.453

Simons, P. R. J. (2000). Towards a constructivist theory of self-directed learning. *Self-Learning*, 1–12.

Singaram, V. S., Naidoo, K. L., & Singh, S. (2022). Self-directed learning during the COVID-19 pandemic: Perspectives of South African final-year health professions students. *Advances in Medical Education and Practice, 13*, 1–10. https://doi.org/10.2147/AMEP.S339840

Singh, C. K. S., Madzlan, N. A., Ong, E. T., Gopal, R., Muhammad, M. M., Shukor, S. S., Mostafa, N. A., Singh, T. S. M., & Maniam, M. (2021). Using synchronous vs asynchronous methods during the COVID-19 pandemic in Malaysia: Preservice and in-service teachers' perspectives. In M. Shohel (Ed.),

E-learning and digital education in the twenty-first century (pp. 1–17). IntechOpen. https://doi.org/10.5772/intechopen.100219.

Smith, J. A., & Eatough, V. (2006). Interpretative phenomenological analysis. In G. Breakwell, C. Fife-Schaw, S. Hammond, & J. A. Smith (Eds.), *Research methods in psychology* (3rd ed., pp. 322–341). Sage.

Steele, J., & Holbeck, R. (2018). Five elements that impact quality feedback in the online asynchronous classroom. *Journal of Educators Online*, 1–5. https://files.eric.ed.gov/fulltext/EJ1199171.pdf

Tunjera, N., & Chigona, A. (2022). Improve pre-service teachers' online learning attendance and accessibility through multiple platforms. *Journal of Education*, 88, 21–34. http://dx.doi.org/10.17159/2520-9868/i88a02

Van der Westhuizen, M. (2020). *Constructivist learning theory and eLearning*. Edge Education. https://edgeeducation.com/constructivist-learning-theory-elearning/

Vygotsky, L. S. (1978). *Mind in society: The development of higher psychological processes*. Harvard University Press.

Co-developing Dialogic Teaching with Digital Technology in Chinese Primary Mathematics Classrooms 11

A Design-Based Approach to Lesson Study

Qian Liu

Introduction

The rapid advancement of digital technology offers rich opportunities to support classroom dialogue where multiple perspectives can be openly shared, critically and creatively linked and synthesised, and new meanings collectively constructed (Major et al., 2018). Research evidence confirms the educational value of productive dialogue in mathematics learning (e.g., Howe et al., 2019; Mercer & Sams, 2006). Due to interconnected factors (e.g., cultural values, school organisation, curriculum, examination), teacher dominance and students' inequitable and passive participation are found in the Chinese primary mathematics classroom dialogue (Liu, 2023). Despite the promising role of digital technology in supporting classroom dialogue (e.g., Cook et al., 2019; Hennessy, 2011), appropriate pedagogy is key to realising the dialogic potential.

DOI: 10.4324/9781003406631-11

Hence, this case study was conducted in two Chinese primary schools, aiming to support mathematics teachers' dialogic teaching with digital technology and Chinese students' active and equitable dialogic participation in primary mathematics classrooms. The case study innovatively employed a design-based research (DBR) approach to tailoring a lesson study (LS) in which seven Chinese teachers from the two schools explored, trialled, and improved dialogic teaching strategies collectively and iteratively while using two digital platforms chosen by them. The shared features and principles (e.g., iteration, collaboration, action and reflection, flexibility, context-based) embedded in DBR and LS theoretically suggest a potential for their integration, thereby developing a mutually beneficial and complementary relationship. In addition to the DBR-led LS model, the case study outlines the procedure, main activities, implementing conditions, and outcomes in detail. Within the DBR, the characteristics and conditions for designing, implementing, and managing a teacher professional development (TPD) programme for dialogic teaching with digital technology are organised into design principles. It is the first attempt to combine DBR and LS in professional learning about technology-mediated dialogic education. The case study offers important implications for teacher educators and educational researchers regarding how to support in-service teachers to conduct inquiry and develop dialogic teaching with digital technology.

Theoretical and Methodological Perspectives

Technology-Mediated Dialogic Teaching

Dialogic teaching is a set of repertoires of pedagogical strategies that highlight the educational values of dialogue and capitalise on it to develop students' thinking and learning. It has five principles: collective, reciprocal, supportive, cumulative, purposeful (Alexander, 2004). Facilitating productive classroom dialogue is a major aim of dialogic teaching. Theoretically productive classroom dialogue includes the following five key features that are synthesised from previous relevant literature and research:

- open teacher initiations;
- participants' extended contributions and elaboration;

162 Qian Liu

- acknowledgement and probing of differences in opinion, ideally offering reasons;
- coordination of different perspectives through explicit links among contributions pursuing common lines of inquiry;
- adoption of a metacognitive perspective on dialogue (Howe et al., 2019).

Productive dialogue has positive effects on mathematics education, including students' improved learning performance (Howe et al., 2019), reasoning and problem-solving skills (Mercer & Sams, 2006), conceptual understanding (Kazak et al., 2015), and enjoyment (Chen et al., 2020). The rapid advancement and increasing ubiquity of digital technologies in education have ignited growing professional and research interest in technology-mediated dialogic teaching (Major et al., 2018). For example, Hardman and Lilley (2023) reported that the use of tablets facilitated South African primary-aged students' exploratory talk and their mathematical reasoning. The dialogic potential of digital technology is greatly attributed to various technological affordances (e.g., visibility, revisiting, multimodality etc.; see more in Major et al., 2018). Some studies explored and exemplified how to enact affordances of a certain technology used to foster classroom dialogue (e.g., Cook et al., 2019; Hennessy, 2011).

However, the dialogic opportunity adds new challenges and complexities to teaching practice, owing to the entangled and mutually shaped relations between context, purpose, values, technology, and pedagogy (Fawns, 2022). Also, there are new challenges faced by teachers, involving technical issues, classroom management, learner inclusion, and instructional design (Major et al., 2018). To support teachers' dialogic approaches to using appropriate digital technology, TPD is crucially important. Therefore, the following sections focus on introducing lesson study, a TPD model, and articulating why and how this should be used with DBR in this case study.

Lesson Study for Teacher Learning and Pedagogy

Lesson study (LS), originated from Japan in the 1870s, is a school-based, practitioner-led, and peer-supported model for professional learning, pedagogical development, student learning, and/or school development. It essentially highlights teacher agency and requires teachers' collaborative inquiry, trials, and reflection. One cycle of LS is normally conducted by a group of three to seven teachers through *planning, teaching/observing, evaluating, and revising* (Xu & Pedder, 2015).

Various adaptations of LS have been developed in different cultural and local contexts. In China, LS was introduced by the Ministry of Education in the 1950s and has been widely used for TPD in Chinese mathematics education (Huang & Han, 2015). The Chinese lesson study (CLS) aims to polish lessons (i.e., effective strategies for teaching a particular subject content or for teaching a type of lesson) through *moke* (磨课, cycles of trialling and refining lesson teaching through repeated teaching with variation, observation, and comparison) (Huang & Li, 2014). CLS, argued by Chen (2017), is bound up with Chinese philosophical and epistemological traditions: a unity of knowing and doing (知行合一) and a tendency of emulating those better than oneself (见贤思齐). With the culture of teaching as a public activity valued (Stigler et al., 2013), Chinese teachers are used to observing others' teaching, being observed by others, and conducting public lessons (Huang & Han, 2015).

One enriched model of CLS is parallel lesson study (PLS; tong ke yi gou, 同课异构), which highlights the development of public research lessons on the same topic through comparison and collaboration between at least two lesson study groups (LSGs) from different schools (Huang & Han, 2015). PLS extends teachers' learning opportunities and brings them into an expanding dialogic space involving multiple and different perspectives from both insiders and outsiders. Teachers can test whether innovative pedagogical practices are applicable and effective in other contexts, in turn facilitating reflection and collective efforts to refine them.

Design-Based Research Approach

Design-based research (DBR) is defined as "a systematic but flexible methodology aimed at improving educational practices through iterative analysis, design, development, and implementation, based on collaboration among researchers and practitioners in real-world settings, and leading to contextually-sensitive design principles and theories" (Wang & Hannafin, 2005, p. 6). DBR prioritises flexibility, collaboration, local adaptation, iteration, and reflection. Furthermore, DBR places greater explicit emphasis on the intertwining of theory and practice and aims to test or develop theory. The anticipated concrete outcomes involve design principles (principles showing *how to*), educational resources, and professional development of participants.

The common features of DBR essentially share those of dialogic practice and successful TPD programmes, namely being open, flexible, context-based, ongoing, and reflective. This suggests a possibility of a DBR approach to TPD for dialogic education. Despite the rare employment of DBR for TPD for dialogic teaching, a few successful initiatives sprouted (e.g., Hennessy et al., 2021; Wilkinson et al., 2017). For example, the Toolkit for Systematic Educational Dialogue Analysis (T-SEDA) (T-SEDA Collective, 2023) was iteratively developed through the DBR approach to support practitioners' self-directed inquiry based on systematic analysis of classroom dialogue and critical peer reflection, resulting in nine versions and their corresponding versions translated into six other languages.

Moreover, there exists an intrinsic link between DBR and LS. They share the dialogic epistemology that views knowledge development as evolving, cumulative, collaborative, and reflective. Linked to pragmatism, both DBR and LS emphasise action and reflection. Other key commonalities include collaboration, partnership, and multiple iterations, which support teachers in exercising collective agency in their own inquiry while engaging in action and reflection (Edwards, 2015). The similarities between DBR and LS from epistemology to operation suggest a potential to coherently combine them as a powerful whole to support teachers' professional growth. Figure 11.1 illustrates a model integrating LS into a

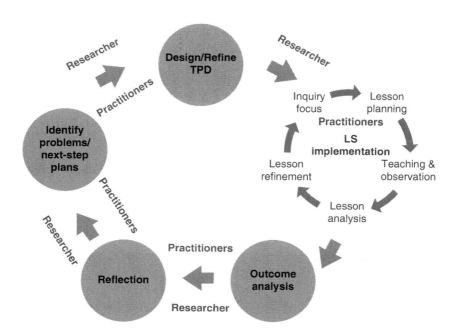

Figure 11.1 Integration of Design-Based Research and Lesson Study

DBR iteration (Liu, 2023). As a driving force, DBR is a systematic, flexible, and collaborative means of tailoring an LS model in a certain context. With LS embedded in DBR, DBR complements LS to jointly contribute to teachers' professional development.

Case Study

Context, Participants, and Technology

The one-year TPD was conducted in two Chinese primary schools from October 2019 to January 2021. Research ethics, as outlined by the British Educational Research Association (2018), was considered and carefully addressed throughout the project. For example, all participating teachers' names reported here are pseudonyms. Due to the COVID-19 pandemic, the schools were closed from February to April 2020. Schools A and B (pseudonyms) are located in an urban area of a city in the southeastern part of mainland China. Both are independent schools accommodating mixed-gender students (aged 6–12). Each class comprises 20–30 students, with four to six seated in a group.

Both schools A and B had similar interests in technology integration and provided infrastructure and equipment support. For instance, all classrooms had Wi-Fi coverage and were equipped with interactive whiteboards. Teachers were provided with laptops or tablets. Students were encouraged to bring tablets from home; schools also provided a few shared digital devices (PCs and tablets) in classrooms. However, the previous TPD activities related to technology integration in the two schools were more like one-shot introductory sessions for demonstrating technical features of those innovative software and/or apps, with only one or two general lesson examples provided, rather than digging into the domain-specific teaching approaches and strategies.

Seven in-service Chinese primary mathematics teachers were organised into two LSGs by school (see Table 11.1). Xia and Zheng volunteered as local school facilitators for their respective LSGs. All of the teachers had previous experience in digital teaching. However, their experience with tablet-integrated pedagogy (involving any digital tools/apps/online platforms/digital resources on the tablet device) was relatively limited. Tablets were initially chosen as a multi-function and children-friendly device type. The teachers further agreed to focus on digital platforms via tablet, with their dialogic intention to support students' active and

Table 11.1 Demographic Characteristics of Participating Teachers

School	Teacher	Gender	Year Level Taught (10/2019-01/2021)	Age (until 2019)	Years of Teaching Mathematics (until 2019)	Prior Experience in Using Tablets in Mathematics Teaching (Until 2019)
A	Lai	F	Y1, Y2 (students' age: 6–7)	25	3	Fewer than 1 year of using tablets
	Sha	M	Y3, Y4 (students' age: 9–10)	28	3	Two years of using tablets
	Xia	F	Y5, Y6 (students' age: 11–12)	28	5	One year of using tablets
	Tu	F	Y5, Y6 (students' age: 11–12)	28	5	Two lessons
B	Chai	M	Y1, Y2 (students' age: 6–7)	24	2	Fewer than one year of using tablets
	Yuan	F	Y1, Y3 (students' age: 6–7 and 8–9)	27	3	Never
	Zheng	F	Y2, Y3 (students' age: 7–8)	44	24	Three years of using tablets

equitable dialogic participation and engagement within and even before or after a lesson. Teachers from School A preferred Padlet, while those from School B chose Zoomabc.

Padlet is an online interactive platform, available as a web-based version or as software on mobile devices, supporting both synchronous and asynchronous communication and collaboration. Users can post ideas in various formats (e.g., text, image, voice, video) from anywhere and at any time. Posts on the same canvas can be viewed, responded to, and evaluated using various rating indicators (e.g., a 'like' sign, a 'thumbs-up' sign, five stars, scores from 1–100) by other users. Zoomabc is an online, multifunctional, and interactive learning platform available as software on tablets, specifically designed for educational use in China. Students' work is automatically saved, and the content can be modified at any time. Additionally, contributions can be easily shared in the 'Class Circle', where posts are displayed chronologically and arranged linearly. Students can browse each other's work, use the 'thumbs up' sign to express agreement or appreciation, and leave either text-based comments or voice messages.

The DBR-Led LS

Overall, this DBR-led LS consisted of three phases: *preliminary phase*, *development phase* (workshops and two cycles of PLS between two LSGs), and *assessment and reflection phase*. In the preliminary phase, the central aim was to understand local institutional and cultural contexts, real problems, and participants' needs, thereby identifying the focal problems and TPD goals and proposing the preliminary design principles. Pre-TPD assessment, including literature reviewing, baseline surveys, consultation, and on-site lesson observations, was conducted. The analyses and results informed and refined the TPD design in the development phase.

The analyses indicated a need to enhance the teachers' theoretical and conceptual understandings about educational dialogue and dialogic teaching. In line with DBR's principles of flexibility and responsiveness, three workshops were delivered in a dialogic manner at each LSG concerning the interconnected areas: classroom dialogue and dialogic teaching, digital technology for dialogue, and systematic analysis of classroom dialogue through the T-SEDA tools and templates. Following the workshops, participants completed an action plan for next-step lesson planning. Following this, two PLS cycles for teachers trialling and co-developing were implemented. Each cycle spanned three months and included (1) establishing and developing ground rules for classroom dialogue using the online platforms individually or collaboratively; (2) individual teaching trials; (3) interim reflective meeting at each LSG; and (4) LS within and between two schools (see Figure 11.2).

In one PLS, one lesson topic was agreed upon by all and then planned collectively in their own LSG. A teacher from each LSG was chosen to deliver the lesson, which was then observed, analysed, and discussed by all the teachers together. Feedback was sought from three or four students in the observed classroom regarding their learning experience and dialogic engagement immediately after the lesson. Students' different gender and the observed different participation level (active or quite) were considered. The recorded two research lessons were shared with the teachers. They were asked to revisit the recorded lesson episodes related to teaching with the platforms. By referring to the T-SEDA's coding framework, individual teachers chose an inquiry focus (e.g., teacher questions, students' responses, teachers' responses to students' online dialogic contributions etc.) and analysed the corresponding parts of the lessons. In addition, they were encouraged to individually reflect on the teaching first along with students' post-lesson feedback and coding results before a collaborative meeting. Following this, all the teachers met together to bring in personal findings and reflection and discuss these with peers collaboratively, resulting in agreed-upon outcomes (e.g., ground rules, useful teaching approaches and strategies, enacted technological affordances), areas for

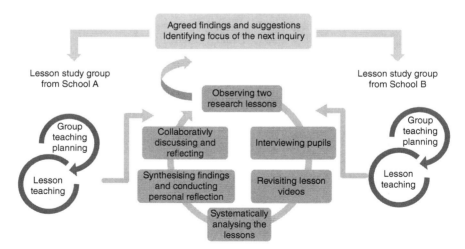

Figure 11.2 Parallel Lesson Study in the Programme

Digital Technology in Chinese Primary Mathematics **169**

further improvement, and the inquiry focus of the next cycle. Moreover, the teachers' perceptions of their TPD participation and suggestions were gained to further inform refinement of the next cycle of PLS.

Lastly, the assessment and reflection phase played a key role in evaluating the TPD's effect on teacher change based on the pre-post comparison, individual teachers' cases, and cross-case analysis. Furthermore, it was essential to synthesise the teaching strategies that the teachers had collectively agreed upon as effective, which can inform future dialogic teaching with digital platforms. Meanwhile, the final design principles were derived through four iterations (see Figure 11.3), acting as practical guidelines for TPD for dialogic teaching with digital technology. However, these principles should be considered in conjunction with their specific contexts and conditions. Adaptation is needed when purposes and contexts are different.

Changes of Teachers and Teaching Practice

After participating in the one-year DBR-led LS, an assessment of teacher change was undertaken through individual questionnaires, interviews, and lesson observations. Firstly, the thematic analysis on individual teachers' pre- and post-programme interviews revealed that their understandings of dialogic teaching became more comprehensive in a relational sense, transforming from a simple interactive format of teacher questioning and student responding to a multidimensional construct. Teachers began to see themselves more as *facilitators* to provide additional opportunities for students to engage with each other's ideas, rather than taking a leading and dominant role in dialogic teaching. They also increased awareness of students' autonomy, active participation, and collective and constructive engagement in dialogue. Teachers highlighted specific features of technology-mediated dialogue, including transcending physical space, sustaining across time, and facilitating inter-animation of students' diverse ideas.

In terms of overall changes in dialogic teaching practice, there was a significant increase in both the proportion of students' high-level participation in dialogue ($z = -2.197$, $p = .028$) and the degree of dialogicality in whole-class teaching ($z = -2.366$, $p = .018$). The coding analysis showed significant improvements in the frequency of *invitations to build on ideas, idea connection, coordination of ideas or agreement*, and *reflecting on dialogue or activity* in teachers' turns and *challenging* in students' turns. Specifically, the DBR-led LS helped the teachers co-develop six key pedagogical strategies iteratively, facilitating

170 Qian Liu

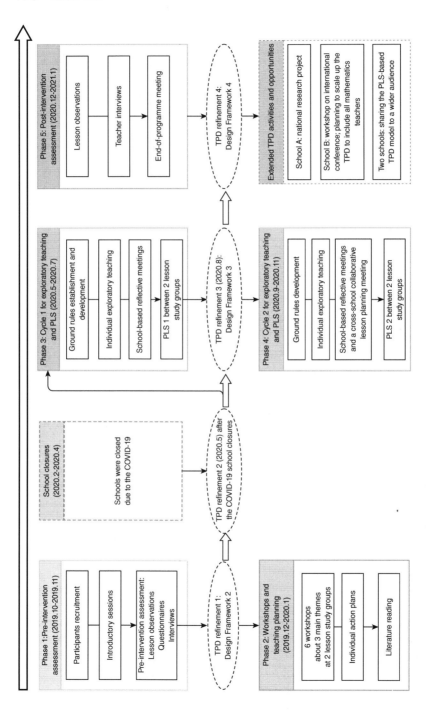

Figure 11.3 Programme Procedure and Main Activities

students' active and equitable participation in dialogue and fostering critical and creative peer engagement with each other's ideas (Liu, 2023).

Furthermore, the teachers reported their enhanced inquiry stance and capability to conduct practitioner-led inquiry in individual interviews after the TPD programme. They frequently reported the following aspects of positive changes: a willingness to trial new methods and take risks; an enhanced sense of integrating research evidence and theory; and habitually adopting critical and reflective perspectives on lessons.

Design Principles of TPD for Dialogic Teaching with Digital Technology

After four iterations (see Figure 11.3), the finalised design principles were refined and then organised into three overarching aspects: TPD design, implementation, and management.

TPD Design

Design Approach and Model

- TPD is designed iteratively in the spirit of DBR and is open to local adaptation based on feedback from teachers and students, as well as provisional findings from lesson observations. TPD documents evidence-based changes in teaching and learning. Changes evidenced during the TPD are made explicitly known to participants.
- TPD incorporates the model of lesson study and encourages teachers to collaboratively undertake practice-based inquiry and critical reflection with peers.

Building Knowledge and Understanding about Educational Dialogue and Dialogic Teaching

- TPD should offer teachers opportunities to understand and learn about the theories and research evidence related to classroom dialogue, making the link between dialogic theory and practice explicit.
- Theory-based introductory workshops incorporate hands-on activities, discursive opportunities, and concrete examples from contexts familiar to teachers to engage them and stimulate reflection.

172 Qian Liu

- TPD provides materials and resources in multimedia formats, which were produced to promote classroom dialogue and include concrete lesson examples from actual classrooms. The materials and resources are open and accessible to teachers and allow for local adaptation.
- TPD introduces ground rules, highlighting their significance in fostering productive dialogue to teachers. Ground rules are incorporated into everyday pedagogical practice and linked to dialogic moves. They need refinement in alignment with different communicative contexts (e.g., online platform, in-person whole-class discussion).

Co-developing Teaching Practices

- TPD emphasises the professional agency of teachers in shaping their dialogic teaching practices, particularly in terms of technology choices and new pedagogical strategies.
- TPD encourages teachers to use analytic tools to systematically scrutinise and reflect on both their own and peers' dialogic practices, testing new approaches and thereby enhancing the quality of educational dialogue.
- TPD encourages teachers to establish and negotiate ground rules with their students and co-develop useful language such as sentence stems in accordance with ground rules.

TPD Implementation

The Whole School Approach and Institutional Support at Multiple Levels

- The implementation of TPD is recognised and supported by the school leadership at the institutional level.
- TPD secures administrative support to coordinate regular group meeting times and some dedicated time for personal inquiry and reflection.
- TPD seeks technical support from schools and external educational technology consultants or technicians.

Local Facilitation

- Each school's TPD implementation is supported by a local facilitator. Ideally, the local facilitator should take the school leadership role and have teaching experience.
- The local facilitator works closely with researchers to discuss content and implementing methods of TPD.
- TPD provides facilitation support to local facilitators.

Digital Technology in Chinese Primary Mathematics **173**

Organisation and Culture Cultivation in LSGs

- An LSG includes three to four motivated teachers who are willing to invest time and effort consistently. The group ideally involves an expert teacher.
- Cultivating a dialogic, supportive, and collaborative culture within an LSG.
- Enhancing teachers' sense of belonging to the supportive community and their ownership of the co-constructed knowledge.
- Strengthening intimate connections amongst teacher participants through regular informal activities.

LS Implementation

- Before an LS, the two LSGs have a collaborative lesson planning meeting to agree on a lesson topic, lesson objectives, inquiry focus, and inquiry questions for a research lesson. Teachers familiarise themselves with the technology used in the other school, not just by understanding its functions, but also by experiencing it firsthand and attempting to integrate it into their own teaching practices.
- Research lessons can be observed through live streaming technology. However, the live observation on site provides an immersive experience and an opportunity to notice details.
- Post-lesson discussions should be goal-orientated, structured, and provide clarity to teachers about the topics of discussion and decisions to be made.
- Employing facilitation strategies to foster teachers' professional dialogue in LS and their dialogic skills in professional contexts.

TPD Management

- TPD makes participants explicitly aware of costs and opportunities of participation and allows them to learn about the relevance of these costs and opportunities to their professionalism and anticipated benefits.
- If adjustments to the TPD are made during the process, the planned changes should be explained and discussed with the facilitators. Other teachers should also be informed, and the reasons for this should be explained.
- TPD provides teacher participants opportunities to publicly report and share their inquiry findings and experience.

Discussion and Conclusion

From this case study, a DBR-led LS model for developing in-service mathematics teachers' dialogic teaching with two digital platforms was proposed and exemplified in the Chinese primary education context. Fundamental to the model is the compatibility between DBR and LS, as well as their complementary relationship. The DBR approach, characterised by *iterative and collaborative design, theory-practice integration, co-development*, and *contextual responsiveness*, contributed to tailoring an LS model to a specific context. For example, an LS normally starts from teaching planning, while the LS employed here had workshops first to build on the teachers' theoretical and practical understandings. This adaptation was based on a better understanding of participants' needs from the baseline data. In addition, DBR increased opportunities for teachers to collaborate with researchers, whereas LS normally takes advantage of peer collaboration among teachers in the same LSG. The researcher-practitioner partnership created a closer connection between theory, research, and practice. For example, the teachers had access to theoretical readings, research evidence, and tools for systematic observation and evaluation, contributing to critical and systematic interrogation of everyday practice and evidence-based and research-informed reflection. Employing LS here is also a cultural response to the Chinese context, as previously discussed in the literature review section. Importantly, LS values teachers' personal and collective agency to develop teaching, which is deemed useful for devising new teaching strategies with new technology.

Furthermore, the combination of DBR and LS fostered the development of teachers' inquiry stance and capability, key to sustainable professional learning. The teachers gained relevant research experience, including identifying and selecting their own inquiry foci, conducting lesson observations and interviews to collect data, systematically analysing classroom dialogue, and interpreting evidence and results. As the traditional Chinese proverb goes, "授人以鱼不如授人以渔" (Give a man a fish and you feed him for a day; teach a man to fish and you feed him for a lifetime). Offering teachers opportunities to engage in the DBR-led LS supported their 'analytic stance' (van Es, 2011), potentially facilitating their ongoing systematic inquiry and making sustained changes. Related to Hughes's (2005) TPD for technology-integrated pedagogy, this DBR-led LS model supported teachers' co-agency to actively exploit potential affordances of the digital platforms they chose to *transform* rather than *replace* or just *amplify* the current teaching practices.

Given the scarcity of successful TPD initiatives for dialogic teaching with digital technology, the case study proposed a DBR-led LS model and showed how this can be applied to design and run an effective, feasible, and sustained technology-related TPD. This was the first attempt to employ an LS model for technology-mediated dialogic teaching in the field. The model can act as a springboard for teacher educators and educational researchers on how to support in-service teachers in integrating technology dialogically into their own contexts. In addition, the study clearly demonstrated the contextual and institutional conditions, TPD procedure, activities within one PLS between two schools, and contributing design principles. These practically show how the model can be locally adapted and implemented in the actual, highly complex, and entangled technology-integrated practice.

When intending to scale up the TPD programme, contextual awareness and purpose-driven adaptation are significantly important. The design principles are not 'what works' items on a rigid checklist; they play a role in informing decisions based on particular conditions, purposes, and technologies used. The outcomes of the case study were not fully attributed to the model. It is important to recognise the inherent advantageous characteristics, such as the voluntary and self-motivated teachers, technological resource support from the schools, and the schools' emphasis on technology integration.

The DBR approach to LS or the DBR-led LS model is suggested to be employed to adapt the TPD programme to diverse contexts (e.g., different subject domains, under-resourced primary schools in China, primary schools in different cultural settings). It encourages a process of productive and mutual adaptation in collaboration with researchers, teacher educators, and teachers to respond to local needs and concerns. It also values teachers' collective agency and critical inquiry in changing practice or developing new practice. Linked to technology integration, teachers have the autonomy to decide on technology type based on their judgement shaped by pedagogical intention and anticipated outcomes. Furthermore, this model highlighting teachers' active trialling and critical inquiry avoids the pitfalls of previous teacher training sessions that marginalised the intertwined relationship between technical affordances, pedagogy, and learning outcomes.

References

Alexander, R. J. (2004). *Towards dialogic teaching: Rethinking classroom talk* (1st ed.). Dialogos.

British Educational Research Association (BERA). (2018). *Ethical guidelines for educational research* (4th ed.). Retrieved October 1, 2023, from https://www.bera.ac.uk/wp-content/uploads/2018/06/BERA-Ethical-Guidelines-for-Educational-Research_4thEdn_2018.pdf

Chen, G., Zhang, J., Chan, C. K. K., Michaels, S., Resnick, L. B., & Huang, X. (2020). The link between student-perceived teacher talk and student enjoyment, anxiety and discursive engagement in the classroom. *British Educational Research Journal, 46*(3), 631–652. https://doi.org/10.1002/berj.3600

Chen, X. (2017). Theorizing Chinese lesson study from a cultural perspective. *International. Journal for Lesson and Learning Studies, 6*(4), 283–292. https://doi.org/10.1108/IJLLS-12-2016-0059

Cook, V., Warwick, P., Vrikki, M., Major, L., & Wegerif, R. (2019). Developing material-dialogic space in geography learning and teaching: Combining a dialogic pedagogy with the use of a microblogging tool. *Thinking Skills and Creativity, 31*, 217–231. https://doi.org/10.1016/j.tsc.2018.12.005

Edwards, A. (2015). Recognising and realising teachers' professional agency. *Teachers and Teaching: Theory and Practice, 21*(6), 779–784.

Fawns, T. (2022). An entangled pedagogy: Looking beyond the pedagogy – technology dichotomy. *Postdigital Science and Education, 4*(3), 711–728. https://doi.org/10.1007/s42438-022-00302-7

Hardman, J., & Lilley, W. (2023). iLearn? Investigating dialogical interaction with tablets in mathematics lessons. *Technology, Pedagogy and Education, 32*(3), 321–335. https://doi.org/10.1080/1475939X.2023.2193194

Hennessy, S. (2011). The role of digital artefacts on the interactive whiteboard in supporting classroom dialogue: Dialogue and IWB artefacts. *Journal of Computer AssistedLearning,27*(6),463–489.https://doi.org/10.1111/j.1365-2729.2011.00416.x

Hennessy, S., Kershner, R., Calcagni, E., & Ahmed, F. (2021). Supporting practitioner-led inquiry into classroom dialogue with a research-informed professional learning resource: A design-based approach. *Review of Education, 9*(3), 1–48. https://doi.org/10.1002/rev3.3269

Howe, C., Hennessy, S., Mercer, N., Vrikki, M., & Wheatley, L. (2019). Teacher-student dialogue during classroom teaching: Does it really impact upon student outcomes? *Journal for the Learning Sciences, 28*(4), 462–512. https://doi.org/10.1080/10508406.2019.1573730

Huang, R., & Han, X. (2015). Developing mathematics teachers' competence through parallel lesson study. *International Journal for Lesson and Learning Studies, 4*(2), 100–117.

Huang, R., & Li, Y. (2014). Developing high-leverage practices in mathematics through exemplary lesson development: A Chinese approach. In Y. Li, E. Silver, & S. Li (Eds.), *Transforming mathematics instruction: Multiple approaches and practices* (pp. 231–254). Springer.

Hughes, J. E. (2005). The role of teacher knowledge and learning experiences in forming technology-integrated pedagogy. *The Journal of Technology and Teacher Education, 13*, 277–302.

Kazak, S., Wegerif, R., & Fujita, T. (2015). Combining scaffolding for content and scaffolding for dialogue to support conceptual breakthroughs in understanding probability. *ZDM, 47*(7), 1269–1283. https://doi.org/10.1007/s11858-015-0720-5

Liu, Q. (2023). *Developing dialogic mathematics with tablet technology in Chinese primary school classrooms: A design-based approach to teacher professional development* [PhD thesis, University of Cambridge].

Major, L., Warwick, P., Rasmussen, I., Ludvigsen, S., & Cook, V. (2018). Classroom dialogue and digital technologies: A scoping review. *Education and Information Technologies, 23*(5), 1995–2028. https://doi.org/10.1007/s10639-018-9701-y

Mercer, N., & Sams, C. (2006). Teaching children how to use language to solve maths problems. *Language and Education, 20*(6), 507–528. https://doi.org/10.2167/le678.0

Stigler, J., Thompson, B., & Ji, X. (2013). This book speaks to us. In Y. Li & R. Huang (Eds.), *How Chinese teach mathematics and improve teaching* (pp. 223–231). Routledge.

T-SEDA Collective. (2023). *Teacher scheme for educational dialogue analysis (T-SEDA) v9 resource pack.* University of Cambridge. Retrieved May 2, 2022, from http://bit.ly/T-SEDA

van Es, E. A. (2011). A framework for learning to notice student thinking. In M. G. Sherin, V. R. Jacobs, & R. A. Philipp (Eds.), *Mathematics teacher noticing: Seeing through teachers' eyes* (pp. 164–181). Routledge.

Wang, F., & Hannafin, M. J. (2005). Design-based research and technology-enhanced learning environments. *Educational Technology Research and Development, 53*(4), 5–23. https://doi.org/10.1007/BF02504682

Wilkinson, I. A. G., Reznitskaya, A., Bourdage, K., Oyler, J., Glina, M., Drewry, R., Nelson, K. (2017). Toward a more dialogic pedagogy: Changing teachers' beliefs and practices through professional development in language arts classrooms. *Language and Education, 31*(1), 65–82. https://doi.org/10.1080/09500782.2016.1230129

Xu, H., & Pedder, D. (2015). Lesson study: An international review of the research. In P. Dudley (Ed.), *Lesson study: Professional learning for our time* (pp. 29–58). Routledge.

Breaking the Digital Divide   **12**

How Tech-Enabled Project-Based Learning Can Level the Playing Field for Marginalized Learners

Liddy Greenaway, Navya Akkinepally, Hiba Rahim, Lauren Lichtman, and Karishma Mhapadi

Introduction

This case study presents lessons learned from the 2022–23 pilot of the Flying Colors program in Uganda. The program, designed to support out-of-school and vulnerable learners, brings together digital learning using Learning Equality's offline-first Kolibri Learning Platform, project-based and playful learning approaches, and social-emotional learning materials from Amal Alliance's Colors of Kindness program. The newly designed curriculum was developed in alignment with the abridged Ugandan curriculum. The pilot aimed to understand the effectiveness of the curated content, educators' ability to facilitate lessons, technology usability, and changes in learning outcomes. Considerations for sustainability and scalability are discussed, together with lessons applicable to similar tech-enabled programs with educators new to blended learning.

The program was jointly developed and implemented by three partner organizations. Hopelink Action Foundation (HAF) Uganda is an organization based in Gulu, Uganda, that focuses on providing mental health

DOI: 10.4324/9781003406631-12

180 Liddy Greenaway et al.

and psychosocial support services, specializing in implementation and pedagogical support.

Learning Equality is a nonprofit organization that provides the Kolibri Learning Platform and pioneers offline-first edtech solutions and support for effective integration of blended learning through edtech. Kolibri is an end-to-end ecosystem of open, adaptable products and tools designed for teaching and learning without requiring connection to the Internet ('offline-first'). It is designed for multiple contexts, with a focus on fostering innovative pedagogy and increasing learning outcomes; increasing the availability of relevant, aligned learning materials; and overcoming infra-structural barriers that prevent equitable access.

Amal Alliance is a nonprofit organization with expertise in social-emotional learning (SEL) and curriculum design. They developed the adaptable Colors of Kindness curriculum that was embedded into the program. Within the context of Flying Colors, SEL refers to the process of acquiring and applying knowledge, attitudes, and skills related to understanding and managing emotions; building positive relationships; showing empathy towards others; effectively handling social interactions; collaborating with others; making responsible decisions; and developing a sense of identity and agency.

Study Context

Flying Colors is a new programmatic intervention that supports SEL and foundational literacy and numeracy (FLN), enabled by technology and project-based learning (PBL). It is a blended learning program, meaning that it combines traditional in-person classroom instruction with digital learning activities using educational technology.

Flying Colors was piloted in 2022–23 in Palabek Refugee Settlement in Lamwo District, Uganda. In-service teachers were recruited and trained to support out-of-school learners who would otherwise be enrolled in grades P3 or P4. Three-quarters of the 714 enrolled learners were refugees, and most were over-age compared to the grade equivalent, ranging from 9–15 years old (P3 learners are typically 7–8 years and P4 are 8–9 years). Flying Colors leverages Learning Equality's Kolibri Learning Platform designed for offline-first teaching and learning, and Amal Alliance's Colors of Kindness program for social-emotional learning.

The initial pilot, funded by The LEGO Foundation, aimed to understand the program's effectiveness in bringing together the blended pedagogical approaches across foundational learning skills and social-emotional competencies and determine whether educators could effectively facilitate lessons with the necessary support, and if the technology was easy to use and navigate. In order to do this, evidence and learning was gathered against the following four evaluation questions:

1. Is the curated content effective and appropriate?
2. Are teachers able to successfully facilitate lessons, and are they appropriately supported to do so?
3. Are teachers and learners able to effectively use the Kolibri Platform?
4. What effect does the program have on student learning outcomes?

The pilot took place across two cohorts of 12 weeks, and was iterative in its design. The first cohort focused on developing and aligning the learning materials with the abridged Ugandan curriculum, as well as offering professional development training for teachers in the integration of Kolibri in a blended learning classroom, playful learning, and PBL and SEL lessons. The program design was iterated on for the second cohort, based on a range of data collected to understand effectiveness and where improvements were needed. The pilot also benefited from the support of Innovations for Poverty Action (IPA) as an evidence partner to guide the learning questions, data collection efforts, and analysis.

Background: Limited Education in Northern Uganda

In Uganda, enrollment in primary school tends to be fairly high. However, a combination of factors, including poverty, child marriage and early pregnancy, domestic labour, child labour, low social skills, and limited school facilities, leads to high drop-out rates in parts of the country (Nabugoomu, 2019), particularly at P4 and significantly by P5 (age 11+). In 2018, the primary net enrollment rate was 91% and the primary completion rate was 51% (EPDC, 2018).

Northern Uganda is also host to a large refugee population. The protracted crisis in South Sudan and widespread displacement has resulted in family breakdowns and high rates of out-of-school children, increasing the pressure on school facilities and increasing the need for dedicated programming focused on the social-emotional and psychological well-being of learners.

In recent years, due to COVID-related school closures, learners who started in P3 and P4 were unable to complete and advance to the next grade in 2020, and an additional year of learning was missed in 2021. It is also known that a significant number of girls aged 13–14 became pregnant during the pandemic, and they had a general unwillingness to return to school. According to the National Planning Authority, an estimated 30% of learners were anticipated to never return to school, and about 3,507 primary schools were likely to close, so initiatives that target the foundational and social-emotional learning needs of these learners, with pathways to re-entry, are critically needed (NPA, 2021). Data collection for Flying Colors confirmed that learners' English literacy levels were lower than expected P3/P4 levels (English is the national language of instruction in Uganda). Limited and highly variable numeracy skills also indicated a need for personalized learning and tailored content.

There have been no information and communications technology (ICT) interventions for primary-level learners in the Palabek refugee settlement, in part due to limited infrastructure, electricity, and Internet connectivity. However, an initial scoping demonstrated high interest and demand for technology, due to increasing needs for digital literacy, limited access to resources and educational materials, and high levels of school drop-outs.

Pedagogical Design of Flying Colors

Flying Colors was developed to address the problems summarized in the previous section. The program takes a multi-faceted pedagogical approach that helps build FLN and SEL through contextually relevant, collaborative, and project-based approaches.

In the context of the Flying Colors program, FLN refers to fundamental literacy skills and strategies involved in reading, speaking, writing, and interpreting language; and basic numeracy skills covering simple numerical concepts such as counting, number sequence, addition, and subtraction. SEL refers to the process of "developing social and emotional competencies in children" (CASEL, 2013), including the skills, behaviors, and attitudes that people need to manage their personal, social, and cognitive behaviors (Yoder, 2014). These skills are important for personal well-being, healthy relationships, academic success, and navigating different social experiences. Flying Colors integrated Colors of Kindness, a holistic SEL hybrid program developed by Amal Alliance, which includes teacher preparation materials and audio podcasts that support teachers to guide learners in building SEL skills through interactive and play-based activities. This content was organized into a channel and made available to learners and teachers via Kolibri, as part of a week-by-week facilitation plan provided by Learning Equality.

The Flying Colors curriculum is aligned to the Ugandan abridged P3 curriculum themes. It is supported by newly developed training and facilitator materials, and leverages existing and new open educational resources (OER) for PBL. It directly responds to the needs of the learning environment, supporting refugee and host community learners that often have limited Internet, and educators with limited SEL and playful learning preparation and limited access to teaching materials.

PBL is an active method of learning through project work that encourages learners to construct their own knowledge by actively engaging in real-world and personally meaningful projects. PBL is acknowledged as contributing to a range of learning outcomes. For example, it is an effective approach for teaching problem-solving and decision-making (Thomas, 2000), and evidence suggests that PBL contributes to SEL outcomes, including the development of identity, agency, and collaboration (Jagers et al., 2021). According to Chen and Yang (2019), implementing PBL for a minimum of two hours per week results in notably improved academic performance among students, compared to using PBL for fewer than two hours per week.

In Flying Colors, PBL was integrated to provide highly tailored and relevant content, incorporating practical, real-world engagement and opportunities for family and community interaction through projects that required dialogue between learners and caregivers. Research has demonstrated that the more caregivers are involved in their children's education, the better their learning outcomes (Zhang et al., 2020).

The blended curriculum was tailored and contextualized to suit the local environment. This was driven by the features of authenticity of projects (Railsback, 2002), including student-centered and student-directed learning; focusing on content relevant to students and observable in their surroundings, addressing real-world problems; involving first-hand investigations, respecting local culture; specific, curriculum-related goals; and encouraging reflective thinking and student self-assessment.

The program also took into consideration the linguistic barriers within the local community. In Uganda, the national language of instruction is English. However, learners spoke different first languages, primarily Acholi and Arabic. Research by the World Bank (2021) indicates that learning in a first language has several positive effects: it is found to enhance learning outcomes in the first language, enhance learning outcomes in a subsequent second language, enhance learning in other academic subjects, and foster the development of other cognitive abilities. It

184 Liddy Greenaway et al.

was therefore important that Flying Colors enabled first language instruction and understanding, while also ensuring materials and content were in English and providing foundational English literacy skills, in alignment with the national curriculum.

To accommodate this, teachers used multilingual instruction while teaching, translating into the local languages where needed. Colors of Kindness content was also adapted to be read in a Ugandan English accent to aid comprehension (following feedback from teachers that the American English accent was difficult to understand). Teachers could then follow the guides with ease and translate hard-to-follow concepts for the learners in the relevant local language. This proved to be a successful solution to addressing the contextual challenges of linguistic barriers.

Teachers were supported through scaffolded training sessions, implemented in a phased manner, as indicated in Table 12.1. Sessions

Table 12.1 Flying Colors Training Plan

Training areas

Phase 1: Month 1–6

- Introduction to PBL
- Introduction to Kolibri, hardware, SEL, and PBL
- Introduction to session structure and lesson planning with Kolibri
- Practice with Kolibri
- Setting up classrooms for implementation – classroom materials, learning space design, classroom management, procedures and routines
- Practice with Kolibri and integrating blended learning
- Practice with SEL
- Practice lesson plan and session structure
- Practice PBL with Kolibri
- Practice Kolibri as a coach
- Practice lesson planning
- Review SEL activities
- Preparing for and creating playful learning materials

Phase 2: Months 7–12

- Introduction to teacher personas – practicing presence, tone, voice, and language for playful learning
- Project-based learning continued training
- Introducing formative assessments with Kolibri and data-informed pedagogy
- Project-based learning continued training
- Introducing differentiation with Kolibri
- Grouping strategies

focused on developing knowledge, skills, and beliefs around PBL, SEL, and blended learning with Kolibri. For example, the session on differentiated learning highlighted its importance and benefits, and equipped teachers to use the grouping feature in Kolibri.

Teachers were supported to jointly facilitate two to four sessions per week, each lasting 80 minutes, encompassing PBL, SEL, and FLN across the different sessions. Figure 12.1 shows the weekly plan provided to teachers.

Weekly planning was aided by lesson plans with activities that teachers could facilitate with or without the Kolibri Learning Platform, and included objectives for the class; time and material requirements; teacher instructions; guidance for implementing a project; and guidance on Kolibri practice, quizzes, and student-centered approaches such as group work.

Integration of technology into the learning environment has been highlighted by multiple researchers as a valuable aspect for teachers implementing a PBL approach (Condliffe et al., 2016). Krajcik and Shin (2014) emphasized that learning environments supported by technological materials can enhance individualized, independent learning, leading to more meaningful educational experiences.

Kolibri acts as a blended learning platform for the program. It hosts and facilitates the use of the content not only for foundational literacy and numeracy but also for social-emotional learning in a single virtual environment. This enables ease of access to resources for both learners and teachers to foster learning in a context such as Palabek, where there is no Internet.

Through Kolibri, educators have access to a coach dashboard (see Figure 12.2) to track student progress, create groups, and assign lessons and quizzes based on the digital resources needed to support learning. In addition, all the content remained available on Kolibri for both learners and educators to access at any time. The focused use of Kolibri to enable PBL, SEL, and FLN was based on the documented improvements in learning outcomes associated with blended learning practice (Khader, 2016).

Technologies Used within Flying Colors

The Kolibri product ecosystem is a suite of open-source software and tools developed for use without requiring the Internet. Learning Equality has been developing Kolibri for more than six years, building on the foundations and lessons learned from deploying our first-generation

186 Liddy Greenaway et al.

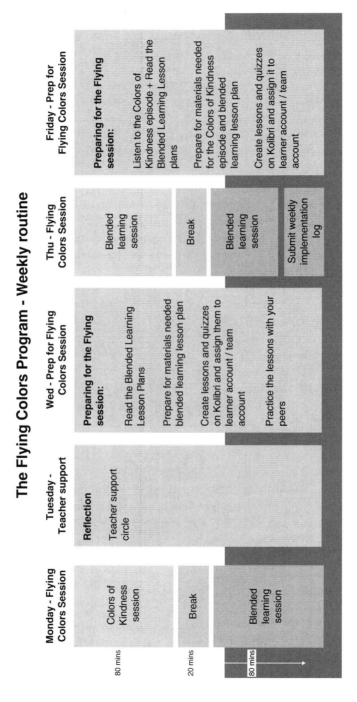

Figure 12.1 Flying Colors Weekly Facilitation Plan

Breaking the Digital Divide

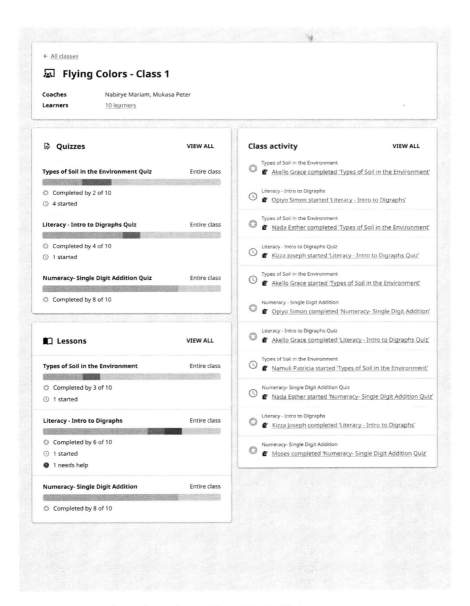

Figure 12.2 Snapshot of Coach Dashboard in Kolibri

platform, KA Lite. The software is built using open-source technologies focused around being adaptable and extensible, having cross-platform and legacy browser support, and running efficiently on low-power devices.

Kolibri supports peer-to-peer data synchronization, which enables Learning Equality to synchronize data generated on end-user devices to local offline servers (such as those in a school) during intermittent connectivity between them. From there, they can sync at some interval to the Internet, or to another device that can be brought somewhere with the Internet to be synced. A typical Kolibri implementation, and the one used for the Flying Colors program, follows a client server model, where devices are connected to a local area network without the use of the Internet. In this way, Kolibri leapfrogs the last-mile problems that prevent effective use of most education technology in disconnected environments, supporting data-driven implementation and asynchronous remote facilitation of learning. By housing content off the Internet, Kolibri also avoids challenges associated with learners accessing non-educational or inappropriate content on connected devices. The Kolibri content library provides a wide range of validated educational resources, and educators have complete control over what learners have access to.

Evaluation of Flying Colors' Effectiveness

To learn and iterate the program, and evaluate whether Flying Colors is relevant, effective, and scalable, evidence was gathered throughout the pilot using a mixed-methods approach.

Methodology: The mixed-methods approach covered a range of surveys, focus group discussions (FGDs), and classroom observations, as listed in Table 12.2, as well as continuous informal feedback from the implementing partner (HAF Uganda). Qualitative attitudes, perceptions, and experiences of teachers and learners were analyzed using thematic coding of interview and FGD data and open text responses elicited from surveys.

Learners' foundational literacy, numeracy, and SEL were measured using surveys administered using a one-on-one interview style approach by a member of staff (Monitoring, Evaluation and Learning Officer) of the implementing partner (HAF Uganda). It is important to note that these assessments and interviews were not conducted by the educators themselves to limit potential bias. The questions used for FLN were based on reliable and valid instruments from the Annual Status of Education

Table 12.2 Data Collection and Analysis Methods

Tool	Measures	Sample Size	Analysis Approach
Teacher surveys at baseline, midline, and endline	• Attitudes towards pedagogical components • Knowledge and confidence • Challenges	• Nine teachers at baseline • Eight teachers at midline and endline	Quantitative and qualitative: • Basic descriptive statistics • Coding of open text responses
Learner cohort pre- and post- surveys	• Foundational literacy and numeracy assessment based on ASER • Adapted Harvard EASEL social-emotional skills assessment • Attitudes and aspirations • Challenges	• 256 matched learner pre-/post- surveys	Quantitative: • Basic descriptive statistics • Paired t-tests • Regression analysis (Pearson's r)
Teacher FGDs	• Teacher attitudes, perceptions, and experiences	• Eight teachers	Qualitative: thematic coding
Learner FGDs	• Learner attitudes, perceptions, and experiences	• 28 learners	Qualitative: thematic coding
Teacher training exit slips	• Training successes and areas for improvement • Knowledge and confidence	• Six teachers at initial training • Six teachers at refresher training	Quantitative and qualitative: • Basic descriptive statistics • Coding of open text responses
Classroom observations	• Implementation	• 26 classroom observations	Quantitative and qualitative: • Matrix score analysis • Coding of open text responses
Kolibri Data Portal	• Teacher and learner log ins and time spent on content	• Collected automatically through Kolibri for all active users	Quantitative: • Basic descriptive statistics • Regression analysis (Pearson's r)

Report (ASER), while the SEL items were adapted from a tool developed by Harvard's EASEL Lab. Quantitative analysis, including basic descriptive statistics, paired t-tests, and regression analysis using Pearson's r, was used to analyze score data.

Data was triangulated where possible, including cross-referencing with Kolibri Data Portal data, which provides real-time reports on content used and time spent on Kolibri for each user, including teachers and learners.

Challenges and limitations: The methodology was largely successful in understanding the process and outcomes of the pilot. By testing in a phased approach and performing rapid analysis, challenges could be identified and addressed to ensure continuous improvement. Nevertheless, some aspects of the data were more reliable than others. Specific challenges and limitations included:

- Limited experience in classroom observations and low capacity for training resulted in poor inter-rater reliability for observations. Low capacity overall also limited the number of observations gathered. Observation data was analyzed in triangulation with other data sources to build a more rounded picture of implementation and teacher training needs.
- Due to inconsistencies in data collection and constraints related to timing and program iteration, post-surveys for Cohort 1 learners were not collected. The process was improved for Cohort 2, and matched responses for pre- and post- responses were successfully collected for 256 Cohort 2 learners (96% of 266 enrolled learners).
- A lack of ongoing data collection with wider stakeholders such as government stakeholders and Head Teachers limited our understanding of buy-in from these groups, which is important for future sustainability. Our evidence partner, IPA, supported data collection in this area, but only at endline, limiting our ability to iterate and improve on wider stakeholder engagement during the pilot.

Findings: The following section summarizes our findings and learning against the four evaluation questions:

1. Is the curated content effective and appropriate?
2. Are teachers able to successfully facilitate lessons, and are they appropriately supported to do so?
3. Are teachers and learners able to effectively use the Kolibri Platform?
4. What effect does the program have on student learning outcomes?

Question 1. Is the Curated Content Effective and Appropriate?

Teachers were positive about the different pedagogical approaches and content incorporated in the program. They identified that blended learning and playful learning approaches were particularly effective for out-of-school refugee children. One teacher commented:

> Incorporating playful learning was one of the best aspects I have experienced . . . because we are dealing with learners who are out of school . . . being a refugee, it's not easy, the trauma they have, and when they were in school we played with them, we did lessons on Kolibri, they were able to be relieved from the trauma.
>
> (Teacher, FGD)

Teachers also identified social and emotional learning as an important contributor to improving learners' confidence, a particular issue they observe in out-of-school refugee children.

Teachers reported several challenges with the content, including the language barrier, as the content was in English (as required by the Ugandan government), but many out-of-school children started with low levels of English proficiency, and the level of the resources for some modules, which were higher than some learners' ability. Nevertheless, most teachers were able to effectively adapt their lessons to the language and abilities of their learners through translation and tailored lesson planning.

Question 2. Are Teachers Able to Successfully Facilitate Lessons, and Are They Appropriately Supported To Do So?

Program data suggests that the majority of teachers were able to facilitate blended lessons effectively. At the beginning of the program, most teachers felt they needed a high or moderate level of support to integrate ICT skills into their teaching practice, but at the end of the program 75% of active teachers said they were very comfortable integrating technology, and 75% said they had the necessary support and resources to do so.

Cohort 2 classroom observations indicated that facilitation improved over time, with a shift in the latter half of implementation towards learners setting up and using technology independently. Across all observations, teachers excelled in engaging learners, encouraging participation, and celebrating students' successes. However, there were several gaps in time management related to technology use and peer-to-peer learning that may have been helped with additional support.

At endline, all teachers reported that Kolibri was easy to use and navigate, and qualitative feedback suggests that most were confident and proficient in using the Kolibri platform, resources, and coach tools. Teachers valued the guided lesson plans and reported that they were easy to use. Some teachers said they felt confident and able to support other teachers to integrate technology. For example, one teacher said:

> I would feel confident to teach other educators Flying Colors because I am well versed; I am able now to plan using the computer, I can also get resources from there without anyone's guidance.
> (Teacher, FGD)

At the end of the program, several teachers said they still needed help with some aspects of facilitation and blended learning, and three of the eight active teachers said they would have benefitted from additional refresher training during the program. Most notably, they asked for additional support in how to facilitate differentiated learning in the classroom. Differentiation was introduced in the final two weeks of the program but was challenging to implement as it involved multiple components, including additional lesson planning, use of Kolibri data insights to group students, and management and communication in the classroom. In the future, teachers would benefit from more intensive support and oversight in this area to improve practices.

Question 3. Are Teachers and Learners Able to Effectively Use the Kolibri Platform?

Teachers were positive about the incorporation of technology into their teaching and the learning environment. They reported that the use of technology equipped them and their learners with resources that enabled better lesson planning, engaged students, and aided social-emotional and foundational learning.

Classroom observations and Kolibri usage data indicated effective use of technology. Teachers made use of Kolibri lesson plans and assigned a variety of Kolibri content to groups of learners. In nine of eleven observed Kolibri lessons, teachers were able to effectively respond to learners' challenges with the technology or resources. Individual learners spent an average of 23 minutes per week using and completing Kolibri content, including videos, documents, exercises, and quizzes, both in and out of assigned lesson plans. It is noted that learners' time using Kolibri was actually greater than this, as learners used the tablets in pairs the majority of the time, but minutes spent could only be recorded under one username.

There were mixed levels of Kolibri implementation in different schools. For example, in one school only three of the expected nine to ten Kolibri numeracy lessons were implemented, and in another school the teachers did not use Kolibri to run Colors of Kindness sessions. Although capacity constraints and competing priorities were a factor, additional support, as well as more oversight and observations, may have helped teachers who felt less confident with the Kolibri Platform. Teachers reported that feedback from observations had been useful and they had applied what they had learned, suggesting this is an important method of support, as well as an evaluative tool.

Question 4. What Effect Does the Program Have on Learning Outcomes?

In focus group discussions, both teachers and learners commented on improvements across a range of competencies, including English literacy, numeracy, social-emotional skills, including self-confidence, socializing, and effective teamwork, and practical skills, such as gardening, that can be applied at home. Learner assessment data demonstrated a significant positive effect on both foundational literacy and numeracy learning outcomes and social-emotional learning outcomes.

Cohort 2 learners started the program with very low literacy levels: half of learners could read a letter and 20% could read a word. However, as shown in Figure 12.3, by the end of the 12-week program, learners' foundational literacy had progressed significantly, with 73% able to read a paragraph and 64% able to read a story. Progression was also seen in numeracy skills, also shown in Figure 12.3. For both literacy and numeracy scores, the difference between the baseline and endline average score was statistically significant at the 95% confidence level, with a very large effect size (see Table 12.3).

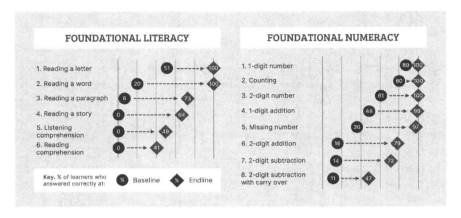

Figure 12.3 Results of Foundational Literacy and Numeracy Assessment, at Baseline and Endline (Cohort 2, n = 256)

Table 12.3 Change in Average Score for Foundational Literacy and Numeracy Assessment (Cohort 2)

Assessment	Mean Score	Number	Standard Deviation	Effect Size (Cohen's d)	A Statistically Significant Difference (t-test, 95%)
Literacy baseline	0.8	256	0.915	2.603	Yes
Literacy endline	4.3	256	1.670		
Numeracy baseline	3.5	256	2.376	1.786	Yes
Numeracy endline	6.9	256	1.264		

A positive correlation was identified between the number of Kolibri sessions implemented in a school and the average proportional increase in numeracy and literacy scores at that school. This suggests that the overall curriculum and teacher engagement contributed positively to foundational learning, learners' confidence in answering learning questions, and/or their ability to recall literacy and numeracy knowledge. A higher proportion of learners also reported feeling comfortable learning reading and Math after participation in the program (see Figure 12.4).

The social-emotional learning assessment indicated a positive increase in learners' self-confidence and self-awareness, as shown in Figure 12.4. Most notably, 89% of learners agreed that they use their imagination,

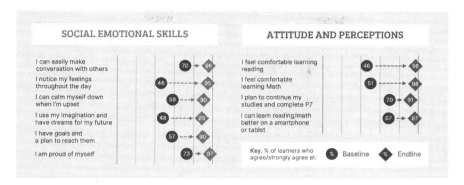

Figure 12.4 Results of Social and Emotional Skills Assessment and Survey on Attitudes Towards Learning, at Baseline and Endline (Cohort 2, n = 256)

compared to 48% at baseline, and 90% agreed they have goals for the future and plans to reach them, compared to 57% at baseline. As with foundational learning, a positive correlation was also identified between an increase in learners' overall SEL scores and the total number of Kolibri sessions implemented in the school, suggesting the holistic program contributes towards SEL outcomes.

Of the 330 learners who successfully completed the first cohort, 322 enrolled back into mainstream primary school after the program (98%).

Conclusions

In conclusion, the Flying Colors program in Uganda demonstrates how tech-enabled project-based learning can bridge the digital divide and provide a level playing field for marginalized learners. The pilot showed statistically significant progress in learners' foundational literacy and numeracy skills and their social-emotional competencies. Teachers embraced the blended learning model, effectively integrating technology into their teaching and engaging students in playful and collaborative learning experiences. Several key challenges and lessons learned were captured, which enables continuous iteration and improvement. The program's positive impact on learners' confidence, overall learning outcomes, and reintegration into education underscores the potential of tailored and contextualized tech-enabled interventions in addressing the diverse needs of marginalized communities. As we strive to create more inclusive and equitable educational opportunities, initiatives like Flying Colors serve as powerful examples in transforming learning experiences and empowering marginalized learners for a brighter future.

Acknowledgements

Our deepest gratitude to our program partners Amal Alliance and Hopelink Action Foundation (HAF) Uganda. Support for the project and research was provided by The LEGO Foundation, with Innovations for Poverty Action (IPA) as our evidence partner.

References

CASEL guide on effective social and emotional learning programs: Preschool and elementary school edition. (2013). CASEL (Collaborative for Academic, Social, and Emotional Learning).

Chen, C. H., & Yang, Y. C. (2019). Revisiting the effects of project-based learning on students' academic achievement: A meta-analysis investigating moderators. *Educational Research Review, 26*, 71–81.

Condliffe, B., Visher, M. G., Bangser, M. R., Drohojowska, S., & Saco, L. (2016). *Project-based learning: A literature review.* MDRC.

EPDC (Education Policy Data Center). (2018). *Uganda: National education profile 2018 update.* EPDC.

Jagers, R. J., Skoog-Hoffman, A., Barthelus, B., & Schlund, J. (2021). Transformative social and emotional learning. *American Educator, 45*(2), 12–17.

Khader, N. S. K. (2016). The effectiveness of blended learning in improving students' achievement in third grade's science in Bani Kenana. *Journal of Education and Practice, 7*(35), 109–116.

Krajcik, J. S., & Shin, N. (2014). Project-based learning. In R. K. Sawyer (Ed.), *The Cambridge handbook of the learning sciences* (2nd ed., pp. 275–297). Cambridge University Press.

Nabugoomu, J. (2019). School dropout in rural Uganda: Stakeholder perceptions on contributing factors and solutions. *Education Journal, 8*(5). Science Publishing Group.

NPA (National Planning Authority) Uganda. (2021). *Towards safe opening of the education sector in Covid-19 times.* http://www.npa.go.ug/wp-content/uploads/2021/09/NPA-on-Reopening-of-Schools-AmidstCOVID19.pdf

Railsback, J. (2002). *Project-based instruction: Creating excitement for learning.* Northwest Regional Educational Laboratory.

Thomas, J. W. (2000). *A review of research on project-based learning.* Technologies de Formation et Apprentissage (TECFA).

World Bank. (2021). *The wealth of today and tomorrow.* World Bank. https://doi.org/10.1596/36725

Yoder, N. (2014). *Teaching the whole child: Instructional practices that support social-emotional learning in three teacher evaluation frameworks.* American Institutes for Research. https://gtlcenter.org/sites/default/files/TeachingtheWholeChild.pdf

Zhang, X., Hu, B. Y., Zou, X., & Ren, L. (2020). Parent-child number application activities predict children's math trajectories from preschool to primary school. *Journal of Educational Psychology, 112.*

A Case Study of an Exemplary Grade 5 Teacher's Experiences When Integrating Technology with Reading-for-Meaning Strategies in a Meaningful Way

13

Janet Condy, Heather Nadia Phillips, and Chantyclaire Tiba

Introduction

Despite the past four Progress in International Literacy Study (PIRLS) (2006, 2011, 2016, 2021) tests assessing South African Grades 4 and 5 learners' levels of reading for meaning, the results continue to show how poorly our learners understand what they read. Yet there is a dearth of research conducted on how primary school teachers themselves understand how to teach critical reading strategies. In 2020, in an attempt to improve this dire situation, the researcher offered a five-day reading-for-meaning (R4M) workshop in conjunction with a local teachers union. The focus was on equipping teachers with relevant classroom literacy instructional practices to encourage higher-order thinking skills. Embedded throughout the workshop were appropriate forms of assessment and

DOI: 10.4324/9781003406631-13

instruction, such as the use of active, participatory and child-centred teaching and learning methods.

Hence the aim of this chapter is to investigate how one exemplary Grade 5 teacher, who attended this workshop, adapted these R4M strategies during COVID-19 and integrates them with technology. We provide recommendations within the lens of the Technology, Pedagogy and Content Knowledge (TPACK) framework on how teachers could effectively integrate the R4M strategies while using technology.

Context

According to a United Nations Educational Scientific Cultural Organisation (UNESCO, 2023) report, there has been an increase from 57% in 2019 to an estimated 70% in 2022 of 10-year-old children in low- and middle-income countries who cannot read and understand a simple text with comprehension. In South Africa, the International Progress in International Reading Literacy Study (PIRLS) conducted in 2021 reported that 81% of Grade 4 learners could not read at the lowest level of 'explicitly stated questions'. From both the UNESCO and the PIRLS studies, it is evident that too many learners do not have the ability to read a text with comprehension. There is evidence that one way in which literacy could be improved is through effective use of technology for teaching and learning (Chin et al., 2019). A considerable number of studies reported an increase in teachers' use of technology during and post-COVID-19 (Winter et al., 2021; Rahayu et al., 2022; Courtney et al., 2022), as many educational institutions have made technology available and accessible. Technology has the potential to enhance teaching and learning and develop learners' critical thinking skills (Chin et al., 2019; Winter et al., 2021) when it is constructively used in the classroom (Berg et al., 2014).

Therefore, teachers have an important role to play in creating an environment that promotes constructive learning. According to Hashim and Aziz (2021), great effort and skill is required by teachers for effective teaching with technology. The challenge is that not enough teachers are using technology in a way that could transform teaching and learning.

Teacher S, an exemplary teacher, teaches at a local school in Cape Town, where, recently, she and her school have won many prestigious awards. In 2022, her school was acknowledged in an international competition as being in the top three schools for the World's Best Schools

Competition for overcoming adversity. Also in 2022, in her own school, she won the award as Top Achiever in Technology and is the current leader for 2023. In that same year, she came in second in the PurpleZA course – a platform for learning different technology skills. She was recognized as a leader on a national scale, where she received a certificate for Google Level 2 achievement in 2023, having completed Level 1 in 2022. In 2021, in order to further equip herself and to stay current with using technology devices in her classroom, she completed a short course on 'Teaching with Technology' at the University of Cape Town.

Teacher S is currently acting Head of Department for the Intermediate Phase and Head of the Natural Science and Technology Department. She is an experienced teacher, having taught for 11 years. Due to her extensive expertise and passion for education, she is a mentor to all Intermediate Phase pre-service teachers who attend her school for teaching practice. In her position as Head of Technology, Teacher S assists her colleagues with any technology-related matters. During and post-COVID-19, she embraced the digital shift and has developed her confidence and competence in her ability to constructively use learner-centred methods to teach with technology.

Problem

The problem experienced in this research is that teachers do not teach with technology in a constructive way that could enhance learning (Pozo et al., 2021). DeCoito and Richardson (2018) believe technology cannot be effective in the classroom without teachers who are knowledgeable about both the technology and its implementation to meet educational goals. Therefore, teachers need to be introduced to ways they could transform their classroom environments with technology. The research question that the researchers sought to answer was: How does an exemplary Grade 5 teacher integrate technology with R4M strategies in a meaningful way?

To collect data, the researchers gave Teacher S an informal semi-structured, open-ended interview schedule before an online interview so she could prepare and plan her responses. Although there were eight questions, the researchers asked many more probing questions to encourage her engagement with them. This informal interview lasted one hour and 11 minutes, after which it was downloaded and professionally transcribed. The researchers used both deductive (theory-driven) and inductive (data-driven) analyses to analyse the data and constantly searched for similarities and outliers (Henning et al., 2004) to develop smaller units of meaning.

In 2019, the researcher received ethical clearance from the university where she worked. During that workshop all participants completed letters of consent, and for this current research project Teacher S completed yet another letter of consent. To protect her identity she will be referred to as 'Teacher S'.

Literature and Theoretical Perspectives

This section focuses on local and international literature pertinent in understanding this study. The discussion focusses on technology and reading for meaning, employing teaching strategies using technology, teachers' role in integrating technology and the benefits of using technology in developing reading for meaning skills. Concluding this section is a discussion on the theoretical framework that underpinned this study.

Technology and Reading for Meaning

The during and post-COVID-19 circumstances rendered technology "an intrinsic aspect of the learning experience" (Hashim & Aziz, 2021, p. 1351). They agree that the use of technologies enhances the language learning processes and are regarded as creative strategies and tools necessary to support and advance language learning. Offering a variety of digital tools can help make teaching languages more accessible to learners since they acquire knowledge in different ways. R4M is one of the most important skills to develop since all learning is based on written material.

Comprehension, according to Kleinsz et al. (2017), can be further developed using computer-assisted programs, which solicit greater motivation and higher levels of attention because of the multimedia approach. Several methods of teaching using digital technology can help students develop their skills, provide opportunities for differentiation and inspire their interest and involvement (Fälth & Selenius, 2022). The infusion of technology has changed the learning environment into one that is alive, engaging, real and very interactive, but it is important to note that technology on its own cannot ensure success in language learning, although it helps to make lessons more exciting and relevant (Hashim & Aziz, 2021).

Employing Teaching Strategies Using Technology

The development of the skill of inference is a crucial part of effective text comprehension and typically is an area with which many learners struggle. When reading a text, different kinds of inferences can be made. Learners are required to tie together a series of assertions that draw on their prior knowledge (Kleinsz et al., 2017) and enable them to make predictions (Capodieci et al., 2020). According to Capodieci et al. (2020), using computer-assisted programs made learners more aware of the reading strategies, and they were able to implement them with greater success during comprehension activities.

The Anticipation Guide is a strategy that has been found to improve reading comprehension during reading and allows learners to get much more detailed information from a text (Antoni, 2017). This strategy entails reading a text aloud, reading a set of statements related to the text and deciding whether they agree or disagree with the statements, or alternatively indicating whether the statements are true or false. Stoetzel and Shedrow (2021) state that through social interactions learners get to the point where they are able to construct their own meaning from the texts and elaborate on their understandings. Using interactive whiteboards when teachers read the text aloud will prompt interaction from learners and result in meaningful discussion. Multimodal and other digital texts can be easily integrated into many strategies with the intention of extending reading experiences positively.

Cooperative learning strategies allow learners to use social interaction to further develop and improve academic performance. The jigsaw method is one such method. Jainal and Shahrill (2021, p. 257) describe the jigsaw method as the following: The process of "(a) choosing a learning material to be covered of the particular subject, (b) preparing questions for the pre- and post-achievement tests, (c) preparing guided questions that iterate important points in the learning material, (d) allocating students into an expert group, and (e) allocating students in forming the jigsaw group". Google Classroom and Google Slides proved to be very successful technological platforms for this strategy. Chang and Benson (2022) revealed their findings and stated that the jigsaw method on these platforms positively influenced individual learning, group learning and collaboration throughout.

The question-and-answer strategy requires good listening skills. ED Puzzle is one technology that can be used to improve listening skills (Egilistiani & Prayuana, 2021). ED Puzzle (alternatively spelt EDpuzzle) is a tool where a video is used, which learners watch. Scores of questions are set for students to answer in the form of quizzes. According to Kuckian et al. (2022), this helps learners to better conceptualise concepts. Programs like ED Puzzle reduce the already heavy workloads of teachers and further have the potential to "intellectually stimulate and empower the learners but position them in a place where they become responsible and accountable for their own learning with limited supervision from the end of the teacher" (Kuckian et al., 2022, p. 1635). In a study by Kuckian et al. (2022), it is reported that teachers are given the opportunity to plan their lessons using video content from multiple sources, develop quizzes and assess learners' performance.

Teachers' Role in Integrating Technology

Ghavifekr and Rosdy (2015) promote greater integration of technology in the teaching of reading and writing since the use of technology has proven to be key to the development of learners' language abilities. The immersion of digital technology on one side does promote learner learning; however, it has proven to be challenging and cumbersome for teachers. Incorporating technology into the daily run of the class does create a challenge since technology is not the expert field of many teachers. Integration must take place, and the mistake many teachers make is to try to directly "transfer the traditional strategies associated with the use of pen and paper to computers and tablets" (Taylor et al., 2020, p. 520). Teachers need to equip themselves to carry out a variety of strategies and use the most up-to-date methods, tools and applications such as Google Classroom, Google Meet, Telegram and WhatsApp (Hashim & Aziz, 2021). It requires teachers to make decisions in terms of when technology is to be used and which applications are suitable, but the research does show that teacher knowledge in this regard is still lacking (Fälth & Selenius, 2022; Hashim & Aziz, 2021).

Benefits of Using Technology in Developing Reading for Meaning Skills

Infusing technology with the various teaching strategies has numerous benefits for both teachers and learners. Kleinsz et al. (2017) suggest that one of the benefits is that learners can get immediate feedback with some programs, and at the same time, because the feedback is provided by a machine, there is less of an emotional charge present, keeping the environment more positive. For teachers this means a reduction in assessing learners' work. Haleem et al. (2022) see the immediate provision of a learning environment, immediate evaluations and the increased engagement as unrivalled benefits.

Added to this, digital learning also cuts costs and allows for better utilisation of resources. Haleem et al. (2022) continue to explain that digital technologies do enhance the development of problem-solving skills and improved comprehension skills. Zhang (2022) contends that the approaches to language teaching and learning have been modified with the use of technology. Computer-based communication connects everyone globally, and this collaboration can only improve learning and promote professional development of teachers.

Theoretical Framework

The framework that guided this study is TPACK (Mishra & Koehler, 2006). According to Mishra and Koehler (2006), for teachers to effectively teach with technology, they must be able to blend these three knowledges: technology, pedagogy and content. Technology Knowledge (TK) is a teacher's ability to use different technological tools for teaching and learning; Pedagogical Knowledge (PK) is how a teacher teaches or imparts knowledge using different methods; Content Knowledge (CK) is the teacher's knowledge about the subject matter to be taught in a particular phase. For teachers to effectively teach with technology, they must be able to teach content using appropriate pedagogical strategies and technology (TPACK).

The three concepts – TK, PK and CK – are combined within the TPACK framework to form TPK, TCK and PCK. TPK is the teacher's ability to choose which pedagogical strategy to use when teaching with a particular technology; PCK is the teacher's ability to choose a particular strategy to teach content; and TCK is a teacher's understanding of what technology to use to teach subject matter. In relation to TPACK, Teacher S was asked during the interview what technology she uses, how she supports learning using technology and if the technology enhances learning experiences for the learners.

Results of R4M Strategies Integrated with Technology

In an attempt to answer the research question: 'How does an exemplary Grade 5 teacher integrate technology with R4M strategies in a meaningful way?' and after inductively and deductively analysing the data, the researchers found there were four examples of R4M strategies that Teacher S adapted to technology. Each strategy has been included in a vignette followed by a discussion on the lessons learnt. For each R4M strategy, the researchers share the technology tool/s used and her comments on how she adapted the technology to her classroom environment. The language used in the comments has not been changed as the researchers wanted to capture her authentic voice.

Vignette 1

Content: R4M strategy – Anticipation Guide; **Technology used:** Whiteboard and sticky notes

Teacher S set learners up to use the whiteboard with sticky notes to employ the Anticipation Guide as a strategy. She shares her experiences:

> the Anticipation Guide I actually use in Natural Science when we are doing a new topic . . . the great thing was when I initially started it was paper-based, but now it's online.

I would write a statement and the children could decide whether they wanted to remain anonymous . . . and they would put little sticky notes around my statement, with their answers on it . . . as soon as the first person puts their little sticky note on, it sparks a kind of popcorn effect . . . I colour co-ordinate . . . all of these answers look fairly similar.

. . . when a person is giving their feedback . . . but they still need to listen, and all they do is they put their devices close by and when another person is giving their answer, it automatically types it in for them. So it eliminates their having to write [on the whiteboard] . . . but they have fun with it.

So I really think, in using those strategies, it's definitely helped the children grow in confidence and in speaking.

Lessons Learnt

One benefit of using technology while employing the Anticipation Guide strategy is collaboration. Teacher S stated that typically her learners are too scared to voice their own opinions, yet they have a wealth of knowledge. She continued saying that in society, people often say: "What's on your mind?" and they feel put down. Because of this, learners are too scared to speak up. Yet using the Anticipation Guide has helped Teacher S's learners grow in confidence and in their speaking. She suggested that using technology flips the teaching and learning around where the teacher is not answering and giving feedback – instead, the learners are asking each other questions and collaborating. According to Taylor et al. (2021, p. 4), "digital technology offers new avenues of meaningful communication and collaboration between teachers and students".

Teacher S builds her learners' self-esteem by giving them a voice, as they had to put sticky notes on the whiteboard (TK). She uses sticky notes to engage learners and involve them in active learning.

Vignette 2

Content: R4M strategy – Jigsaw; **Technology used**: Zoom, break-out rooms and Google Slides
    Teacher S set the class up in Zoom and continues:

Step 1: Break-out rooms with the children . . . and they discussed their topic.
Step 2: Google Slides, which your little group has, and you need to contribute a particular slide and collectively, you are then doing one presentation.
Step 3: And then we'd come back to the collective group.
Step 4: And I'd check in with everyone that they understood, were there any questions that they needed to ask me.
Step 5: Send them back into a different break-out room to discuss and give feedback.

Lessons Learnt

One of the benefits that Teacher S experienced when using technology for the jigsaw activity was that she needed to be mindful that everything is reading and everything is comprehension. Technology does not take away that skill from learners – they still need to comprehend, whether the question is on a screen or whether the question is on paper, it's the same. They need to read it, they need to comprehend and they need to give the answer in an interactive way.

Teacher S recommends that when using Google Slides as a collaboration tool, each person has their slide to work on; it gives everyone the sense of helping one another, but you still have ownership of your own work. This ownership of the work leads to higher self-esteem and helps learners create a more positive mindset around school and learning (Jainal & Shahrill, 2021). This is an activity in which everyone collaborates and Teacher S monitors everyone's participation. Haleem et al. (2022) concurs that using Google Slides as a technological tool gives real-time and immediate feedback. Teachers can monitor their learners' work, making the teacher-learner relationship more participatory. Regarding the TPACK model, Teacher S was competent in the use of technology, as she was able to put together a Zoom lesson, use Google Slides and break-out rooms.

Vignette 3

Content: R4M strategy – Inference and predicting; **Technology used**: Google suite – Miro, whiteboard, jamboard and videos

I use Miro which is basically like a whiteboard and also a jamboard which is connected to the Google suite. I used it for creating different predictions.

. . . we did a whole predicting of a text and my children absolutely love it when we have story time and we have to do predictions.

I'd start with the cover and I'd ask the children: "What do you think this is about?" And once again, there were actually certain parts where I did pre-recordings [of videos] for those that were not necessarily able to be in the classroom. I'd tell them: "Okay, pause

---

here, you jot down what you think your prediction is and then when you are ready, continue."

When we did the predicting of texts . . . I'd ask my children to write down their ideas on their whiteboard. And what they would then do is they could submit that to me and I would have access to it, and depending on the type of lesson, I could actually collate all of the whiteboards together and the children could then see – as an overall . . . I had a similar thought to this one and this one and this one.

Lessons Learnt

For this literacy activity of inferencing and predicting, Teacher S used a number of technological tools from Miro to Google Suites Jamboard. She mentioned the benefits of using these tools are that she could monitor the learners' pace of work on one screen, and she could flip through their work without them knowing. She could collate all the predictions of the texts and share them with her learners, and they could see, anonymously, what predictions other learners had written and discuss them as a whole class. Haleem et al. (2022) reiterate that technology can be a very powerful collaborative tool in the teaching and learning environment.

Teacher S knew how to use a variety of technology to transform her lesson (TK) and make it fun. By using technology, she was able to have a holistic understanding of her learners' knowledge about the content (CK) that she taught.

Vignette 4

Content: R4M strategy – Questioning; **Technology used**: Google Classroom – EDPuzzle, video and whiteboard

So what EDPuzzle does, is it allows you to pause the video at any point and then to ask your question. And if the child feels that they need to go back they just press – go back – and view again or listen again, and then answer the questions. I use prompting questions so much in class and I always tell them "But why?". . . they need to be able to motivate it and it sparks this whole thing in class because the

> person that actually gave the statement might know [the answer] they kind of back each other up and they support one another in class.
>
> So that gets them very excited – you continue to prompt them . . . you are forcing them to dig deeper and even if they don't have an automatic answer, they're still processing and they're thinking.
>
> "But why?" and they have to write it down on their whiteboard, and then everyone shows me their whiteboards and I see you know, so the two of you have a kind of a similar thought . . . and then you get them to discuss their train of thought . . . you are forcing them to dig deeper and even if they don't have an automatic answer, they're still processing and they're thinking.
>
> . . . that's sparking their creativity and it's sparking . . . just a little bit of deeper thinking than just – this is the answer.
>
> . . . but always trying to extend them, and extending them is not by putting it on a device. That's not extending their thinking.

Lessons Learnt

In Vignette 4, Teacher S expresses the need to extend her learners' critical thinking skills. At the same time she warns that creating critical thinking is not just putting information on devices; it is about creating innovative and collaborative activities on your devices, as you are not always there to guide them. To prevent wasting learners' and the teacher's time navigating around devices during your lessons, Teacher S recommends that one should play around with the technological tools before your lessons to find out everything that you need to know about how they work. Taylor et al. (2020) states that the introduction of technology into daily lessons has become a challenge to many teachers, but what is important is that teachers take the time to equip themselves with the necessary knowledge of the tools and the implementation skills of the digital tools they would like to use in their classroom.

Teacher S is equipped and skilled in the use of EDPuzzle (TK). In order to reinforce learners' understanding of subject matter, she used EDPuzzle, which allows her to pace lessons (PK). During lessons, she paused videos and asked learners questions (PK) to deepen their understanding of subject matter (CK). Teacher S is at level 3 of the SAMR model – modification – as she has mastery of EDPuzzle, using it in an innovative way to enhance learning.

Teacher S mentioned that one of the benefits of using Google Classroom is that instead of having to search for the learners' work all the time, she can see their work at the same time as they are forced to share their work with the teacher, and she can see the levels of questions they are asking. Another benefit of using Google Classroom is that the teacher can set up her tasks and rubrics as self-marking. Rubrics as an assessment tool, according to Goodwin and Kirkpatrick (2023), raise the value of learning for learners. This tool, according to Ríos-Lozada et al. (2022), allows learners to track their own tasks and that of others, understand the purpose of their learning, know where they are and what they want to achieve.

Conclusions

These four vignettes provide evidence that Teacher S is constantly challenged by using technology to improve and extend her students' critical thinking abilities, by preparing activities that are collaborative and fun with opportunities for her learners to speak, which in turn improves their confidence levels. The use of technology has added a much-needed dimension in her classroom. It has increased motivation levels in her classroom, and Carstens et al. (2021, p. 106) claims that "the more motivated learners are to learn something new, the more likely they are to retain the material".

Teacher S believes that reading and comprehension skills are embedded across all subjects she teaches. Since her school is in the top three World's Best Schools in overcoming adversity, she prepares all her activities with differentiation in mind. With all of this experience of incorporating technology into her everyday teaching, Teacher S says she is beginning to understand her role as a teacher better. Carstens et al. (2021, p. 106) explains "teachers now take learners on a journey, learning with them instead of teaching them". Teacher S does not teach technology in isolation, but she is able to blend technology, pedagogy and content knowledge, which is required for meaningful teaching and learning with technology.

Since Teacher S was known to one of the researchers, all three researchers worked independently in an attempt to identify and interpret the emerging themes from the transcribed data. In a discussion we agreed on the themes that would answer the research question. By writing like this, and being careful with the words we used, we avoided issues of bias. This small research project was limited to interviewing one exemplary teacher who integrated R4M strategies to use with technology in her class. However, the data provided was explicit and in-depth, which showed that she was teaching more meaningfully.

Recommendations

Teacher S recommended that "teachers need to be mindful of learners' eyes and brains and them becoming too anti-social". Teachers need to work smarter and not harder and need to have patience when using technology. Educators are not going to get everything right immediately, and they need to be kind to themselves and take one step at a time. Therefore, professional development training should start from the most basic to complex technology. It is recommended that experts are used who are knowledgeable on how to blend content, pedagogy and technology and show teachers practical examples.

Teacher S recommends that teachers need to be mindful of having a good balance between using technology effectively and still having the other skills that learners need. Educators do not want to take away from writing completely, because with screen time there is still a need to develop the learners' verbal and vocabulary skills and create opportunities for asking probing questions and having discussions. Teachers need to build their learners' confidence to speak, as this develops their confidence.

References

Antoni, D. (2017). The effect of "anticipation guide strategy" and students' reading interest on students' reading comprehension. *English Language Teaching and Research, 1*(1), 65–76.

Berg, S., Benz, C. R., LasleyII, T, J., & Raisch, C. D. (2014). Exemplary technology use in elementary classrooms. *Journal of Research on Computing in Education, 31*(2).

Capodieci, A., Cornoldi, C., Doerr, E., Bertolo, L., & Carretti, B. (2020, April 23). The use of new technologies for improving reading comprehension. *Frontiers in Psychology, 11*, 751.

Carstens, K. J., Mallon, J. M., Bataineh, M., & Al-Bataineh, A. (2021). Effects of technology on student learning. *Turkish Online Journal of Educational Technology-TOJET, 20*(1), 105–113.

Chang, W. L., & Benson, V. (2022, July 9). Jigsaw teaching method for collaboration on cloud platforms. *Innovations in Education and Teaching International, 59*(1), 24–36.

Chin, C. K., Munip, H., Miyadera, R., Thoe, N. K., Ch'ng, Y. S., & Promising, N. (2019, September 17). Promoting education for sustainable development in teacher education integrating blended learning and digital tools: An evaluation with exemplary cases. *EURASIA Journal of Mathematics, Science and Technology Education, 15*(1), 1–17.

Courtney, S. A., Miller, M. E. S., & Gisondo, M. J. (2022). The impact of COVID-19 on teachers' integration of digital technology. *Contemporary Educational Technology, 14*(4).

DeCoito, I., & Richardson, T. (2018). Teachers and technology: Present practice and future directions. *Contemporary Issues in Technology and Teacher Education, 18*(2), 362–378.

Egilistiani, R., & Prayuana, R. (2021). Students' responses through the use of ED puzzle as an application in achieving listening comprehension. *LINGUISTS: Journal of Linguistics and Language Teaching, 7*(2), 63–74.

Fälth, L., & Selenius, H. (2022, September). Primary school teachers' use and perception of digital technology in early reading and writing education in inclusive settings. *Disability and Rehabilitation: Assistive Technology*, 1–10. https://doi.org/10.1080/17483107.2022.2125089

Ghavifekr, S., & Rosdy, W. A. W. (2015). Teaching and learning with technology: Effectiveness of ICT integration in schools. *International Journal of Research in Education and Science (IJRES), 1*(2), 175–191.

Goodwin, R., & Kirkpatrick, R. (2023). Using rubrics to improve writing skills: A study in Kuwait. *Language Testing in Asia, 13*(1), 1–17.

Haleem, A., Javaid, M., Qadri, M. A., & Suman, R. (2022). Understanding the role of digital technologies in education: A review. *Sustainable Operations and Computers, 3*, 275–285.

Hashim, Z. B., & Aziz, A. A. (2021, September 23). The use of technology in teaching reading comprehension before and during the pandemic. *International Journal of Academic Research in Business and Social Sciences, 11*(9), 1345–1379.

Henning, E., van Rensburg, W., & Smit, B. (2004). *Finding your way in qualitative research*. Van Schaik Publishers.

Jainal, N. H., & Shahrill, M. (2021). Incorporating Jigsaw strategy to support students' learning through action research. *International Journal on Social and Education Sciences, 3*(2), 252–266.

Kleinsz, N., Potocki, A., Ecalle, J., & Magnan, A. (2017). Profiles of French poor readers: Underlying difficulties and effects of computerized training programs. *Learning and Individual Differences, 57*, 45–57.

Kuckian, S., Joe, A., & Anil, V. (2022). Utilization of ED puzzle: An interactive tool in teaching practices. *International Journal of Special Education, 37*, 1633–1647.

Mishra, P., & Koehler, M. J. (2006). Technological pedagogical content knowledge: A framework for teacher knowledge. *Teachers' College Record, 108*(6), 1017–1054.

Pozo, J., Echeverría, M. P., Cabellos, B., & Sánchez, D. L. (2021, April 29). Teaching and learning in times of COVID-19: Uses of digital technologies during school lockdowns. *Frontiers in Psychology, 12*. https://doi.org./10.3389/fpsyg.2021.656776

Progress in International Reading Literacy. (2021). *South African preliminary report.* https://www.up.ac.za/media/shared/164/ZP_Files/2023/piirls-2021_highlights-report.zp235559.pdf

Rahayu, S., Rahmadani, E., Syafitri, E., Prasetyoningsih, L. S. A., Ubaidillah, M. F., & Tavakoli, M. (2022). Teaching with technology during COVID-19 pandemic: An interview study with teachers in Indonesia. *Education Research International*, 1–9. https://doi.org/10.1155/2022/7853310

Ríos-Lozada, R. N., Guevara-Fernández, J. A., Carranza-Dávila, R. G., Ramirez-Delgado, J. G., & Hernández-Fernández, B. (2022). Google classroom in educational service: A systematic review. *Journal of Positive School Psychology, 6*(2), 1634–1639.

Stoetzel, L., & Shedrow, S. J. (2021, April 29). Making the move online: Interactive read-alouds for the virtual classroom. *The Reading Teacher, 74*(6), 747–756.

Taylor, D. B., Handler, L. K., FitzPatrick, E., & Whittingham, C. E. (2020). The device in the room: Technology's role in third grade literacy instruction. *Journal of Research on Technology in Education, 52*(4), 515–533.

Taylor, M., Fudge, A., Mirriahi, N., & de Laat, M. (2021). *Use of digital technology in education: Literature review*. Prepared for the South Australian Department for Education on behalf of The Centre for Change and Complexity in Learning, The University of South Australia.

United Nations Educational Scientific Cultural Organisation. (2023). *Celebrations in 2023*. http://www.unesco/en/days/literacy

Winter, E., Costello, A., O'Brien, M., & Hickey, G. (2021, April 28). Teachers' use of technology and the impact of Covid-19. *Irish Educational Studies, 40*(2), 235–246.

Zhang, W. (2022). The role of technology-based education and teacher professional development in English as a foreign language classes. *Frontiers in Psychology, 13*.

Effects of a Professional Development Programme for Teaching and Learning in Digital Environments from the Perspective of Teachers

14

Case Study from Finland

Sini Kontkanen, Satu Piispa-Hakala, Susanna Pöntinen, and Teemu Valtonen

Introduction

Our society is digitalised, and digital technology has become increasingly integrated into various educational levels. However, digital teaching and learning practices remain complex (Erstad et al., 2021; Kontkanen et al., 2016; Pöntinen & Räty-Záborszky, 2020), and the need for the professional development (PD) of teachers has grown significantly (Instefjord & Munthe, 2017; Kontkanen et al., 2023). Previous studies indicate that teachers lack digital qualifications; typically, in-service training programmes focus mainly on technical aspects rather than on pedagogical aspects and lack a connection to school contexts (Fernández-Batanero et al., 2020). Recognising that high-quality PD is crucial for promoting teachers' learning (Borko et al., 2010), this research aims to

DOI: 10.4324/9781003406631-14

Characteristics of a High-Quality PD Programme

PD is essential support for teachers' aspiration for advancement. The objective of a high-quality PD programme should be to build wide capacity to understand and implement strategies and innovative pedagogies (Borko et al., 2010; Stein et al., 1999). Several studies emphasise the importance of time and structuring of PD (Philipsen et al., 2019; Postholm, 2012). This is in line with Voogt et al. (2015), who suggest that teachers need to be provided with an active, agentic role for a long period to enable them take individual and collective responsibility of design and learning from the process. Moreover, teaching programmes need to support teachers' reflective activities (Postholm, 2012), focusing on the use and experiences of new areas of PD and to trigger their professional visions (Sherin & Russ, 2014).

Darling-Hammond et al. (2017) emphasise the role of coaching and expert support in successful PD. This includes the sharing of expertise and targeting the special needs of the teachers. Expert scaffolding has proven to be efficient in supporting the implementation of new methods or technologies and to deepen teacher reflection (Voogt et al., 2015). PD programmes should also support active teacher learning by coaching and collective problem-solving (Borko et al., 2010), and programmes are more efficient when participants influence the development process (Sancar et al., 2021). As Postholm (2012) suggests, the goal of PD should be learning to learn and becoming self-regulated in the process of learning and PD. Moreover, Voogt et al. (2015) suggest that collaborative design is a means to support teachers' PD. Borko et al. (2010) also emphasise the meaning of professional learning communities as well as collective and collaborative learning environments.

PD and learning need to be situated within a meaningful context and be connected with everyday teaching activities. The participation of teachers in creating concrete artefacts, such as digital learning materials and environments, enables them to actively shape the teaching and learning activities employed (Voogt et al., 2015). The situated nature of PD better acknowledges the existing context for new innovations and

216 Sini Kontkanen et al.

practices (Philipsen et al., 2019). This implies that PD should involve continuous and long-term activities that are sustainable over time (Borko et al., 2010). It should provide teachers with opportunities to engage in the cycles of reflection and experimentation to improve learning and teaching in digitalised environments. Cooperative practices can provide opportunities for the emergence of different informal communities that are valuable support and sources for the PD of teachers (Macià & García, 2016).

Research Questions

To ascertain how to provide effective support for in-service teachers in enhancing their digital teaching and learning practices, this study aimed to investigate teachers' perception and experiences of the long-term PD programme. We addressed the following research questions:

RQ1: How do teachers perceive and evaluate a long-term PD programme?
RQ2: What effect does a long-term PD programme have on the PD of teachers?

Research Context

Case studies are useful for investigating complex, dynamic phenomena situated in particular contexts (Yin, 2009). This design was useful since the special context of this study was a Finnish professional specialisation programme called Learning and Teaching in Digitalised Environments (60 ECTS). The programme is a university-level training for in-service teachers and was designed to meet the needs of curriculum reform and teacher competence to implement it for students at all levels of education (Piispa-Hakala et al., 2023). As information and communications technology (ICT) and media literacy are considered highly important, it has become crucial to support the development of students' ICT and media skills within school settings (Ilomäki et al., 2016; Vahtivuori-Hänninen et al., 2014). A general educational objective for students is to be able to critically evaluate information and create new knowledge, both individually and in groups. Consequently, the role of teachers in supporting students' social and collaborative working skills and communal modes of studying using ICT is deemed important. These are applied and reframed in the

Effects of a Professional Development Programme 217

Finnish national core curriculum and the strategy for the development of teacher education (Lavonen, 2020).

The programme was introduced in 2016 as a new method to deepen the expertise of in-service teachers. From the outset, it was planned and structured to be a specialisation programme that emphasised PD. The programme's objective was to build broad capacity to understand the pedagogies of educational technology, which implies establishing settings in terms of content and organisation (see Figure 14.1). The programme was scheduled for a longer duration than traditional in-service trainings (approximately two years) and the format varied from seminars, workshops, and virtual platforms to tasks implemented as part of a participant's everyday work.

To meet the needs of participating teachers, the programme was rather flexible and personally tailored. This was ensured by creating a PD plan (PDP) according to the programme curriculum. PDPs were discussed with a personal academic mentor. Participants also underwent

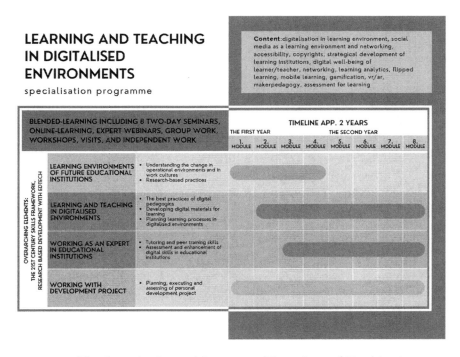

Figure 14.1 The Organization and Structure of Learning and Teaching in Digitalized Environments Specialization Program

218 Sini Kontkanen et al.

continuous tutoring or coaching by the programme staff throughout the programme. Collective and collaborative digital learning environments (Sharepoint, Teams) were a crucial part of the specialisation programme.

In terms of content, the core of the programme involved combining research-based knowledge on the pedagogies of educational technology to the development of everyday teaching practices in the field. The role of the programme was to proactively respond to the competence requirements arising in the educational field. The programme aimed to support teachers in developing their digital competence, particularly exploring digitalised learning as well as teaching based on research and the pedagogical perspective. The two-year programme comprised multiform modules related to the use of technology in education. During the programme, participants had eight two-day seminars at the university campus; they also studied on a virtual platform and participated in webinars.

One-third of the programme involved a development project, which was implemented in the participant's own work environment. These projects were practical research-based tasks, and the aim was to pedagogically develop the adequate use of educational technology in the selected level and environments. The project context varied from the classroom level to the school/institution or municipal level.

Data and Analysis

Our research data was taken from teachers' semi-structured interviews (n = 28), which were conducted at the end of the professional training programme. Interviews functioned also as teachers' expert auditions in the programme. The duration of one interview ranged from 45 minutes to 1 hour. Interviewed teachers (the whole cohort) participated in the programme during the years 2017–2021. Participants were experienced teachers, most of whom had teaching experience for more than ten years. The unit of analysis was aspects that in-service teachers mentioned as meaningful for their PD. Interviews were analysed using theory-guided content analysis (cf. Elo & Kyngäs, 2008), identifying features related to the effectiveness of training programmes presented by Kirkpatrick and Kirkpatrick (2016). The model comprises four levels to evaluate the outcomes of the training programme (Kirkpatrick & Kirkpatrick, 2016):

1 The reaction level determines the level of participants' immediate reactions and satisfaction with the training programme. Assessing their perceptions of the training content, delivery methods, and overall experience are examples of areas to be evaluated.
2 The learning level measures the extent to which participants have acquired knowledge, skills, and abilities as a result of the training.
3 The behavioural level examines the transfer of learning from the training programme to the workplace. This includes assessing whether participants have applied the skills and knowledge they have acquired to their tasks and whether there have been changes in their behaviour or performance.
4 The results level assesses the impact of the training on career development and future orientation.

Two researchers first conducted the analysis, independently coding units of analysis and locating them in the levels of Kirkpatrick and Kirkpatrick's (2016) model. Thereafter, the research team met to discuss their individual classifications and reached a shared understanding. The final categorisation of the data is presented in the figure above (Figure 14.2).

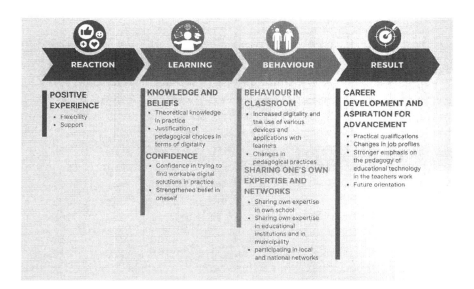

Figure 14.2 Categorisation of the Data According to Levels of the Model Presented in Kirkpatrick and Kirkpatrick (2016)

Results

Reaction Level

Overall, the training was a positive experience, according to teachers. The responses of the interviewees emphasised the flexibility of the training tasks according to the individual situations of each participant. In addition, the teachers felt that they had received sufficient and timely support from the instructors; support was also received from peers. These elements created a safe atmosphere in the programme. This safe atmosphere was able to develop during the long-term programme. The responses of certain teachers highlighted the challenges of working life and the fact that their work communities or supervisors did not provide sufficient support. Teachers who were supported by their leaders and work community to participate in the programme (time resource and content support) experienced the programme as particularly successful.

Learning Level

Knowledge and Beliefs

All of the teachers felt that their understanding of the theoretical principles of educational use of technology had increased during the training. A few teachers found that they were more capable of applying theoretical knowledge in practice and described their expertise as having deepened. Moreover, teachers understood the scope of digitalisation in education and that they could not fully master all aspects of it independently. They considered that a better overview of the possibilities and limitations of educational technology use helped them to make and explain pedagogical decisions. The following examples clearly reveal the importance of changes in teachers' ability to apply theoretical knowledge to justify pedagogical choices in terms of digitality:

> Instead of just tinkering around, I have strong pedagogical knowledge and theoretical basis on which to base my work. Somehow, I feel that it has been the biggest thing that I have developed during these studies. I have received confirmation on how everything is worth doing.
>
> (TEACHER_1_12)

Effects of a Professional Development Programme **221**

I was hoping that this training would justify digitalisation and its use, support for what makes sense, and which direction should we take in the municipality. I have received a lot of those answers. By studying, participating in learning tasks, and hearing examples and experiences from other municipalities, I have been able to use them in my own work. So, development is not just related to this digital issue, but somehow to the overall development of schools and basic education. (TEACHER_1_05)

Confidence

Teachers described that their confidence had increased during the programme, which improved both their personal and professional growth as well as their decision-making skills in handling unforeseen or challenging situations. A few teachers mentioned that after completing the training, they became more confident when attempting to identify workable digital solutions in practice.

There has been a great improvement in skill level and self-esteem. It makes you more willing to try and more able to cope if the technology doesn't work. Often, if you've planned something and it doesn't work, you get frustrated. But when you have more skills, you can broaden the scope of planning. You know where to look for tips, know-how, and knowledge.

(TEACHER_3_04)

Thus, it was evident for the teachers that there are multiple viewpoints to consider when developing digital practices. Their increased confidence helped them to continue trying even if they did not manage to find the best practices when using digital tools and applications the first time. Their increased confidence resulted from a strengthened belief in themselves. A few teachers said that the courage to express their own opinions and, hence, to function as active members in the school community increased after completing the training. This encouraged several teachers to contact digital experts for pedagogical assistance. A significant indication of increased self-confidence among the teachers was their ability to implement effective career strategies. The training they received empowered and inspired them to become stronger and more enthusiastic regarding their personal and professional development.

Behaviour Level

Behaviour in Classroom

The programme brought concrete changes to classroom work for numerous teachers. Teachers reported that the training increased digitality and the use of various devices and applications with learners in the classroom. These concrete digital experiments were guided by both the tasks performed in the programme and the teachers' increased courage to use digital tools as part of their own teaching.

> My pedagogy has changed, and that's thanks to the program. I now use technology and applications easily. I ask for help. Before, I didn't dare because I wasn't an expert. Now, I have the courage to integrate this into my work.
>
> (TEACHER_1_09)

In addition to increasing digitality, the teachers described the changes in their own pedagogical practices. Student orientation, functionality, and giving up frontal education are examples of these. The teachers felt that they were applying what they had learned in the programme and combining technology with their own pedagogy. The development project implemented in education was also considered to provide support for classroom work. Activities related to the flipped learning were also mentioned. A few teachers said they received positive feedback from the students' guardians regarding the new teaching methods.

> You have just stated the objective for which I applied for the programme. The approaches and guidance or coaching I received gave me the keys to move away from a teacher-led [pedagogy] and building knowledge together with the students. That's how it's done in digital environments!
>
> (TEACHER_1_08)

The development project implemented in the training also affected the concrete activities of the school in numerous ways. As their development projects, teachers worked on, for example, the digital skills calendar of their schools or planning for the educational use of ICT, developed their school's assessment culture and tool, and created a student agent model

Effects of a Professional Development Programme   **223**

for the school. In general, the school's ICT equipment was actively used in the programme and more ICT equipment was acquired for the school.

Sharing One's Own Expertise and Networks

The interviewees indicated that throughout the programme, they learned to share their expertise with others in their own work community. Teachers considered it important that colleagues use digital tools in teaching and that they provide close support for colleagues when they encounter digital issues. A majority of teachers also trained peers and held workshops on various devices and digital pedagogical skills in their schools or municipalities. Teachers who had attended the training also shared information on the various information channels of schools – for example, about flipped learning and their own development project. As part of the programme, teachers also mapped and assessed the digital tools of their own work communities, teachers' digital skills, and attitudes towards digitalization.

> One of the main lessons has been that we do the assignments in the same way that we are expected to do them with the students. Another is that I am no longer afraid to put my own knowledge and ideas out there, or to publish my own work. When you share material, you get more ideas from there.
> (TEACHER_1_08_)

> I've checked applications with a colleague and showing how something works and suggesting if you could use it if it helped.
> (TEACHER _1_10)

Teachers also brought their own expertise to educational institutions and municipalities, including bridging the gap between educational staff and administration. They presented skills gained in the programme in various development work groups – for example, in connection with planning a new school, developing curriculum work, developing municipal tutoring, and creating dynamic assessments. The interviewees indicated that they intend to continue their development project after the training and become involved in developing the school's digital practices.

224 Sini Kontkanen et al.

> [Expertise] has increased. I am listened to. It has already been seen that electronic systems are useful.
>
> (TEACHER _1_04)

> When the municipal ICT curriculum has begun to be drawn up, I was asked for my opinion. And that is a good step forward.
>
> (TEACHER _2_02)

Further, the interviewees also indicated that participating in local and national networks increased. The importance of networking emerged, both in terms of sharing one's own expertise, gaining new knowledge, and obtaining peer support. Educated teachers saw that their networks had grown and expanded with the programme, and their courage to network also increased. Moreover, teachers expanded their networks among their own educational institutions, municipalities, and in nearby municipalities. They also became active on a variety of social media channels and networks and began engaging with national experts.

> I actively follow experts in the field, and I have gained more people to follow through training.
>
> (TEACHER _1_070

> There have been experts in the program, and we have interviewed experts and participated in various webinars, and I have become familiar with the people behind the scenes. I didn't know anything about them before. Now I dare to email and contact them if I need help. And I know how to maintain my professionalism in the future.
>
> (TEACHER _1_02)

Results Level

Career Development and Aspirations for Advancement

The practical qualification of numerous teachers had changed during and with the programme. The programme led to a teacher obtaining a permanent teaching position or getting a fixed-term job at a new school. A few of them considered the programme as a guarantee for them to get a job as a teacher in the future. For a few teachers, training was a means to obtain an official certificate of their own competence in the field of teaching and learning in digital environments.

> I am about to get a permanent job as a teacher. That was one of the reasons to applied for the programme. To get a certificate for all my skills. The municipality paid part of the fee, even though I didn't have a permanent job, they wanted to engage me. And now I'm getting a permanent job.
>
> (TEACHER _1_05)

For a large number of teachers, the programme changed their job profile in some manner. Some had moved from the traditional work of teachers to being leaders of various projects or expert teachers in their own educational institution or municipality.

> I have moved on to project work. The director of education said that there could be similar jobs available after the project if I wanted them. So, I'm not going back to teaching. I think the position came about as my expertise has grown tremendously. Before the program, I would not have even dared to expect such a proposal.
>
> (TEACHER _1_04)

For some, the programme led to a stronger emphasis on the pedagogy of educational technology alongside or incorporated into the teacher's work. The participants work include increased use of educational technology. They acted as areal mentors in their own municipality or as the ICT executives of their school.

> I would say that this has strengthened my belief [in the future] a lot, given me guidance on where to go and what I want to achieve in my working life.
>
> (TEACHER _3_10)

A few teachers described their future orientation. The programme provided them the courage to see themselves in a role other than that of a traditional teacher. They hoped to play an expert role in their own municipality or educational institution. The training had also made them enthusiastic for further training and development in areas related to technology, such as coding or ICT systems, at the university level or even doing a doctoral dissertation on one of the topics of the development project. One teacher said he found a direction during the programme that he wants to take as a teacher, and many of them found enthusiasm for the continuous development and renewal of work in the current position.

Discussion and Conclusion

The aim of this case study was to examine the effectiveness and functioning of the practices of the PD programme based on participating teachers' experiences. This was done by analysing 28 teacher interviews with qualitative theory-guided content analysis, following Kirkpatrick and Kirkpatrick's (2016) evaluation model. Overall, the programme for the teachers was effective and of high quality. The teachers had a positive experience of the programme in all the levels of Kirkpatrick and Kirkpatrick's (2016) evaluation model. Our research reveals that the teachers were active participants; they constructed new understandings of theoretical knowledge offered in the programme. Furthermore, our results clearly revealed that teachers situated PD experiences in multiple contexts: classrooms, educational institutions, municipalities, and national networks. Participating teachers stated change in their professional paths. According to Borko et al. (2010), these are signs of a high-quality PD programme.

In the light of results, it appears that the specialisation programme presented in this study is a potential means to implement high-quality in-service training in the field of teaching and learning in digital environments. In line with Darling-Hammond et al. (2017), our result emphasises that creating a supportive environment for teachers' learning is critical. In the programme, a variety of formats of collaboration, communication, and ongoing support clearly supported the teachers' learning and active participation. Because a high-quality PD programme's objective should be built on teachers' wide capacity to understand and implement strategies and new or innovative pedagogies (Borko et al., 2010; Stein et al., 1999), the programme succeeded in this aim.

Fernández-Batanero et al. (2020) argued that PD programmes improve teachers' technical skills, but connecting digital aspects to school contexts remains rare. This is slightly different than our result: even though teachers reported developed skills with technology, the results indicated that the teachers' research-based overview of digital possibilities and restrictions improved. Their behaviour in classroom changed, as they applied more digital methods of working in teaching and learning practices and engaged in student-centred pedagogy.

Further, sufficient time to absorb what has been learned has been considered an important factor for PD (Philipsen et al., 2019; Postholm, 2012). The development project and associated small-scale tasks (creating, e.g., digital artefacts) and a reflection on them during the programme made it possible to deliver training information to the work community and networks. According to Macià and García (2016), cooperative practices in informal communities provide valuable support for teachers' PD. Most likely, this gradual sharing of one's own learning during the training may have been one strategy that strengthened the teachers' confidence in their own abilities.

Further, the interview data suggests that teachers' self-reported experiences of the PD programme were positive. As teachers participated in the programme on a voluntary basis, it is difficult to assess the impact of their beliefs and motivation on the results of this study. Moreover, the context of the study is unique: the PD programme was implemented in Finland, where teacher education is based on research (Niemi et al., 2018). Two of the researchers involved in the study were also members of the programme staff. These aspects made it difficult to conclude whether the results would be the same among teachers from different backgrounds. However, the purpose of a case study is not to generalise findings across populations but to inform theory by examining constructs and phenomena in the context in which they occur (Yin, 2009). Therefore, the case study method is well suited for this study. As Borko et al. (2010) point out, context is an essential part of PD that often cannot be separated from teacher outcomes.

Teachers mainly expressed positive perceptions of the effectiveness of education, but some participants pointed out areas for development. Some teachers were left without support from their work community to complete their education. In the future, emphasis should be placed on the active participation of teachers' work communities in the programme. One teacher had not shared much information about the content of the programme with others in her work community. This would require more systematic encouragement. According to another teacher, cooperation among the participants could be improved, especially in terms of technical matters. The third participant longed for deeper knowledge of programming during the training. Individual needs should be better considered in such PD programmes, although this can be challenging due to the diverse field of digital learning.

One of the strengths of this study is that the results reflect all levels of Kirkpatrick and Kirkpatrick's (2016) model and not only the lower levels (reaction and learning) (Cahapay, 2021). Further, examining the effectiveness of PD programmes (Borko et al., 2010) by combining interview data with actual classroom observation data would improve the credibility of the results and, hence, could be an important step for future research.

In conclusion, the PD programme was effective, personally relevant to the teachers, and purposeful for the development of work communities. After the program, the teachers were able to direct their own work tasks more meaningfully, expand their job profiles, and even move on to entirely new kinds of work responsibilities. These changes in teachers' job profiles indicate the rich development of the work communities as an outcome of the PD programme.

References

Borko, H., Jacobs, J., & Koellner, K. (2010). Contemporary approaches to teacher professional development. *International Encyclopaedia of Education, 7*(2), 548–556.

Cahapay, M. B. (2021). Kirkpatrick model: Its limitations as used in higher education evaluation. *International Journal, 8*(1), 135–144.

Darling-Hammond, L., Hyler, M. E., & Gardner, M. (2017). *Effective teacher professional development.* Learning Policy Institute.

Elo, S., & Kyngäs, H. (2008). The qualitative content analysis process. *Journal of Advanced Nursing, 62*(1), 107–115.

Erstad, O., Kjällander, S., & Järvelä, S. (2021). Facing the challenges of "digital competence" a Nordic agenda for curriculum development for the 21st century. *Nordic Journal of Digital Literacy, 16*(2), 77–87.

Fernández-Batanero, J. M., Montenegro-Rueda, M., Fernández-Cerero, J., & García-Martínez, I. (2020). Digital competences for teacher professional development: Systematic review. *European Journal of Teacher Education,* 1–19.

Ilomäki, L., Paavola, S., Lakkala, M., & Kantosalo, A. (2016). Digital competence – an emergent boundary concept for policy and educational research. *Education and Information Technologies, 21,* 655–679.

Instefjord, E. J., & Munthe, E. (2017). Educating digitally competent teachers: A study of integration of professional digital competence in teacher education. *Teaching and Teacher Education, 67,* 37–45.

Kirkpatrick, J. D., & Kirkpatrick, W. K. (2016). *Kirkpatrick's four levels of training evaluation.* Association for Talent Development.

Kontkanen, S., Dillon, P., Valtonen, T., Renkola, S., Vesisenaho, M., & Väisänen, P. (2016). Pre-service teachers' experiences of ICT in daily life and in educational contexts and their proto-technological pedagogical knowledge. *Education and Information Technologies, 21*, 919–943.

Kontkanen, S., Pöntinen, S., Kewalramani, S., Veresov, N., & Havu-Nuutinen, S. (2023). Children's digital competence in early childhood education: A comparative analysis of curricula. *Eurasia Journal of Mathematics, Science and Technology Education, 19*(1), em2215.

Lavonen, J. (2020). Curriculum and teacher education reforms in Finland that support the development of competences for the twenty-first century. In F. M. Reimers (Ed.), *Audacious education purposes: How governments transform the goals of education systems* (pp. 65–80). Springer.

Macià, M., & García, I. (2016). Informal online communities and networks as a source of teacher professional development: A review. *Teaching and Teacher Education, 55*, 291–307.

Niemi, H., Lavonen, J., Kallioniemi, A., & Toom, A. (2018). The role of teachers in the Finnish educational system: High professional autonomy and responsibility. In H. Niemi, A. Toom, A. Kallioniemi, & J. Lavonen (Eds.), *The teacher's role in the changing globalizing world* (pp. 47–61). Brill.

Philipsen, B., Tondeur, J., Pareja Roblin, N., Vanslambrouck, S., & Zhu, C. (2019). Improving teacher professional development for online and blended learning: A systematic meta-aggregative review. *Educational Technology Research and Development, 67*, 1145–1174.

Piispa-Hakala, S., Korhonen, T., Kontkanen, S., Veermans, M., Järvinen, J. P., Lahti, A., Sormunen, K., & Valtonen, T. (2023). Luokanopettajan ammatillinen toimijuus opetuksen digipedagogisessa kehittämisessä. [Class-teachers' professional agency in developing digital pedagogy]. In S. Kontkanen, S. Piispa-Hakala, & S. Havu-Nuutinen (Eds.), *Oppimisen muuntuvat maisemat* (pp. 319–348). Suomen Kasvatustieteellinen Seura.

Pöntinen, S., & Räty-Záborszky, S. (2020). Pedagogical aspects to support students' evolving digital competence at school. *European Early Childhood Education Research Journal, 28*(2), 182–196.

Postholm, M. B. (2012). Teachers' professional development: A theoretical review. *Educational Research, 54*(4), 405–429.

Sancar, R., Atal, D., & Deryakulu, D. (2021). A new framework for teachers' professional development. *Teaching and Teacher Education, 101*, 103305.

Sherin, M. G., & Russ, R. S. (2014). Teacher noticing via video: The role of interpretive frames. In B. Calandra & P. Rich (Eds.), *Digital video for teacher education: Research and practice* (pp. 11–28). Routledge.

Stein, M. K., Smith, M. S., & Silver, E. (1999). The development of professional developers: Learning to assist teachers in new settings in new ways. *Harvard Educational Review, 69*(3), 237–270.

Vahtivuori-Hänninen, S., Halinen, I., Niemi, H., Lavonen, J., & Lipponen, L. (2014). A new Finnish national core curriculum for basic education (2014) and technology as an integrated tool for learning. In H. Niemi, J. Multisilta, L. Lipponen, & M. Vivitsou (Eds.), *Finnish innovations and technologies in schools* (pp. 21–32). Brill Sense.

Voogt, J., Laferriere, T., Breuleux, A., Itow, R. C., Hickey, D. T., & McKenney, S. (2015). Collaborative design as a form of professional development. *Instructional Science, 43*, 259–282.

Yin, R. K. (2009). *Case study research: Design and methods* (Vol. 5). Sage.

What Is Important in Applying ICT to Classroom Practice in Schools

15

Wakio Oyanagi

Introduction

During the COVID-19 pandemic, schools encountered situations that they had never experienced before. Darling-Hammond et al. (2020) and Brushwood and Bimm (2021) identified the issues raised by COVID-19 and explained what could be learned from them and what educational activities should be considered in the future. Huck and Zhang (2021) also systematically reviewed reports and studies on how schools and teachers responded from March–July 2020, when schools around the world closed when COVID-19 started. These articles pointed out that it was only when COVID-19 was contained and we started conducting our daily lives that we realized what we had taken for granted. Additionally, they describe how schools responded to COVID-19 in the initial months to ensure the safety and security of their students and stopped them from learning. It also describes the role of information and communications technology (ICT) in educational activities.

We also used the database to analyze how elementary and secondary education had been facing COVID-19 since 2020, while using technology. The Education Resources Information Center (ERIC), an online library sponsored by the Institute of Education Sciences of the U.S. Department of Education, was used to search for relevant articles from 2020 that

DOI: 10.4324/9781003406631-15

included "COVID-19," "Elementary and Secondary Education," and "Technology Use in Education" in their abstracts. Peer-reviewed articles were surveyed. As a result, 110 articles were retrieved. Among the 110 articles, 57 dealt with distance education, 41 with barriers, 35 with teacher attitudes, 28 with access to computers, 23 with the teaching method, 15 with learner engagement, 14 with equal education, and 11 with educational change.

For instance, Yanoski et al. (2021) and White et al. (2022) demonstrated how an ICT environment can contribute to the safety and security of students when they have been stopped from learning. They identified what was required of schools, administrators, and teachers, as well as what responses were effective in bridging these regional gaps. Burgin et al. (2022) pointed out the importance of examining student engagement in distance learning and bringing needs and voices into consideration in lesson design. Naff et al. (2022) found that the home environment, socioeconomic status, and previous mental health or disability diagnosis had an impact while addressing the effects of COVID-19 on the mental health of PK–12 students. Administrators should focus on the well-being of children and teachers, carefully examine their emotions, and be agile in advancing policies with teachers on how to respond to crisis situations (Kwatubana & Molaodi, 2021; Wilson, 2021; Farhadi & Winton, 2022). Yıldız and Göçen (2022) examined teachers' opinions on leadership and guidelines for teachers' behavior to survive in turbulent times and attempted to identify what teachers should do in response to the new normal.

Thus, the articles published over the past three years confirm that elementary and secondary education, through its response to COVID-19, has become more confronted with the digital divide and the students' mental health care that exists in the region and the importance of the attitude and role of principals and teachers in facing these issues. Through our research with ERIC, we found that since COVID-19 started, the use of ICT in schools has been discussed in detail as a response to various problems, with references to ICT as a tool for guaranteeing learning and close communication. However, we did not find many references to the use of ICT for data application in solving various problems.

In Japan, the use of ICT in schools has partially changed since 2020 in response to the COVID-19 pandemic. Japan's Ministry of Education, Culture, Sports, Science, and Technology (MEXT) has been recommending the use of one-to-one terminals, advanced technologies such as artificial intelligence, virtual reality, augmented reality, as well as metaverses in education, and the collection and usage of educational data. However, although ICT has been used in schools to guarantee learning, improve teaching methods, and facilitate close communication among teachers, students, and parents, less attention has been paid to the use of educational data. Clarifying how ICT has been used in schools in Japan would lead to an understanding of the relationship between the use of ICT in education and educational data, which was not found in the ERIC database.

Therefore, this study discusses Japanese efforts to address the trends and emerging issues of ICT use and teachers' attitudes toward its use in schools in 2020. In the following sections, we describe the educational policy pursued by the Japanese educational government in relation to ICT use in schools before and after 2020. Next, we explain the changes in ICT use in schools in 2020. Using the results of a questionnaire survey, we discuss how teachers feel about the use of educational data in relation to the use of ICT in schools. Finally, what is required to ensure that education using ICT for this purpose is implemented in schools and is discussed from the viewpoint of teacher education. The relationship between the international trends mentioned and Japan's efforts are discussed.

Japanese Education Policy Related to ICT Use in Schools Around 2020

Since 1947, the Ministry of Education in Japan (now the Ministry of Education, Culture, Sports, Science and Technology) has revised and published courses of study and curriculum standards for elementary and secondary education almost every 10 years. In 2018, soon after the most recent courses of study were published, the ICT environment in Japan's schools was fragile and in critical condition, with a large disparity in the state of development among regions. In December 2019, the government decided to integrate one terminal per student with a high-speed and high-capacity communication network for each student to achieve the goals of the new courses of study. This was named the Global Innovation Gateway for All-Schools Initiative (GIGA). The GIGA schools initiative was implemented partially because the spread of COVID-19 in 2020 revealed Japan's lagging digitalization of the education sector. The installation of an educational terminal for elementary and junior high school students was completed in March 2021 (96.1%).

A nationwide period of school closure was initiated in March 2020 owing to COVID-19. It lasted for approximately three months. During this period, face-to-face classes were not available. However, from June

2020 onward, schools were not closed all at once at the national level, and face-to-face classes began at the discretion of the local boards of education. Until the GIGA schools initiative in 2020, teachers often used ICT to present teaching materials and summarize lessons. In most schools, there was no environment in which each student had access to a terminal during regular classes, and students had limited opportunities to use ICT as a learning tool. However, while face-to-face teaching was limited, there was a need to use ICT as a communication tool for close contact with students and their parents as well as for the psychological care of students. Through these experiences, the challenges in the school environment and school initiatives that were unthinkable in pre-2020 schools were revealed. New operational issues (environment and methods) have become apparent in the process of using a learning environment sequentially established through the GIGA school initiative as a tool for learning activities and communicating with students and their families.

How did children, instructors, and parents who used these environments from 2020 to July 2021, when the impact of COVID-19 was so high, feel about the initiative? The "Results of the Questionnaire Survey of instructors on the GIGA School Concept and Future Direction" (September 3, 2021, Updated January 31, 2022) by the "Digital Agency, Ministry of Internal Affairs and Communications, MEXT, and Ministry of Economy, Trade and Industry" reported relevant results. The survey on these results was based on an analysis of the results of the Digital Agency's "Questionnaire for Instructors on the GIGA School Concept" and "Questionnaire on Tablets" for children, implemented from July 1–31, 2021. The educational survey on GIGA in schools comprised nine questions, and 42,333 responses (from faculty, staff, parents, etc.) were collected. The school children's survey on tablets comprised three questions, and 217,077 responses were received.

Regarding the children's opinions on the problems they face when using terminals such as tablets, many reported that the school network is slow, difficult to operate, and influenced by usage. As children progress from elementary school to junior and senior high school, they tend to be more specific about their communication environment. Regarding the importance of using tablets, elementary school students tended to have more opinions about following rules and listening to teachers' opinions, whereas junior and senior high school students tended to have more opinions about increasing opportunities for use, information literacy, and communication environment. Some respondents also reported that they

What Is Important in Applying ICT to Classroom Practice **235**

preferred not to use tablets and that there were relaxed and strict opinions regarding restrictions on tablet use.

Conversely, in terms of adults' opinions regarding the issues they experienced about learners (students), teachers and staff reported that they also experienced issues related to the network environment and teaching methods. Moreover, parents reported concerns regarding using the tablets for purposes other than learning. As for the challenges faced by teachers and staff, approximately 60% of the teachers and staff felt that the workload was unevenly distributed among certain teachers and staff with high literacy levels. Approximately 50% of the respondents reported that they did not know how to use ICT effectively in their subject areas, whereas approximately 40% expressed concern that the ICT environment for teachers and staff was not well maintained. In addition, in the free answers to the survey, many respondents reported the need for ICT training. The most reported concern regarding the issues they felt about schools and other related institutions was the sense of challenge in digitization of documents and surveys. Teachers and staff reported concerns regarding the lack of networking and other on-site systems to promote tablet use. Many parents reported that the school's overall educational policy and communication methods were not digitized and were based on phone calls and paper.

In response to these statements, a summary of these results reiterates that the purpose of GIGA and the digitization of education is to use digital means to unlock the potential of children to become creators of an increasingly changing society and to provide education that meets the needs of diverse groups of children. The summary further stated that in the current situation, the spread of COVID-19 – distance/online education using ICT – is extremely crucial to "keep children learning, even in times of emergency." It was also noted that not all issues could be solved at once, and that some items required further study, such as the improvement of school network environments as well as the maintenance and updating of teacher and staff terminals, and items that have pros and cons, such as filtering restrictions. The ministries and agencies concerned continued to study these issues, and those items that required further promotion were included in the "New Priority Plan," to be approved by the Cabinet by the end of FY2021. Government ministries and agencies worked as 'one team' and persistently monitored issues while listening to the voices of those involved in the education system.

As the GIGA school initiative had advanced the realization of a one-child-one-device environment, it has become evident that other issues

236 Wakio Oyanagi

must be resolved, environmentally and effectively, as described earlier. In addition to responding to these issues, the MEXT has begun to take on the challenge of realizing "personalized, self-regulated, and collaborative learning," which will bring out the potential of all children. For this purpose, it was decided that the effective use of educational data was necessary and that specific studies were needed on the measures required to promote such usage. It was stated that the purpose of using educational data was to examine each student's situation from multiple perspectives based on such data, and to enable detailed support to maximize each student's ability in each educational activity, such as learning guidance, student guidance, classroom management, and school administration. It was also stated that existing cutting-edge technologies should be effectively combined and used in education according to their intended purposes.

What Changes Have Occurred in the Use of ICT in Schools Around 2020

How has ICT been used in schools in the context of educational policy development related to ICT in 2020 and in response to COVID-19?

Oyanagi (2023) analyzed the changes in efforts in 2020 for the Japan Association for Educational Technology (JAET), the largest organization in Japan, where teachers interested in adopting ICT in Japanese schools reported their practices and exchanged information at the end of October each year. The JAET is a practical research organization for schoolteachers, education-related companies, and researchers. Schoolteachers present their reports on classroom and school practices, exchange the results of their practical research, and aim for professional growth. Reports on educational practices are submitted but not peer-reviewed by the organization or researchers. Therefore, the influence of publication bias by researchers is minimal, and what teachers practice is reported (https://jaet.jp/paper/). Oyanagi (2023) extracted the following practice reports by investigating the teachers reported at the JAET conference, taking into account the fact that new courses of study were announced in 2018 and fully implemented in 2020, and the fact that one terminal per student under the GIGA school concept was introduced in elementary and junior high schools ahead of schedule due to COVID-19 from 2020.

In 2018, the new curriculum guidelines were announced; in 2020 the one-per-pupil environment of the GIGA school concept was deployed in schools, partially due to COVID-19; and in 2021 the face-to-face and distance classes were conducted in schools using that environment concurrently. Japan follows a school calendar schedule in which the new school year begins in April and ends in March the following year. Therefore, teachers often report on the practices they have been promoting since April each year at the JAET conference in October of the same year or present their practices up to the previous year. To investigate how the impact of Japan's education policy on ICT and the GIGA school initiative has changed the way teachers use ICT in their classrooms and schools, the practice reports of 2017 and 2018 as well as 2020 and 2021 were discussed. The survey included practical reports and articles published by the JAET in 2017 (121 papers), 2018 (130 papers), 2020 (84 papers), and 2021 (87 papers).

To analyze practice reports and other data, Oyanagi (2023) decided to use the PICRAT model, which allowed us to analyze trends in the use of ICT in the classroom from teachers and students' ICT perspectives. The PICRAT model by Kimmons et al. (2020) was used to analyze reports on educational practice research in Japan in 2020. This model proposed a framework for reflecting on technology integration from teachers' and students' perspectives. In terms of teacher use, this study discusses: (1) educational practices that simply replace existing teaching methods with ICT and digital content (replaces), (2) educational practices that capitalize on the functions of ICT and digital content (amplifies), and (3) educational practice papers that make creative use of ICT and digital content to improve teaching, or use them in ways that have not been done in the past and are aimed at new methods or content (transforms).

Additionally, in terms of the use of ICT by students, this study discusses: (1) the use of ICT based on passive learning activities (passive), (2) the use of digital content and ICT to encourage students to interact with teaching materials and learn in an interactive way (interactive), and (3) the use of digital content and ICT to generate new ideas as artwork, make proposals based on their ideas and findings, and participate in society by working on projects (creative). Kimmons et al. (2020) had arranged the three utilization types of teachers and three types for students as a matrix and represented their model with nine boxes.

As a result, the number of presentations (number of reports and articles analyzed) in 2020 and 2021 decreased because of the impact of COVID-19 and the shift to online conferences compared to 2017 and 2018. Therefore, Oyanagi (2023) counted the number of papers corresponding to the analyzed items in the total number of papers for each year and analyzed the increase or decrease in the number of papers as a percentage. The following overall trends were identified:

1 The use of ICT by teachers was higher for replaces than for other items.
2 The use of ICT by teachers was lower in the use of transforms than for other items.
3 The use of ICT by students was higher for passive and interactive than for other items.
4 The use of ICT by students was lower for creative than for other items.

Oyanagi (2023) also identified that the number of educational practices that emphasize creativity were still not very large from an overall perspective, but the percentage of such creativity-oriented educational practices increased slightly after 2020. The impetus for these educational practice papers stems from the fact that the contents of their reports make programming a crucial theme. This was because activities such as creating animation and music using programming were possible in the classroom and remotely. Compared to the 2017 and 2018 reports, the 2020 and 2021 reports showed an increase in the percentages of Replace-Passive, Amplifies-Passive, Replace-Interactive, Replace-Creative, and Amplifies-Creative. Although it is nearly impossible to identify educational practices aimed at transformation, creative educational practices have emerged. However, the survey results did not mention the use of educational data.

Teachers' Attitudes Toward ICT Use Initiatives in Schools Since 2020

These results were based on an analysis of the themes and interests of the presentations made by teachers who, by 2021, actively used ICT in their schools and their own classes and who were willing to exchange them with teachers from around the country at the JAET conference.

In the following section, we discuss the results of this research on the current state of ICT use in schools and classrooms, including efforts in 2022, when face-to-face instruction were the norm.

The participants in the survey were elementary school teachers from City A. In Japan, elementary school teachers have made more progress than secondary school teachers have in using ICT in their classes. We selected teachers with three years of experience working for the school because we wanted them to respond to the question about their experience since 2020, when the school environment changed. We decided that it was necessary for the purpose of this study to identify how teachers were using ICT in Japan, so we asked elementary school teachers to cooperate. City A is a large city that includes mountainous and urban areas, and we requested their cooperation because we believed that, as a city in Japan, the location of its schools was unbiased and representative. All study participants provided informed consent, and the study design was approved by the appropriate ethics review board. Forty teachers in leadership positions and 177 teachers in their third year of service who accepted to participate in the survey were requested to complete the questionnaire in early June 2023. However, only 20 teachers in leadership positions and 80 in their third years of service responded to this deadline. Table 15.1 shows the results of a survey conducted on the use of ICT in schools using the following six questions among teachers in leadership

Table 15.1 Use of ICT in Schools

	Teachers in Leadership Positions ($n = 20$)		Teachers in Their Third Year of Employment ($n = 80$)	
	Average	*Standard Deviation*	*Average*	*Standard Deviation*
Q1. Teachers' use of ICT in the lessons	4.2	0.62	4.19	0.80
Q2. Students' use of ICT in the lessons	4.15	0.67	4.14	0.79
Q3. Teachers' use of ICT in school affairs	4.15	0.59	3.95	0.74
Q4. Utilizing various survey information on students to understand students	3.65	0.81	3.78	0.86
Q5. Utilizing various survey information on students to improve lessons	3.6	0.60	3.76	0.82
Q6. Need for teacher training on the use of educational data	4.15	0.75	3.86	0.91

positions during teacher training and in their third year of employment. Participants were asked to respond to the questions rated on a five-point scale, with five being very positive and one being very negative.

The results showed that teachers in the two positions rated the school in the same way regarding the use of ICT by teachers and students in the classroom in Q1 and Q2. However, in Q4 through Q6, teachers in both positions gave lower ratings to the school's efforts to use educational data than in Q1 and Q2. Teachers in leadership positions were willing to consider the need for training in the use of educational data in schools, but teachers in their third year of service were somewhat reluctant to actively promote such training.

At the end of June, we requested 177 teachers in their third year of employment who had already participated in the survey to self-evaluate their use of ICT. Consequently, 132 teachers responded to the deadline.

Table 15.2 shows that there is a difference between the school's efforts and one's own efforts in Q2, " Student's use of ICT," and Q5, "using survey information to improve lessons," and that there are variations in the responses. Looking at the results of Q7 and Q8, it can be understood that the respondents were more negative, on average, to conduct their own surveys to improve their lessons and classroom management than the results of the other question items. The standard deviation is also larger than that of the other questions, so it can be interpreted that there is a tendency for variation in response among teachers.

According to the "free answers" of teachers in their third year of employment, it was evident that they tend to consider the "use of ICT in teaching as well as learning activities" and the "use of educational data using ICT" to be two different things. The tendency has become evident that "ICT use in teaching and learning activities" was understood as an initiative that contributes to the improvement of teaching and learning, and "ICT use of educational data" is considered as an initiative to evaluate students.

In summary, ICT was used as a tool to guarantee learning, support learning activities, and support school affairs in 2020, although these are the results of a survey conducted in City A in Japan. However, teachers have not focused on the use of educational data acquired in learning and communication activities using one terminal per student in a cloud environment with a high-speed network. It has become evident that in addition to the fact that teachers' lack of interest in the use of educational data in the first place, they lack awareness or recognition that the use of ICT and educational data are closely related. The MEXT has been actively promoting the use of educational data and advanced technology since 2021, but it was thought that the situation had not been fully communicated to teachers.

What Is Important in Applying ICT to Classroom Practice **241**

Table 15.2 Comparison of School Initiatives and Own Initiatives Regarding ICT Use

	About initiatives at the school where you work; teachers in their third year of employment (n = 80)		About your own efforts; teachers in their third year of employment (n = 132)	
	Average	Standard Deviation	Average	Standard Deviation
Q1. Teachers' use of ICT in the lessons	4.19	0.80	4.18	0.80
Q2. Students' use of ICT in the lessons	4.14	0.79	3.71	1.04
Q3. Teachers' use of ICT in school affairs	3.95	0.74	4.02	0.97
Q4. Utilizing various survey information on students to understand students	3.78	0.86		
Q5. Utilizing various survey information on students to improve lessons	3.76	0.82	3.17	1.21
Q6. Need for teacher training on the use of educational data	3.86	0.91		
Q7. Conducting self-designed surveys to understand how students are doing in order to improve lessons			2.86	1.25
Q8. Conducting self-designed surveys to understand how students are doing for classroom management			3.2	1.14

What Is Required for More Effective Use of ICT in Classroom Practice at Schools

Therefore, what initiatives are required to rethink what we have taken for granted in schools, respond to various issues using ICT, use ICT functions for creative learning activities, relate ICT use to educational data use, and apply it to classroom practice? It makes sense to have students encounter these issues during teacher training and to closely relate teacher training and in-service education. To answer this question, we believed that the concepts of technology integration and infusion are relevant in educational activities.

Borthwick et al. (2020) moved from the idea of promoting the integration of technology into the teacher preparation curriculum to proposing the prospect of systematically building a new culture of teacher preparation through five spaces, in universities and among the teacher instructors involved. Thus, they used the concepts of technology integration and infusion to explain the four pillars of their approach (Graziano et al., 2023; Jin et al., 2023; Sprague et al., 2023; Warr et al., 2023; Williams et al., 2023). We were interested in this theoretical framework because the idea of technology infusion has implications for teacher preparation education and for promoting teachers' professional learning in schools. We thought it is meaningful to learn about the relationship between the use of ICT and educational data and its meaning throughout the entire training curriculum from the time of teacher training to challenge ourselves and make us reevaluate what we took for granted from our prior school education experience, to consider student learning by capitalizing on the new environments, and to think about the relationship between the use of ICT and educational data and its meaning.

Conclusions

This study attempts to clarify how ICT and educational data use in schools were promoted in 2020 through Japanese case reports. Although this study is a case report from Japan, it reveals certain aspects of cultural transformations in schools, the emergence of barriers as the learning environment changes, and advancements in the process of integrating technology into classrooms.

Consequently, many schools and teachers have gained an environment in which one device per student is available in the wake of the COVID-19 pandemic and positive initiatives from the Minister of Education. To ensure the safety and security of students and to improve their academic performance, ICT is used. Teachers who used ICT as a teaching tool in the past are now trying to use it as a learning tool for creative learning. However, the classification and organization of teachers' practice reports revealed that the number of schools and teachers taking on the challenge of educational transformation remains small. A survey of teachers in one city revealed that the use of educational data, which has not been seen in ICT-enabled practices in elementary and secondary education in international surveys, has not been observed in Japan. This was because teachers were not interested in the use of educational data in the first place, and they did not understand the relationship between the use of ICT and educational data. To tackle these issues, this study has summarized that it is necessary to start with the reform of the teacher preparatory curriculum and that the concept of technology infusion may be significant for this reform.

References

Borthwick, A. C., Foulger, T. S., & Graziano, K. J. (Eds.). (2020). *Championing technology infusion in teacher preparation: A framework for supporting future educators.* International Society for Technology in Education.

Brushwood, R., C., & Bimm, M. (2021). Children, schooling, and COVID-19: What education can learn from existing research. *Journal of Teaching and Learning, 15*(2), 3–20.

Burgin, X. D., Daniel, M. C., & Wasonga, T. A. (2022). Teachers' perspectives on teaching and learning during the pandemic in the United States. *Educational Process: International Journal, 11*(3), 122–140.

Darling-Hammond, L., Schachner, A., Edgerton, A. K., Badrinarayan, A., Cardichon, J., Cookson, P. W., Jr., Griffith, M., Klevan, S., Maier, A., Martinez, M., Melnick, H., Truong, N., & Wojcikiewicz, S. (2020). *Restarting and reinventing school: Learning in the time of COVID and beyond.* Learning Policy Institute.

Farhadi, B., & Winton, S. (2022). Ontario teachers' policy leadership during the COVID-19 pandemic. *Canadian Journal of Educational Administration and Policy, 200,* 49–62.

Graziano, K. J., Foulger, T. S., & Borthwick, A. C. (2023). Design pillars for technology-infused teacher preparation programs. *Contemporary Issues in Technology and Teacher Education Journal, 23*(1). https://citejournal.org/volume-23/issue-1-23/general/editorial-design-pillars-for-technology-infused-teacher-preparation-programs

Huck, C., & Zhang, J. (2021). Effects of the COVID-19 pandemic on K-12 education: A systematic literature review. *Educational Research and Development Journal, 24*(1), 53–84.

Jin, Y., Clausen, J. M., Elkordy, A., Greene, K., & McVey, M. (2023). Design principles for modeled experiences in technology-infused teacher preparation programs. *Contemporary Issues in Technology and Teacher Education, 23*(1).

https://citejournal.org/volume-23/issue-1-23/general/design-principles-for-modeled-experiences-in-technology-infused-teacher-preparation

Kimmons, R., Graham, C. R., & West, R. E. (2020). The PICRAT model for technology integration in teacher preparation. *Contemporary Issues in Technology and Teacher Education, 20*(1). https://citejournal.org/volume-20/issue-1-20/general/the-picrat-model-for-technology-integration-in-teacher-preparation

Kwatubana, S., & Molaodi, V. (2021). Leadership styles that would enable school leaders to support the wellbeing of teachers during COVID-19. *New Challenges to Education: Lessons from Around the World. BCES Conference Books, 19,* 106–112.

Naff, D., Williams, S., Furman-Darby, J., & Yeung, M. (2022). The mental health impacts of COVID-19 on PK-12 students: A systematic review of emerging literature. *AERA Open, 8*(1), 1–40. https://doi.org/10.1177/23328584221084722

Oyanagi, W. (2023). A case study on the transformation process of technology use around 2020. In E. Langran, P. Christensen, & J. Sanson (Eds.), *Proceedings of society for information technology & teacher education international conference* (pp. 820–825). Association for the Advancement of Computing in Education (AACE).

Sprague, D. R., Zumpano, N. M., Richardson, J. W., Williamson, J., & Gray, L. (2023). Technology infusion and the development of practice: The quest to create digitally-able teachers. *Contemporary Issues in Technology and Teacher Education, 23*(1). https://citejournal.org/volume-23/issue-1-23/general/technology-infusion-and-the-development-of-practice-the-quest-to-create-digitally-able-teachers

Warr, M., Driskell, S., Langran, E., Mouza, C., & Schmidt-Crawford, D. (2023). Curriculum design for technology infusion requires a continuous collaborative process. *Contemporary Issues in Technology and Teacher Education, 23*(1). https://citejournal.org/volume-23/issue-1-23/general/curriculum-design-for-technology-infusion-requires-a-continuous-collaborative-process

White, S., Harmon, H., Johnson, J., & O'Neill, B. (2022). In-the-moment experiences of rural school principals in the COVID-19 pandemic. *The Rural Educator, 43*(2), 47–59.

Williams, M. K., Christensen, R., McElroy, D., & Rutledge, D. (2023). Teacher self-efficacy in technology integration as a critical component in designing technology-infused teacher preparation programs. *Contemporary Issues in Technology and Teacher Education Journal, 23*(1). https://citejournal.org/volume-23/issue-1-23/general/teacher-self-efficacy-in-technology-integration-as-a-critical-component-in-designing-technology-infused-teacher-preparation-programs

Wilson, A. (2021). Emotionally agile leadership amid COVID-19. *School Leadership Review, 15*(2). https://scholarworks.sfasu.edu/slr/vol15/iss2/1

Yanoski, D. C., Gagnon, D., Schoephoerster, M., McCullough, D., Haines, M., & Cherasaro, T. L. (2021). *Variations in district strategies for remote learning during the COVID-19 pandemic (REL 2021-118)*. U.S. Department of Education, Institute of Education Sciences, National Center for Education Evaluation and Regional Assistance, Regional Educational Laboratory Central. Retrieved September 18, 2023, from http://ies.ed.gov/ncee/edlabs

Yıldız, Ş. S., & Göçen, A. (2022). Teachers' views on leadership in the new normal. *Asian Journal of Distance Education, 17*(1), 1–16. https://doi.org/10.5281/zenodo.5979709

A Dialogic Design-Based Research Partnership Approach

Developing Close-to-Practice Educational Technology Theory in Kenya

Louis Major, Rebecca Daltry, Asad Rahman, Daniel Plaut, Mary Otieno, and Kevin Otieno

1. Introduction

Design-Based Research (DBR) is a systematic approach that combines previous research insights, iterative use in real-world settings, data collection, analysis, evaluation, and re-design to inform the development of educational 'products' (Smørdal et al., 2021). Collaborating with teachers and others is crucial in DBR to generate practical knowledge applicable in real-world contexts (Roschelle & Penuel, 2006). In DBR, design and research are intertwined, with design being research-based and research being design-based (Bakker, 2019). Co-design and collaboration play a crucial role in the research process, facilitating the exploration of educational problems and the advancement of contextually sensitive theory and design principles (diSessa & Cobb, 2004).

This chapter presents and critically reflects on the implementation of innovative DBR involving Kenyan pre-primary teachers and other partners over two consecutive school years (2022–2023). The focus of this

DOI: 10.4324/9781003406631-16

This chapter has been made available under a CC-BY-NC-ND 4.0 license.

study was the iterative evaluation of a 'digital personalised learning' (DPL) tool to develop close-to-practice theory about its integration into classroom practice. Research on DPL has primarily focused on its technological implementation, overlooking the pedagogical perspective (Vanbecelaere & Benton, 2021). Studies mainly explore DPL as a 'supplementary' intervention, separate from regular instruction, rather than aligned with the curriculum or integrated into classroom practice (Major & Francis, 2020; Major et al., 2021). UNICEF (2022) suggests potential for low-cost approaches aligning DPL with teachers' practices, while previous research indicates potential benefits of using technology to support teachers (Heinrich et al., 2020; Piper et al., 2015). DBR was thus a suitable approach to investigate the integration of a DPL tool into classroom practice, due to its focus on iterative development and evaluation in real-world contexts and its capacity to address the unique challenge of exploring the integration of DPL in classroom instruction through close collaboration and co-creation between researchers and practitioners.

Reported DBR had two key objectives. First, it aimed to promote teacher-researcher engagement in DBR by utilising a dialogue-informed 'intermediate theory building' framework (Hennessy, 2014). There is growing recognition across education research, policy, practice, and community groups regarding the importance of establishing authentic educational partnerships (The Collaborative Education Research Collective, 2023). The flexibility and adaptability of DBR as a methodological framework holds promise in fostering meaningful educational cooperation. To ensure successful DBR, it is essential to prioritise engaging key educational actors from the outset (Hall, 2020). However, managing such relationships can present challenges (Cukurova et al., 2019). This DBR study intended to bridge the gap between theoretical concepts and practical implementation by facilitating research closely aligned with real-world practice and fostering effective collaboration between teachers and researchers. The adoption of an intermediate theory-building approach aimed to recontextualise emergent theory, bridging the gap between scholarly and practical perspectives, in order to create an intermediate formulation presented in accessible language.

Second, the study aimed to enhance inclusivity by implementing strategies to broaden the concept of partnership in DBR. This involved an *integrated* approach encompassing a range of partners – including a leading EdTech developer, educational researchers and other specialists, and innovation and policy experts – at different stages of the co-design and research process. The approach builds on calls for further guidance

248 Louis Major et al.

on creating inclusive and expansive DBR partnerships (Mercier et al., 2022) – especially for research on educational technology (EdTech) in low- and middle-income countries (LMICs), where DBR demonstrates significant promise and utility (Amukune et al., 2023; Laleka & Rasheed, 2018), but may rarely be used in practice (Hennessy et al., 2022).

2. Defining the Problem Space

2.1 Complexities Undertaking Design-Based Research (DBR)

Although still regarded as a methodological newcomer by some in the research community, DBR has gained international recognition as a prominent framework for the systematic development of educational technology and associated pedagogical methods. However, the implementation of DBR poses challenges due to its inherent 'messiness' (Buhl et al., 2022). Issues that can limit DBR and create uncertainty have been discussed elsewhere (e.g., Henriksen & Ejsing-Duun, 2022). These include the potential adverse impact of researchers on research trustworthiness (Barab & Squire, 2004); challenges in bounding the temporal scope of studies (although DBR as part of a doctoral study remains feasible; e.g., Herrington et al., 2007; Martin, 2022); there being little distinction between DBR and implementation studies (due to limited commitment to genuine theoretical development; Fowler et al., 2022); and difficulties in sustaining implementation and widespread adoption after the main DBR phase (McKenney & Reeves, 2018).

The focus of this chapter is on examining the role of collaboration and partnership in DBR, and how to potentially address and overcome associated challenges to enhance our understanding of DPL applied in LMICs. This inquiry encompasses two dimensions: (1) identifying new strategies to effectively facilitate 'close-to-practice' research and foster collaboration between EdTech researchers and teachers, and (2) developing a more comprehensive and inclusive understanding of the concept of 'partnership' in EdTech-related DBR.

2.1.1 Challenges in Promoting Meaningful Engagement between Teachers and Researchers

Engaging teachers as co-researchers aims to enhance the relevance and applicability of DBR findings. DBR values the craft knowledge and

A Dialogic Design-Based Research Partnership Approach **249**

instincts of teachers, incorporating both outsider (etic) and insider (emic) perspectives through researcher-teacher collaboration to understand the issues at hand (McKenny & Reeves, 2018, p. 14). However, teacher involvement presents challenges, for instance, due to their limited research experience and other professional commitments (Anderson & Shattuck, 2012; Penuel et al., 2015).

A common critique of DBR is its perceived similarity to practitioner-oriented action research (Lewin, 1946). Although both approaches intend to effect change and improve learning outcomes, there are distinctions (Hall, 2020). DBR aims for practical improvements within the context of learning (a 'proximal contribution' such as a classroom), while also generating new conceptualisations of learning through theoretical contributions and design principles (a 'distal contribution') (Hall, 2020; McKenney & Reeves, 2018). In contrast, action research tends to focus on achieving positive changes in a specific context without emphasising wider theoretical development (Bakker, 2019).

DBR aims to 'bridge the gap' between educational practice and theory; however, there is uncertainty surrounding the best means of achieving this goal, and effective approaches remain unclear (Hall, 2020). This raises questions about how to maximise the contribution of teachers as co-researchers, not only to enhance educational outcomes in a specific study context, but to make a broader contribution to the wider body of research knowledge (in a way beyond what is typically achieved in action research). Establishing new ways to engage and collaborate with teachers during DBR would, therefore, be valuable in facilitating more effective co-design and co-creation that makes a wider contribution to knowledge (Holflod, 2022).

2.1.2 Extending Understanding of Practitioner Collaboration in DBR

Although teachers play a central role in DBR, DBR partnerships can extend beyond their participation alone, but this is less common (Tinoca et al., 2022; Zheng, 2015). Various experts, and learners, can provide useful input during DBR (McKenny & Reeves, 2018, p. 180). Other participants might include EdTech developers, software engineers, innovation specialists, industry experts, educational coaches, consultants, instructional designers, intermediaries, leaders, and others within the educational system (Minichiello & Caldwell, 2021; McKenny & Reeves,

2018). Such collaborators may play specific roles as 'co-researchers', contributing at different project stages (Zamenopoulos & Alexiou, 2018). Involving diverse expertise can enhance the effectiveness of DBR and foster collective creativity (Gallagher & Fazio, 2019; Sanders & Stappers, 2008). Such breadth of knowledge, experience, and know-how has the potential to act as the catalyst behind DBR innovation and discovery, in addition to further consolidating the link between research and practice (Minichiello & Caldwell, 2021).

However, the potentially entangled and contradictory interests of participants involved in DBR can complicate matters (Buhl et al., 2022). Researchers lack guidance to assist them in creating inclusive and expansive DBR partnerships that involve others beyond teachers (Mercier et al., 2022). There is also the scope to draw on new approaches in DBR that have traditionally been applied elsewhere. This includes methods such as 'user journey mapping', which provides practical and usable insights from teachers, and the lean startup process, which helps align assumptions within diverse teams (that may include developers and implementers) (Ries, 2011). Incorporating such approaches in a collaborative 'just-in-time' fashion during DBR may be advantageous.

Enhancing DBR outcomes might be achieved by involving stakeholders from diverse contexts in an interactive process at different stages of the DBR process. However, this raises the question (Buhl et al., 2022): What is an appropriate model for engaging stakeholders at different phases of DBR and when is optimal? Factors related to the effective coordination of such collaboration have to be considered.

3. Research Context and Theoretical Foundations

3.1 Research Aims and Setting

Reported research involved undertaking DBR to investigate the implementation of the EIDU (https://eidu.com/) DPL tool in Kenyan pre-primary classrooms. While EIDU's implementation in Kenya began in 2016, the research team's involvement commenced in 2021, demonstrating the adaptability of DBR to support ongoing implementation as well as the start-up design of EdTech. Reported DBR nonetheless coincided with a significant milestone: EIDU's preparation for nationwide DPL delivery aligned with the Tayari structured pedagogy (SP) programme. The classroom integration of EIDU intends to support pre-primary learning and teaching in two ways. Firstly, mapped to Kenya's pre-primary competency-based curriculum for learners aged 4 to 6, it delivers adaptive DPL using quality content from providers including onebillion (e.g., evaluated by Pitchford et al., 2019). Secondly, devices aid teachers with digitised materials and lesson guides from Tayari, demonstrated to enhance pre-primary learning outcomes (Piper et al., 2018; Sitabkhan et al., 2022). Tayari lesson plans are mapped to units of DPL content, enabling learners to engage with activities that link to that day's lessons.

However, there remained unanswered questions about the optimal implementation of such a DPL model aligned with structured pedagogy (henceforth referred to as EIDU's "DPL-SP" model), as opposed to the more common 'supplementary' DPL outside of teacher-led instruction (see Section 1.1). To bridge the gap between theory and practice, it was considered necessary to develop a more expansive understanding of DBR that emphasised dialogue. This was especially pertinent, considering that the DBR was taking place after several years of implementation, rather than at its inception, but also at a time of change to the implementation model. Hence, a dialogic approach to DBR involving a multidisciplinary team was considered valuable for consolidating learnings from the initial years of implementation, together with innovative strategies to further improve the model.

DBR was conducted between May 2022 and November 2023 and involved 74 teachers across two Kenyan counties, Mombasa and Kiambu. Teachers had varying years of teaching experience, and class sizes ranged from 10 to 100. One EIDU device was initially used in each classroom, although a second was introduced due to emergent DBR findings revealing this to be potentially valuable. As of 2023, EIDU is used by approximately 200,000 monthly active learners across 4,000 Kenyan pre-primary schools (Friedberg, 2023).

3.2 The Research Team

The DBR represented a partnership among teachers, researchers, education stakeholders, and a technology developer. The team was assembled through EdTech Hub (edtechhub.org) – a global research and innovation partnership committed to promoting evidence-based decision-making in EdTech – in close collaboration with Women Educational Researchers of Kenya (WERK). This brought together teachers and experts from a range of disciplines to collaboratively and creatively generate and apply

252 Louis Major et al.

evidence: researchers from universities in the UK and Kenya; innovation experts experienced in user testing and rapid iteration; education specialists with extensive knowledge of DPL evidence; and local technical consultants experienced in addressing system-wide implementation challenges specific to the context. The multidisciplinary nature of the research team was further enhanced through close collaboration with EIDU, the implementation partner and technology developer.

Although the distinct role of the research team was recognised – as an independent facilitator of dialogue and evidence building, as opposed to an active stakeholder in the DPL-SP implementation – close collaboration between all parties was deemed essential for the exchange of diverse perspectives throughout the DBR process.

3.3 Dialogic Theoretical Foundations

Dialogue, conceptualised as the interanimation of multiple 'voices' in an extended sense, that goes beyond the analysis of 'just talk' or interaction alone, serves as a theoretical foundation for the developed DBR strategy (Trausan-Matu et al., 2021). Adopting co-creation methods is increasingly associated with a 'dialogic turn' in educational research, featuring dialogue-based approaches to generate knowledge and encourage change (Olesen et al., 2018). This perspective considers knowledge as emerging from a collective dialogue between diverse stakeholders collaboratively producing meaning and not as something transmitted from expert(s) to participant(s) (Holflod, 2022). Applicable here is 'boundary crossing' as a dialogical phenomenon (Akkerman & Bakker, 2011). Dialogic space theory is also relevant, as this proposes that establishing a shared dialogic space enables the exchange of diverse perspectives, leading to new learning opportunities through the 'interanimation' of different voices (Trausan-Matu et al., 2021; Wegerif & Major, 2019). A dialogic approach to DBR might facilitate a more complex, multi-voiced, open-ended, and constructive process of co-creation; one that intentionally aims to continuously incorporate stakeholders' diverse ideas and perspectives, and contribute to the development and experimentation of learning designs (Holflod, 2022).

To operationalise these constructs, the DBR strategy was rooted in an 'intermediate theory building' framework. This is intended to enhance teacher-researcher engagement to bridge the research-practice gap. Another objective was to boost inclusivity and collaboration by establishing

A Dialogic Design-Based Research Partnership Approach **253**

an 'integrated' partnership approach as part of the DBR process. In doing so, the DBR model aimed to address calls to maximise teachers' contributions as co-researchers (Hall, 2020), in addition to offering a more expansive DBR implementation strategy (Buhl et al., 2022).

3.3.1 Intermediate Theory Building

Intermediate theory building is a participatory research approach in which teachers and researchers act as 'co-inquirers', establishing a bridge between educational theory and educational settings (Hennessy & Deaney, 2009; Hennessy, 2014). Differing from practitioner-led action research and academic-led approaches characterised by data gathering, this reconceptualises the roles of practitioner and researcher (Hennessy & Deaney, 2009). Intermediate theory building can facilitate the joint construction of analytical frameworks that elicit and codify "the explicit and implicit, initial and evolving theories and expectations of the different individuals involved" (Hennessy & Deaney, 2009, p. 1765).

An understanding of intermediate theory building underpins reported DBR. A methodological strategy built around a co-learning partnership between teachers and researchers was developed, using the classroom as a practical testing ground for pedagogical assumptions related to DPL integration (Hennessy, 2014). For instance, as discussed in Section 4.5, data was sorted and coded to bridge teachers' and researchers' views, with findings discussed in relation to "a priori" theories (of both) on integrating education technology into LMIC contexts.

3.3.2 An Integrated Approach to Partnership

Understanding of co-learning partnerships also extended beyond the relationship between teachers and researchers to incorporate a wider 'dialogic design' perspective. This emphasises complex stakeholder relationships and promotes sharing, listening, and interaction for effective collaboration involving multiple participants (Manzini, 2016). In addition to teachers and researchers, other participants were involved as 'co-enquirers', enabling synergy and exchange by drawing on scholarly and craft knowledge (Hennessy & Deaney, 2009).

Core principles guided the partnership process. Regular consultation and dialogue were key to prioritising strategies to enhance learning and

254 Louis Major et al.

exchange opportunities among all contributors to the research. Other strategies included identifying common ground in intervention goals and beliefs in effective implementation and evaluation approaches, as well as recognising differing concerns (such as researchers prioritising methodological rigour and practitioners considering time constraints; McKenny & Reeves, 2018, p. 210). Throughout, DBR was seen as facilitating a dynamic collaborative process, rather than primarily being a means to report design outcomes (Svihla & Reeve, 2016). This partnership strategy builds on research highlighting the necessity for both homogeneous and heterogeneous perspectives in DBR, conceptualised as continuous explorations of differences and tensions in boundary-crossing co-creation (Holflod, 2022).

4. An Integrated DBR Partnership Approach

Figure 16.1 provides an overview of the key phases and multidisciplinary methods, explaining their purpose and outcomes. While this DBR approach emphasised continuous dialogue and was inherently sequential, with each phase building upon the previous, it nonetheless retained the iterative, cyclical characteristics typical of DBR (Bakker, 2019).

Phase	Purpose	Outcomes
1. Scoping and initiating dialogue (May 2022)	For the research team to establish the foundations for co-design and collaboration with all key education and implementation stakeholders.	Co-creation by integrated team initiated and methods for the foundational phase developed.
2. Foundational phase of integrated multi-disciplinary methods (June-July 2022)	Integrating mixed-methods research and innovation strategies, to understand key stakeholders' perspectives of the DPL-SP model, and collaborate on solutions to identified challenges.	Qualitative data is thematically analysed and descriptive statistics are generated from quantitative data. Internal review of evidence conducted to validate insights, inform future research methods development, and shape collective understanding of contextual and implementation challenges.
3. Implementation iteration workshop #1 (Aug 2022)	For the research team to share findings with the implementing partner and collaboratively identify priority areas for improvement and future DBR cycles.	Co-learning lesson study phase is designed to address three priority areas of the implementation model identified as requiring more evidence.
4. Iterative, co-learning phase of lesson study (Oct-Nov 2022)	The co-learning approach of lesson study for teachers and researchers to collaboratively plan, implement, reflect upon and analyse different methods of integrating the DPL-SP model in the classroom.	Rigorous sorting and categorising of the data corpus, including deductive and inductive thematic coding and analysis, to integrate teacher and researcher perspectives and produce validated insights to shape the DPL-SP model and wider learnings about DPL implementation.
5. Implementation iteration workshop #2 (Nov 2022)	For the research team to share findings with the implementing partner and collaboratively identify priority areas for improvement and future DBR cycles.	Changes made to the implementation model (including two application design changes and the introduction of an additional device to classrooms), and other areas for future research agreed upon.
6. Innovation sandbox (April-Nov 2023)	Innovation research to improve an identified key issue in the model (equality of use).	Continuous learning alongside teachers and implementers to identify effective strategies to improve equality of use as the EIDU model scales across Kenya.
7. Evaluating practical and theoretical contributions (Nov 2023-Feb 2024)	Using DBR as the foundation for large-scale, quantitative research to assess the impact of the improved EIDU DPL-SP model on learning outcomes.	The development of both proximal and wider theory about the integration of DPL-SP in classrooms.

Figure 16.1 Overview of the Integrated DBR Partnership Approach

4.1 Scoping and Initiating Dialogue

A scoping phase was initiated to establish the dialogic foundations for co-design and collaboration. This aimed to address an inherent challenge: that the inception and funding for the study had been secured by researchers, in consultation with the implementation partner. Otherwise, there was a risk of perpetuating a common critique of social science research: that when research is conceived in the Global North but implemented in the Global South, it may not reflect the realities or priorities of the implementation context (Haelewaters et al., 2021).

The scoping phase focused on enabling informal dialogue and partnership between different stakeholders, by aligning priorities and establishing 'ground rules'. Recognising the distinct role of the research team to facilitate and convene collaboration, researchers engaged separately with teachers, headteachers, early-childhood development officers (ECDOs), county government officials, and EIDU colleagues, exploring the existing EIDU DPL-SP model from stakeholders' perspectives. The subsequent foundational cycle was based on emerging priorities, such as starting with collaborative effort to identify the strengths and challenges of the current DPL-SP model.

4.2 Foundational Phase of Integrated Multidisciplinary Methods

Data collection began with a foundational DBR cycle that combined 'traditional' mixed-methods research with innovation strategies. This integration approach had two main objectives: understanding stakeholders' perspectives on the DPL-SP model and collaborating on possible solutions to identified challenges.

Established data collection methods were first utilised. Key informant interviews (KIIs) and focus group discussions (FGDs) were conducted with teachers (7 FGDs), headteachers (6 KIIs), ECDOs (6 KIIs), and EIDU colleagues (6 KIIs). These identified the perceived benefits and challenges of EIDU, such as a perceived positive impact on learners' attendance and motivation in class but challenges with managing the battery life of the Android device. Direct observations (13 full school days) and indirect observations (94 videos of DPL use) complemented the KIIs and FGDs, by facilitating researchers' observational analysis of the DPL-SP model in practice. This mixed-methods strategy developed a foundational

256 Louis Major et al.

understanding of the current use of EIDU's DPL-SP model, to collaborate with teachers most effectively in future phases of the DBR.

This initial mixed-methods research was followed by two *innovation* workshops with 22 teachers, involving a 'user journey mapping' strategy, to transition from reflecting on challenges with the current DPL-SP model to identifying possible solutions. First, synthesising data from the KIIs, FGDs, and observations, 'as is' user journeys – mapping teachers' current use of the DPL-SP tool in classrooms – were constructed and provided to teachers for feedback. Critically engaging with the 'as is' user journey through collaborative discussion in the workshops, teachers then proposed an 'ideal' user journey with new ideas for implementation and usage of EIDU's DPL-SP tool.

By integrating traditional data collection approaches with innovative tools such as a user journey map, the DBR process addressed common limitations associated with non-participatory research methods, resulting in valuable and unique insights. Although DBR inherently focuses on co-creation, the tools and processes introduced from innovation methods (which stem from technology and software development) were particularly helpful in furthering co-creation with the users of the EIDU technology (teachers), enabling them to conceptualise their use of this tool and, informed by DBR data, conceptualise improvements to their engagement with it.

4.3 Implementation Iteration Workshop 1

The implementation iteration workshops (see also Section 4.5) facilitated productive dialogue amongst research partners. Ahead of the first workshop, qualitative data was thematically analysed and descriptive statistics were generated from quantitative data, out of which a set of recommendations were formed. A 'strength of evidence framework' was then used, to ensure all findings were traceable and triangulated across the integrated approach, and to determine recommendations according to the depth of evidence and stakeholders' priorities.

The outcomes of the workshops were twofold: first, when evidence from the DBR aligned with prior learnings by the implementation team, immediate improvements were made to the DPL-SP implementation model; second, when analysis suggested new areas for improvement that required further iteration, additional rounds of DBR were designed and undertaken.

4.4 Iterative, Co-learning Phase of Lesson Study

Having pinpointed areas of the DPL-SP model that required further evidence to develop an optimal implementation approach – specifically, the number of devices in the classroom, the time at which the device is used during the school day, and the way in which learners are selected to engage with the DPL tool – a co-learning approach between teachers and researchers was designed. This involved employing an adapted form of lesson study (Fernandez & Yoshida, 2004), which is a teacher professional development approach characterised by practitioner interaction within a dialogic space of professional learning (Warwick et al., 2016). Having discussed the findings of the foundational phase of DBR, teachers and researchers followed the lesson study framework of planning, implementing, reflecting, and analysing: following a co-planning workshop, two weeks of iterative implementation took place in six classrooms alongside daily teacher-researcher observations and reflections; two further workshops then focused on collaborative reflection and analysis. Classrooms were viewed as a practical space to test pedagogical assumptions regarding the integration of DPL, through the systematic framework of lesson study that fostered teacher-research collaboration.

4.5 Implementation Iteration Workshop 2

A second implementation iteration workshop (see Section 4.3) followed rigorous sorting, thematic coding, and analysis of the full lesson study data corpus to integrate teacher and researcher perspectives. There were two tangible outcomes from this workshop. First, changes were made to the DPL-SP model, including two design changes to the EIDU application and the introduction of an additional device to classrooms. Second, equality of DPL use was highlighted as a priority area for future DBR phases.

4.6 Innovation Sandbox

EdTech Hub Sandboxes are utilised to create a space within a wider system for testing new products, interventions, or pedagogical approaches. Their purpose is to validate assumptions and demonstrate progress towards a particular goal, serving as a preliminary step before potential wider implementation (Simpson et al., 2021).

258 Louis Major et al.

A sandbox was therefore initiated as the next phase of DBR to identify effective approaches for learner selection that might promote equal device usage. Interventions were designed with EIDU field staff liaising with teachers to surface existing ways in which they promoted equality of usage. A holistic set of reinforcing interventions was introduced into classrooms (e.g., a usage tracking poster for learners and a usage 'logbook' for teachers). Interventions were introduced into 20 schools in two districts, with 'critical beliefs' – key assumptions about the intervention to be tested throughout implementation – collaboratively co-created by teachers and learners.

The sandbox was split into two 'sprints', with a 'review' phase for iteration. To gather data, researchers observed classes in and out of lessons, and then undertook teacher and ECD Officer interviews to capture feedback on the interventions' impact and viability. In addition, quantitative data linked to equality of usage was collected from EIDU's platform. This data sought to directly measure and improve the outcomes of developed interventions on equality of usage (i.e., it focuses on addressing a specific goal within the broader DBR project) and to inform future integration of the EIDU DPL-SP model in classrooms throughout Kenya as EIDU scales.

4.7 Evaluating Practical and Theoretical Contributions

The iterative nature of the DBR enabled the development of 'proximal' theory and design principles to inform EIDU's DPL-SP model, resulting in practical improvements to the software design, ratio of device-to-learner, and provision of teaching support (Daltry et al., in preparation). Through the application of complementary methods underpinned by dialogic foundations, this research has also made a wider 'distal' contribution to educational research (Hall, 2020). For instance, in addition to generating intermediate theory and transferrable design principles to inform other implementations of DPL in LMICs, the improved DPL-SP model became the basis for rigorous quantitative research – including an ongoing randomised controlled trial and large-scale software evaluation – to assess the impact of the improved model on learning outcomes (Major et al., 2023). This addresses a common critique of DBR, which suggests it neither sustains outcomes beyond the time and budget constraints of the project nor expands ideas and designs on a broader scale (Buhl et al., 2022).

5. Conclusion

In this chapter, we have examined collaboration and partnership in DBR through a dialogic lens. At points a 'high level' overview has been provided, meaning there is potential for further in-depth exploration, particularly in terms of data collection and analysis strategies. However, critical reflection on the reported DBR strategy highlights the potential value of its dialogic theoretical foundations.

One strength of DBR is its adaptability to evolve (Campanella & Penuel, 2021). The reported DBR strategy is innovative as it combines dialogic theory with an integrated partnership approach. This allowed the gap between theory and practice to be bridged by maximising teachers' contributions as co-researchers, shaping both changes to the DPL-SP implementation model and the design of future research cycles. It also facilitated research closely aligned with real-world implementation – for instance, the ability to investigate the integration of Tayari into EIDU's DPL model early in its adoption, before scaling the model nationally – in addition to fostering inclusivity and collaboration among an expanded research team.

The value of reflexive practice has been highlighted to develop and strengthen the application of DBR (Buhl et al., 2022), which in the case of this DBR approach centred around the nuanced role of the research team within the teacher-research partnership. While the co-learning objectives of methods like lesson study and the innovation sandbox boosted inclusivity and collaboration in the research process, the research team recognised their distinct role in facilitating and convening collaboration across all the participating stakeholders. Although this meant that teachers were not involved in every aspect of the research process, as might be the 'ideal' in participatory research paradigms (Ospina et al., 2021), the research team were able to create a dialogic space that bridged a gap both between multiple stakeholder voices and broader DPL theory. This has served to strengthen the design and delivery of EIDU's DPL-SP model prior to a nationwide rollout, through the contribution of multiple voices in refining the approach.

The limited context of the reported DBR is recognised. While successful in generating practical recommendations for integrating DPL and Tayari within select Kenyan pre-primary classrooms (i.e., a more 'proximal contribution'; Hall, 2020; McKenney & Reeves, 2018), the contribution to wider educational practice and theory is still being developed, given that research is ongoing. The impact of the approach will continue to be evaluated, including in terms of sustained implementation, through large-scale quantitative research evaluating the impact of the improved DPL-SP model on learning. This chapter provides a foundation to inform similar projects and contributes to the ongoing use of DBR in LMICs and other EdTech settings, which has been underutilised so far. The presented approach represents a preliminary step towards addressing challenges previously identified in the literature. We welcome dialogue with other researchers to explore the broader applicability and transferability of this approach in other contexts.

References

Akkerman, S. F., & Bakker, A. (2011). Boundary crossing and boundary objects. *Review of Educational Research*, *81*(2), 132–169.

Amukune, S., Barrett, K. C., Szabó, N., & Józsa, K. (2023). Development and application of FOCUS app for assessment of approaches to learning in 3–8-year-old children in Kenya: A design-based research approach. *International Journal of Early Childhood*, *55*(1), 69–87.

Anderson, T., & Shattuck, J. (2012). Design-based research: A decade of progress in education research? *Educational Researcher*, *41*(1), 16–25.

Bakker, A. (2019). *Design research in education: A practical guide for early career researchers*. Routledge.

Barab, S., & Squire, B. (2004). Design-based research: Putting a stake in the ground. *The Journal of the Learning Sciences*, *13*(1), 1–14.

Buhl, M., Hanghøj, T., & Henriksen, T. D. (2022). Reconceptualising design-based research: Between research ideals and practical implications. *Nordic Journal of Digital Literacy*, *17*(4), 205–210.

Campanella, M., & Penuel, W. (2021). Design based research in educational settings: Motivations, cross-cutting features, and considerations for design. In Z. A. Philippakos, E. Howell, & A. Pellegrino (Eds.), *Design-based research in education: Theory and applications* (pp. 3–22). Guilford Publications.

The Collaborative Education Research Collective. (2023). *Towards a field for collaborative education research: Developing a framework for the complexity of necessary learning*. The William and Flora Hewlett Foundation.

Cukurova, M., Luckin, R., & Clark-Wilson, A. (2019). Creating the golden triangle of evidence-informed education technology with EDUCATE. *British Journal of Educational Technology*, *50*(2), 490–504.

Daltry, R., Major, L., Otieno, M., Otieno, K., & Hinks, J. (In preparation). *Integrating digital personalised learning into pre-primary classroom practice: A teacher-researcher multiple-case study partnership in Kenya* [Working title].

diSessa, A. A. & Cobb, P. (2004). Ontological innovation and the role of theory in design experiments. *Journal of the Learning Sciences, 13*(1), 77–103.

Fernandez, C., & Yoshida, M. (2004). *Lesson study: A Japanese approach to improving mathematics teaching and learning* (1st ed.). Routledge.

Fowler, S., Cutting, C., Fiedler, S. H., & Leonard, S. N. (2022). Design-based research in mathematics education: Trends, challenges and potential. *Mathematics Education Research Journal*, 1–24.

Friedberg, A. (2023, July 20–22). *A sequential Bayesian approach to educational A/B testing utilizing the ELO rating algorithm*. Learning at Scale.

Gallagher, T. L., & Fazio, X. (2019). Multiple layers: Education faculty reflecting on design-based research focused on curricular integration. *Qualitative Research in Education, 8*(1), 27–59.

Haelewaters, D., Hofmann, T. A., & Romero-Olivares, A. L. (2021). Ten simple rules for Global North researchers to stop perpetuating helicopter research in the Global South. *PLOS Computational Biology, 17*(8).

Hall, T. (2020). Bridging practice and theory: The emerging potential of design-based research (DBR) for digital innovation in education. *Education Research and Perspectives, 47*, 157–173.

Heinrich, C. J., Darling-Aduana, J., & Martin, C. (2020). The potential and prerequisites of effective tablet integration in rural Kenya. *British Journal of Educational Technology, 51*(2), 498–514.

Hennessy, S. (2014). *Bridging between research and practice: Supporting professional development through collaborative studies of classroom teaching with technology.* Brill.

Hennessy, S., D'Angelo, S., McIntyre, N., Koomar, S., Kreimeia, A., Cao, L., Brugha, M., & Zubairi, A. (2022). Technology use for teacher professional development in low-and middle-income countries: A systematic review. *Computers and Education Open, 3*, 100080.

Hennessy, S., & Deaney, R. (2009). The impact of collaborative video analysis by practitioners and researchers upon pedagogical thinking and practice: A follow-up study. *Teachers and Teaching: Theory and Practice, 15*(5), 617–638.

Henriksen, T. D., & Ejsing-Duun, S. (2022). Implementation in design-based research projects: A map of implementation typologies and strategies. *Nordic Journal of Digital Literacy, 17*(4), 234–247.

Herrington, J., McKenney, S., Reeves, T. C., & Oliver, R. (2007). *Design-based research and doctoral students: Guidelines for preparing a dissertation proposal.* Ed Media.

Holflod, K. (2022, June 25–July 3). Co-creating playful learning designs for interprofessional higher education: Dialogic perspectives on design-based research. In D. Lockton, S. Lenzi, P. Hekkert, A. Oak, J. Sádaba, & P. Lloyd (Eds.),

DRS2022: Bilbao. https://dl.designresearchsociety.org/drs-conference-papers/drs2022/researchpapers/55/

Laleka, S. M., & Rasheed, K. (2018). Design-based research in education: A prolific approach to applied research in developing countries. *Journal of Research & Reflections in Education, 12*(2), 136–154.

Lewin, K. (1946). Action research and minority problems. *Journal of Social Issues, 2*(4), 34–46.

Major, L., Daltry, R., Otieno, M., Otieno, K., Zhao, A., Hinks, J., Sun, C., & Friedburg, A. (2023). *Randomised controlled trial protocol: Digital personalised learning to improve literacy & numeracy outcomes in early-grade Kenyan classrooms* [Study Protocol]. EdTech Hub.

Major, L., & Francis, G. A. (2020). *Technology-supported personalised learning: Rapid evidence review.* EdTech Hub.

Major, L., Francis, G. A., & Tsapali, M. (2021). The effectiveness of technology-supported personalised learning in low-and middle-income countries: A meta-analysis. *British Journal of Educational Technology, 52*(5), 1935–1964.

Manzini, E. (2016). Design culture and dialogic design. *Design Issues, 32*(1), 52–59.

Martin, K. (2022). *Using mobile phones to enhance small group dialogic learning: A design based approach to educational innovation in Rural East Africa* [PhD thesis, Faculty of Education, University of Cambridge].

McKenney, S., & Reeves, T. (2018). *Conducting educational design research.* Routledge.

Mercier, E., Lawrence, L., Ahn, J., Wegemer, C., Benichou, M., Kali, Y., Hod, Y., Borge, M., Gomez, K., Lee, U., McKenney, S., Poortman, C., & Arce-Trigatt, P. (2022). Mapping the complexities and benefits of research-design partnerships. In C. Chinn, E. Tan, C. Chan, & Y. Kali (Eds.), *Proceedings of the 16th international conference of the learning sciences-ICLS 2022* (pp. 1794–1801). International Society of the Learning Sciences.

Minichiello, A., & Caldwell, L. (2021). A narrative review of design-based research in engineering education: Opportunities and challenges. *Studies in Engineering Education, 1*(2), 31–54.

Olesen, B. R., Phillips, L. J., & Johansen, T. L. R. (2018). Når dialog og samskabelse er mere endplusord. I. B. R. Olesen, L. J. Phillips, & T. R. Johansen (Reds.), *Dialog og samskabelse: Metoder til en refleksiv praksis* (pp. 11–37). Akademisk Forlag.

Ospina, S. M., Burns, D., & Howard, J. (2021). Introduction: Navigating the complex and dynamic landscape of participatory research and inquiry. In D. Burns, J. Howard, & S. M. Ospina (Eds.), *The Sage handbook of participatory research and inquiry* (pp. 3–16). Sage.

Penuel, W. R., Allen, A.-R., Coburn, C. E., & Farrell, C. (2015). Conceptualizing research–Practice partnerships as joint work at boundaries. *Journal of Education for Students Placed at Risk (JESPAR), 20*(1–2), 182–197.

Piper, B., Jepkemei, E., Kwayumba, D., & Kibukho, K. (2015). Kenya's ICT policy in practice: The effectiveness of tablets and e-readers in improving student outcomes. *FIRE: Forum for International Research in Education, 2*(1), 3–18.

Piper, B., Sitabkhan, Y., & Nderu, E. (2018). Mathematics from the beginning: Evaluating the Tayari preprimary program's impact on early mathematics skills. *Global Education Review, 5*(3), 57–81.

Pitchford, N. J., Chigeda, A., & Hubber, P. J. (2019). Interactive apps prevent gender discrepancies in early-grade mathematics in a low-income country in sub-Sahara Africa. *Developmental Science, 22*(5), e12864.

Ries, E. (2011). *The lean startup: How today's entrepreneurs use continuous innovation to create radically successful businesses.* Currency.

Roschelle, J., & Penuel, W. R. (2006). Co-design of innovations with teachers: Definition and dynamics. In *Proceedings of the 7th international conference on learning sciences* (pp. 606–612). International Society of the Learning Sciences.

Sanders, E. & Stappers, P. J. (2008). Co-creation and the new landscapes of design. *CoDesign, 4*(1), 5–18.

Simpson, L., Carter, A., Rahman, A., & Plaut, D. (2021). *Eight reasons why EdTech doesn't scale: How sandboxes are designed to counter the issue* [Position Paper]. EdTech Hub.

Sitabkhan, Y., Jukes, M. C. H., Dombrowski, E., & Munialo, I. (2022). *Differentiated instruction in multigrade preprimary classrooms in Kenya* (Publication No. OP-0084-2212). RTI Press.

Smørdal, O., Rasmussen, I., & Major, L. (2021). Supporting classroom dialogue through developing the talkwall microblogging tool: Considering emerging concepts that bridge theory, practice, and design. *Nordic Journal of Digital Literacy, 16*(2), 50–64.

Svihla, V., & Reeve, R. (2016). Untold stories. In V. Svihla & R. Reeve (Eds.), *Design as scholarship: Case studies from the learning sciences* (pp. 1–10). Routledge.

Tinoca, L., Piedade, J., Santos, S., Pedro, A., & Gomes, S. (2022). Design-based research in the educational field: A systematic literature review. *Education Sciences, 12*(6), 410.

Trausan-Matu, S., Wegerif, R., & Major, L. (2021). Dialogism. In U. Cress, C. Rosé, A. Wise, & J. Oshima (Eds.), *International handbook of computer-supported collaborative learning* (pp. 219–239). Routledge.

UNICEF. (2022). *Trends in digital personalized learning: Landscape review – taking stock of personalized learning solutions in low and middle-income countries* (N. M. Castillo, T. Adam, A. Alam, G. Alrawashdeh, & P. Tiwari, Eds.). UNICEF.

Vanbecelaere, S., & Benton, L. (2021). Technology mediated personalized learning for younger learners: Concepts, design, methods and practice. *British Journal of Educational Technology, 52*(5), 1793–1797.

Warwick, P., Vrikki, M., Vermunt, J. D., Mercer, N., & van Halem, N. (2016). Connecting observations of student and teacher learning: An examination of dialogic processes in lesson study discussions in mathematics. *ZDM, 48,* 555–569.

Wegerif, R., & Major, L. (2019). Buber, educational technology, and the expansion of dialogic space. *AI & Society, 34*(1), 109–119.

Zamenopoulos, T., & Alexiou, K. (2018). *Co-design as collaborative research.* Bristol University / AHRC Connected Communities Programme.

Zheng, L. (2015). A systematic literature review of design-based research from 2004 to 2013. *Journal of Computers in Education, 2,* 399–420.

Contextualised e-Learning Interventions for HEIs in Resource-Constrained Environments

The Case of an African University

Caroline Magunje

Introduction and Background of the Study

Integrating technology for curriculum delivery has become imperative for higher education institutions (HEIs), and more so since COVID-19 has emphasised the inevitable need to accept e-learning as a mode of delivery in all levels of education. Teacher educators within HEIs find themselves in a more complicated position since they must not only integrate technology into curriculum delivery, but they must also ensure adequate capacitation of student teachers, who must be equipped with the appropriate knowledge and skills to integrate technology in teaching and learning in their classrooms.

This chapter is a case study based on a research study of a pan-African university based in Zimbabwe that sought to integrate technology for curriculum delivery amidst challenges associated with sub-Saharan Africa (SSA), such as scanty electricity supply, poor internet infrastructure, lack of national e-learning policies, and resistance towards

DOI: 10.4324/9781003406631-17

e-learning by actors, among other things (Eltahir, 2019; Kasse & Balunywa, 2013; Sakala, 2019). The department of education within the institution mainly enrol practicing educators who enrol for postgraduate degrees in education. Students in these programs are therefore adult working learners, thus, to cater for them the university ran block release programs. These programs are run during school holidays, when teachers are free from their work commitments. Block release programs are usually associated with poor pedagogy where students are forced to sit for long hours of note-taking and risk information overload with very minimum interactive and collaborative activities that lead to 21st-century skills (Barkley, 2010).

The institution therefore sought to increase the flexibility of educators in block release programs and to extend its reach within Africa and beyond through blended and online programs. To initiate this process, however, the institution had to ensure that not only teacher educators in the department of education but also the institution itself were ready and adequately prepared to offer technology-enhanced programs. However, like most countries in SSA, Zimbabwe faces several socioeconomic challenges that hinder e-learning adoption.

The Association of African Universities (2020) reported that the advancement of ICTs in SSA over the past 20 years elevated the anticipation for a higher technology level that would encourage a cost-effective technique of resolving the challenges of access to education. According to Munyanyi (2021), HEIs in Zimbabwe have invested heavily in ICTs and their infrastructure relative to budget allocations. The researcher, as a teacher educator of a digital literacy course in one of the block release programs at the university under study, noticed very good smartphones amongst students and how most of them could easily acquire laptops from South Africa when they understood their importance. Thus, blended and online programs are possible in the Zimbabwean context when students have the required digital literacy skills, technological devices, internet, and the curriculum has been redesigned for the mode of delivery.

Given the unique challenges of developing contexts and the internal resistances within a university, the objective of this study is:

> To evaluate interventions put in place at a higher education institution to support the integration of technology for curriculum delivery by teacher educators.

Actor Network Theory

The chapter focuses on Actor Network Theory's (ANT) four moments of translation, which are: problematisation, interessment, enrolment, and mobilisation (Callon, 1990; Latour, 1999). The actor network is built from the coming together of heterogenous actors, including both human and non-human actors, within a particular context. Through this symmetrical analysis, ANT gives technology and policies the same value as humans without weakening the status of humans through the stabilisation of heterogeneous actor networks that make up organisations and society (Latour, 1999). In this study, the trajectory towards the network involved bringing together various actors within a university that included management as the network builder, and teacher educators, ICT staff, e-learning staff, and the non-human actors in the form of the e-learning policy and technology.

The problematisation stage is the initial stage where a network builder identifies a problem and conceptualises a solution (Law, 1999). In this study the problematisation stage occurred when university management identified problems associated with block release programs within the university context and proposed e-learning as a solution. The interessment stage follows, which entails the network builder building the network and seeking alliances by advocating and convincing other actors of the solution, in this case adopting e-learning as a mode of delivery in the university context (Callon, 2017). Management as the network builder in the interessment stage sought the support of other actors in the university network that would promote and work towards adopting e-learning as a mode of curriculum delivery within the university.

The enrolment stage is the third moment of translation, which is a result of the success of the first two stages where the network of alliances is stabilised, and other actors accept the interests as laid down by the lead actor (Latour, 1999). When teacher educators and other actors within the university network begin to show interests and consider e-learning as a possible mode of curriculum delivery, then the university would have reached the enrolment stage. Finally, the mobilisation stage, which is the amalgamation of the stabilisation of the network of alliances, occurs as the proposed solution is accepted by most actors and the spokesperson's legitimacy is established (Callon, 1986). This is the stage within the university network when e-learning has been accepted by all actors and has become an established mode of curriculum delivery.

ANT is useful in identifying actors within the context of the university under study that act and are acted upon from problematisation to mobilisation as the actors interact and negotiate within the network. The theory allows the research to examine the university network as it sought to bring the heterogenous actors together to forge alliances and provide interventions that would lead to the successful integration of technology.

Literature Review

Faculty Resistance to Innovation and the Need for e-Learning Professional Development

Despite external, internal, institutional, cultural, and personal factors on which institutional adoption of innovation is dependent, HEIs in developing contexts are forced to embrace e-learning opportunities in unconducive environments that are still heavily dependent on traditional practices (Becker et al., 2017; Gachago & Sykes, 2017). Dagada and Chigona (2013) highlighted that there are several threats to the integration of technology for curriculum delivery in HEIs due to cultural factors, which include faculty resistance to innovation and change and negative attitudes towards technology. However, for e-learning to be successful, teacher educators must accept it.

Ng'ambi et al. (2016) highlighted a shortage of satisfactory training of higher education educators in the proper use of technology to advance learning outcomes and the need for a "culture shift" among instructors to accept participatory approach to curriculum delivery, to be among the main hindrances in the integration of technology for curriculum delivery in developing contexts. According to Elatihir (2019), training lecturers in pedagogical and technological knowledge should be a huge part of continuous professional development. This could contribute to e-learning adoption, especially for those educators who resist the mode of delivery due to a lack of knowledge in the area.

ICTs in Sub-Saharan Africa

According to the World Bank (2018), Zimbabwe is a developing nation with severe inequalities with a national average poverty headcount rate of a paltry USD 1.90 per day. Starr-Glass (2011) highlighted that issues such as lack of funding to purchase technology infrastructure, among other things, contribute to the challenges that developing contexts face in the integration of technology in curriculum delivery. Aung and Khaing (2015) assert that the establishment and provision of ICT tools and network infrastructure are the biggest challenges affecting the meeting of e-learning preconditions in developing contexts. Universities should, therefore, set up technological infrastructure that include adequate bandwidth, learning management systems, and web conferencing systems to provide efficient and effective e-learning (Porter et al., 2014).

Methodological Considerations

The study is based on the interpretive paradigm, which is based on the notion that truth and knowledge are subjective, in addition to being culturally and historically situated (Ryan, 2018). The qualitative case study approach enabled the researcher to trace and follow the sequential flow of events taking place in the university context (Amaratunga et al., 2002). With the assistance of the e-learning department, purposive sampling was used to ensure participants directly involved in the integration of technology in the university context were involved in the study.

Using semi-structured interviews, the study involved 12 participants comprising a member of the university management, faculty dean, and two heads of the department, one ICT, and one e-learning support staff, and six teacher educators who were introduced to e-learning across a period of five years. Valuable data on the strategies adopted to ensure the integration of technology in the university was provided by participants in leadership roles. Teacher educators provided useful information on how the introduction of e-learning in the university context created tensions and how acceptance was achieved in the university context. The ICT staff contributed useful information on the issues pertaining to technology, whilst e-learning support staff provided data on the training and support they provided by the e-learning department. Data was analysed according to themes from the literature and ANT.

Ethical protocols of the researchers' institution on research involving human subjects, as well as the protocols of the university under study were adhered to, to safeguard human participants from any harm as well as to protect their dignity. To maintain confidentiality and anonymity, interviewees were referred to as "participants" and were identified by numbers rather than using their real names, when direct quotes are used in the findings section.

Findings and Discussion

ANT is used in this study as a lens to fully explore how an institution, in a complex socio-economic developing context in Zimbabwe, initiated and sought to establish e-learning as a mode of delivery in the university context to accommodate practising teachers who sought to advance their studies. The empirical study identified the following as the main human and non-human actors in the integration of technology for flexible delivery: management as the network builder, teacher educators as indispensable actors, support staff in the ICT Department and the e-Learning department, and technology in the form of data/internet.

Problematisation: Network Builder Identifying e-Learning as a Solution and Actor Resistance

Management (Vice Chancellor and Deputy Vice Chancellor) or network builder identified the limited flexibility offered to adult learners in block release programs as a problem in the university context. For practising educators seeking to advance their studies, e-learning is an ideal mode of delivery as it can provide flexibility without the need to leave the workplace to pursue further studies (Thurab-Nkhosi, 2018). The following participant highlighted that:

> So, he (Vice Chancellor) kept pushing for e-learning. He wanted to increase flexibility so that students can access learning materials wherever they are at convenient times to the learner.
>
> (Participant 7)

The participant shows how the network builder advocated for e-learning based on increased flexibility, especially for adult learners. Online learning allows students to work anywhere and anytime, whilst block release programs force students to leave work, family, and other responsibilities to attend classes during a block session (Magunje & Chigona, 2021).

Management's solution of replacing the block release program with e-learning programs was faced with resistance from mostly teacher educators, who were indispensable actors in the network that management as the network builder was trying to build. One of the main challenges of the integration of technology for curriculum delivery in HEIs is the fact

Contextualised e-Learning Interventions for HEIs **271**

that they must contend with a lukewarm reception by stakeholders and sometimes outright rejection (Ogunlela & Ogunleya, 2015).

> It was still something that was completely new to us and the way it was cascaded from the top management to the faculty level, was not clear and we were still living in the dark and in doubt.
>
> (Participant 2)

> Some understood e-learning but most of us believed it will never work.
>
> (Participant 11)

The participants' utterances show that although a few teacher educators understood e-learning, most of them lacked clarity on e-learning and were sceptical of the mode of delivery. Participant 2 described the lack of clarity as "dark," portraying the depth of doubt and powerlessness teacher educators felt in the problematisation stage of the ANT's translation process.

Interessment: Contextualised Interventions

Establishment of an e-Learning Department

The absence of pedagogical skills and technical capability required to set up and uphold e-learning departments affect staff development in developing contexts (Kasse & Balunywa, 2013). Thus, to equip teacher educators with the required e-learning skills and knowledge and to counter the resistance in the university context, management as the network builder facilitated the establishment of an e-learning department.

> Even when people embrace e-learning, they needed proper training for them to become online teachers. . . . There was a need for re-orientation of lecturers' skills and teaching methods so they could be effective in e-learning.
>
> (Participant 7)

A participant in management recognised the need to re-orient teacher educators in terms of skills, knowledge, and attitude to prevent a situation

272 Caroline Magunje

where they just transfer face-to-face teaching methods to online environments. Bali and Caines (2018) highlighted that the lack of prior online teaching experience leads to the transfer of traditional approaches to the online classroom, perpetuating proven ineffective face-to-face classroom approaches. Training of teacher educators, as indispensable actors, was therefore used as an empowerment tool by the network builder to strengthen the university network in technology-enhanced curriculum delivery.

The role of the e-learning department was appreciated by teacher educators in the university network, as supported by the following comment by a participant:

> They follow proper e-learning pedagogies, they conduct regular continuous training, and they are ready to advise lecturers on what to do.
>
> (Participant 9)

The advanced shift from technology-oriented to pedagogy-oriented planning demands the transformation of mindsets and the required change in practice that emphasise student-centred learning in e-learning settings by educators (Kong et al., 2017). By providing continuous constant training and support in online learning, the e-learning department was instrumental in transforming the mindsets of teacher educators.

Increasing Teacher Educators' Internet Access

The high cost of internet access is one of the main challenges of a developing context that affected e-learning in the university network. Participant 3 highlights this challenge in the university context:

> Challenges like the cost of data and bad networks, . . . the e-learning infrastructure at country level is bad.
>
> (Participant 3)

The availability and accessibility of technology is essential in e-learning. Lack of funding to purchase technology infrastructure is one of the major challenges that affect e-learning in developing contexts (Eltahir, 2019; Kasse & Balunywa, 2013). Whilst the network builder had little control over the overall internet infrastructure of the country, they ensured that teacher educators were connected to the internet on and off campus. A member of the ICT department highlighted that:

> Initially we provided educators with modems. We installed them in every household which gave lecturers unlimited access to the internet because the modem is the most expensive component.
>
> (Participant 10)

By providing internet modems for teacher educators to be able to work from home, the network builder provided a required intervention for e-learning to succeed in the university context. Internet (technology) is an integral actor in e-learning.

Threats in the Interessment Stage

Where an actor-network's stability is threatened by other actors or external actors, the relationships linking actors may be weakened, after which an actor-network can fail and potentially disappear (Rivera & Cox, 2016). Despite the provision of e-learning professional development, there were still elements of resistance towards the mode of delivery in the university network.

Age as a Hindrance to Technology-Enhanced Curriculum Delivery

One of the issues raised by lecturers as actors in the university network is that of age. Fischer et al. (2014) highlighted that older lecturers usually have limited interaction with technology and are reluctant to develop the required e-learning skills as they are comfortable with their traditional teaching experience.

> The support unit was doing its best, but the problem was age. Older people are not keen to use technology, [and] the younger lecturers were already using it.
>
> (Participant 4)

> some of us were born before computers, so the issue of computers is not easy.
>
> (Participant 8)

The teacher educators viewed age as a hindrance to the adoption of technology for curriculum delivery, inferring that elderly teacher educators are not keen on adopting e-learning and were not open to the new mode of delivery and lacked digital skills. The participants believe that e-learning adoption is easier for younger teacher educators because they are already comfortable with technology. Zalat et al. (2021) observed that younger academic staff generally use technology in their daily lives compared to older lecturers, and hence they are more receptive and willing to increase their abilities using e-learning technology.

Lack of Digital Literacy Leads to Technophobia

According to Sukumaran (2019), HEIs face hindrances to e-learning success due to the failure of educators to acclimatise to e-learning transformation quickly, as reported by the following participants:

> Another challenge was technophobia. Students know more about technology than educators. They [educators] were afraid to make mistakes and embarrass themselves. So, educators resisted e-learning. They found excuses to avoid the training.
>
> (Participant 5)

The participant highlights teacher educators' fear in using technology as they compare themselves to students who are usually techno-savvy, and as a result they shy away from receiving much needed e-learning training. The information age has, however, made the need to acquire technological skills imperative for educators. According to Dron (2022), educators have no choice when it comes to acquiring the skills to use technology in teaching since education is always enacted through technology.

Enrolment Stage

Enrolment is the third phase of the moment of translation, which depicts a positive result of the success of the first two stages, leading to a network of alliances, which is stabilised when other actor(s) accept the interests as laid down by the network builder (Callon, 1986). However, in this phase, the network builder (management) and their alliances (e-learning

Contextualised e-Learning Interventions for HEIs **275**

department) must address the threats to the network that arose in the interessment stage. The enrolment stage involves "negotiations, trials of strength and tricks that accompany the interessment and enable them to succeed" (Callon, 1986, p. 221).

Mitigating Threats in the University Network through Continuous e-Learning Training

The threats to the network in the study were mainly technophobia due to age-related issues and lack of digital skills. UNESCO Statistics (2015) observed that most educators in educational institutions in developing countries do not have the basic skills required to use e-learning tools, as there is a dearth of training and professional development to integrate technology for curriculum delivery. To resolve the threats of technophobia in the university network, the network builder – through its alliance, the e-learning department – used trials of strengths through continuous training to restore stability in the university network.

> The continued training from the support department has helped. We have more workshops, and some are online. They also offer one-on-one sessions. We were not resisting per se, but it was fear of technology for sometimes it was because of age, but because of the training we are catching up.
>
> (Participant 6)

The participant appreciates the efforts of the e-learning department in ensuring teacher educators were empowered with e-learning knowledge and skills, thereby dispelling technophobia in e-learning adoption. Mostert and Quinn (2009) highlighted the importance of HEIs to respond to challenges associated with moving from traditional-based learning to e-learning through the provision of staff development with emphasis on the professionalisation of educators.

Acceptance of e-Learning as a Flexible Mode of Delivery

In ANT, enrolment of actors in the university network takes place when there is acceptance of e-learning among actors, i.e., when actors have identified and gained certain benefits from the 'idea' or 'solution' introduced

276 Caroline Magunje

in the network. Teacher educators' attitudes toward e-learning changed as they realised favourable benefits in the mode of delivery, as highlighted in the following statement by the participant:

> E-learning is ideal for our students because they don't have to travel; you can interact with them from anywhere, and I also found it exciting most of all.
>
> (Participant 1)

Becker et al. (2017) noted how perceptions towards online learning have been changing favourably in recent years, as increased numbers of educators view it as a viable option compared to some methods of face-to-face learning. The following statement from a teacher educator shows acceptance of e-learning by a teacher educator:

> The major benefit was gaining access to students who would otherwise fail to come to campus. Many students in online classes are working . . . and being Pan African, we were able to get students from beyond the borders.
>
> (Participant 9)

The teacher educator appreciates the affordances of technology in teaching and learning for adult working students, thereby confirming his enrolment into the e-learning actor network. E-learning is an ideal mode of delivery as it provides adult learners with access and much-needed flexibility in learning, as one does not need to leave the workplace to pursue further studies but can still access flexible learning requirements and instruction (Bates & Sangra, 2011).

Mobilisation Stage: Stability in Online Programs

According to Callon (1986), the final moment of translation is the amalgamation of the stabilisation of the network of alliances, as the proposed solution is accepted by most actors, and the spokesperson's legitimacy is established. In the mobilisation stage, online and blended learning are fully running, with all the relevant actors in the university network connected and in agreement, and other actors besides the network builder become spokespersons in the university network.

Contextualised e-Learning Interventions for HEIs **277**

> We are thinking of a global campus; we have increased our enrolments to other African nations.
>
> (Participant 12)

The participant shows that the university has managed to increase access to the university programs by enrolling students from beyond Zimbabwe. Online courses provide a market without borders for HEIs with no need for campus infrastructure, with the educators providing guidance in the learning experiences (Crawford & Jenkins, 2017; Sadeghi, 2019). Unlike block release programs, which limit enrolments to Zimbabwe, e-learning enabled the university to enrol students from across Africa. The actors portray a state of stability within the university network as e-learning has been fully embraced as a mode of delivery in the university network.

Conclusion

HEIs in developing contexts face different challenges compared to their counterparts in the developed world. Embracing e-learning as a mode of delivery is a huge milestone in a developing context as it increases the flexibility of practising educators and adult working learners seeking higher qualifications. The unique challenges faced by HEIs in developing contexts as they strive to integrate technology for curriculum delivery demands that they provide timely contextualised interventions specific to their institutions.

Emphasising e-learning professional development is therefore an important intervention for HEIs as they seek to integrate technology into curriculum delivery. Professional development ensures that teacher educators are capacitated with the required pedagogical and techno-logical knowledge so they can be effective online facilitators. Diligent professional development ensures the provision of timely interventions, such as extra support to curb resistance that might arise due to technophobia.

By accentuating the role of each actor in an e-learning actor network, HEIs in developing contexts can identify the weak links as actors strive to come together to ensure successful e-learning implementation. Whilst data and internet connectivity might not be a big issue in well-developed contexts, they can be a huge hindrance to e-learning in the developing contexts. HEIs should therefore provide interventions that address the issues in their context. The provision of data to teacher educators had a positive effect in the university network, leading to the successful integration of technology in teaching and learning. The study has shown that e-learning adoption is not a one-size-fit-all issue; it requires an institution to carefully consider its requirements, challenges, and demands to provide adequate contextually relevant interventions that meets their needs.

References

Amaratunga, D., Baldry, D., Sarchaar, M. & Newton, R. (2002). Quantitative and qualitative research in the built environment. *Work Study*, *51*(1), 17–31.

Association of African Universities. (2020). *Over 1, 500 university lecturers receive training under the ACE project*. Retrieved October 11, 2022, from https://blog.aau.org/over-1-500-university-lecturers-receive-training-under-the-ace-project/

Aung, T. N., & Khaing, S. S. (2016). Challenges of implementing e-learning in developing countries: A review. In *Genetic and evolutionary computing: Proceedings of the ninth international conference on genetic and evolutionary computing, August 26–28, 2015, Yangon, Myanmar* (Vol. II, pp. 405–411). Springer International Publishing.

Bali, M., & Caines, A. (2018). A call for promoting ownership, equity, and agency in faculty development via connected learning. *International Journal of Educational Technology in Higher Education*, *15*(1), 1–24.

Barkley, S. G. (2010). *Quality teaching in a culture of coaching*. R&L Education.

Bates, A. T., & Sangra, A. (2011). *Managing technology in higher education: Strategies for transforming teaching and learning*. John Wiley & Sons.

Becker, S. A., Cummins, M., Davis, A., Freeman, A., Giesinger, C. H., Ananthanarayanan, V., & Wolfson, N. (2017). *NMC horizon report: 2017 library edition*. The New Media Consortium.

Callon, M. (1986). The sociology of an actor-network: The case of the electric vehicle. In *Mapping the dynamics of science and technology: Sociology of science in the real world* (pp. 19–34). Palgrave Macmillan.

Callon, M. (1990). Techno-economic networks and irreversibility. *The Sociological Review*, *38*(1_suppl), 132–161.

Callon, M. (2017). Some elements of a sociology of translation: Domestication of the scallops and the fishermen of Saint-Brieuc Bay. *Logos (Russian Federation)*, *27*(2), 49–94.

Crawford, R., & Jenkins, L. (2017). Blended learning and team teaching: Adapting pedagogy in response to the changing digital tertiary environment. *Australasian Journal of Educational Technology*, *33*(2), 4.

Dagada, R., & Chigona, A. (2013). Integration of e-learning into curriculum delivery at university level in South Africa. *International Journal of Online Pedagogy and Course Design (IJOPCD)*, 3(1), 53–65.

Dron, J. (2022). Educational technology: What it is and how it works. *AI and Society*, 37(1), 155–166. https://doi.org/10.1007/s00146-021-01195-z

Eltahir, M. E. (2019). E-learning in developing countries: Is it a panacea? A case study of Sudan. *IEEE Access*, 7, 97784–97792. https://doi.org/10.1109/ACCESS.2019.2930411

Fischer, H., Heise, L., Heinz, M., Moebius, K., & Koehler, T. (2014). E-learning trends and hypes in academic teaching. Methodology and findings of a trend study. In *Proceedings of the International Conference e-Learning 2014 – Part of the Multi Conference on Computer Science and Information Systems* (pp. 63–69). MCCSIS 2014.

Gachago, D., & Sykes, P. (2017, September). Navigating ethical boundaries when adopting digital storytelling in higher education. *Digital Storytelling in Higher Education: International Perspectives*, 91–106. https://doi.org/10.1007/978-3-319-51058-3

Kasse, J. P., & Balunywa, W. (2013). *An assessment of e-learning utilization by a section of Ugandan universities: Challenges, success factors and way forward* (Vol. 15). International Conference on ICT for Africa. https://www.academia.edu/25231473/An_assessment_of_e_learning_utilization_by_a_section_of_Ugandan_universities_challenges_success_factors_and_way_forward

Kong, S.-C., Looi, C.-K., Chan, T.-W. & Huang, R. (2017). Teacher development in Singapore, Hong Kong, Taiwan, and Beijing for e-Learning in school education. *Journal of Computers in Education*, 4(1), 5–25.

Latour, B. (1999). On recalling ANT. *The Sociological Review*, 47(1), 15–25.

Law, J. (1999). After ANT: Complexity, naming and topology. *The Sociological Review*, 47(1), 1–14.

Magunje, C., & Chigona, A. (2021). E-learning policy and technology-enhanced flexible curriculum delivery in developing contexts: A critical discourse analysis. *Critical Studies in Teaching and Learning (CriSTaL)*, 9(2), 83–104.

Mostert, M., & Quinn, L. (2009). Using ICTs in teaching and learning: Reflections on professional development of academic staff. *International Journal of Education and Development Using ICT*, 5(5), 72–84.

Munyanyi, R. (2021). *A critical analysis of the implementation of e-learning platforms at selected public universities in Zimbabwe*. Durban University of Technology. https://openscholar.dut.ac.za/bitstream/10321/3921/3/MunyanyiR/Phd/thesis/Final/9December2021.pdf

Ng'ambi, D., Brown, C., Bozalek, V., Gachago, D., & Wood, D. (2016). Technology enhanced teaching and learning in South African higher education – a rearview of a 20 year journey. *British Journal of Educational Technology, 47*(5), 843–858. https://doi.org/10.1111/bjet.12485

Ogunlela, V. B., & Ogunleye, B. O. (2015). Promoting quality assurance practices for ODL programmes in West African higher education institutions: The role of RETRIDAL. *International Open and Distance Learning Journal, 1*(1).

Porter, W. W., Graham, C. R., Spring, K. A., & Welch, K. R. (2014). Blended learning in higher education: Institutional adoption and implementation. *Computers & Education, 75*, 185–195.

Rivera, G., & Cox, A. M. (2016). An actor-network theory perspective to study the non-adoption of a collaborative technology intended to support online community participation. *Academia Revista Latinoamericana de Administración, 29*(3), 347–365.

Ryan, G. (2018). Introduction to positivism, interpretivism and critical theory. *Nurse Researcher, 25*(4), 14–20.

Sadeghi, M. (2019). A shift from classroom to distance learning: Advantages and limitations. *International Journal of Research in English Education, 4*(1), 80–88.

Sakala, L. (2019). *Resistance to the implementation of learning management systems by teacher educators in higher education in a developing country context.* University of Cape Town. http://hdl.handle.net/11427/30345

Starr-Glass, D. (2011). Military learners: Experience in the design and management of online learning environments. *MERLOT Journal of Online Learning and Teaching, 7*(1), 147–158. http://jolt.merlot.org/vol7no1/starr-glass_0311.htm

Sukumaran, S. D. (2019). The influence of change management and e-learning in Malaysian private higher education institutions. *Pertanika Journal of Science and Technology, 27*(2), 897–910.

Thurab-Nkhosi, D. (2018). Implementing a blended/online learning policy on a face-to-face campus: Perspectives of administrators and implications for change. *Journal of Learning for Development, 5*(2).

UNESCO Statistics. (2015). *Teachers and educational quality: Monitoring global needs for 2015.* UNESCO.

World Bank Group. (2018). *Poverty and equity brief: Sub Saharan Africa-Zimbabwe.* http://povertydata.worldbank.org/poverty/country/ZWE

Zalat, M. M., Hamed, M. S., & Bolbol, S. A. (2021). The experiences, challenges, and acceptance of e-learning as a tool for teaching during the COVID-19 pandemic among university medical staff. *PLoS ONE, 16*(3 March), 1–12. http://dx.doi.org/10.1371/journal.pone.0248758.

Threading Together Digital Technology Integration Perspectives Across the Globe

18

Agnes Chigona, Nyarai Tunjera, and Helen Crompton

Digital Technology Integration Perspectives Across the Globe

The 21st-century skills requirements coupled with the COVID-19 pandemic imposed new demands on teaching and learning processes. The promise and potential of using technology in education are now rapidly becoming apparent, and the COVID-19 pandemic indeed highlighted the necessity for technology in education and for educators to understand the tools available, how to effectively integrate the technologies into teaching and learning (Crompton et al., 2023), and the affordances they can provide beyond the non-digital options.

This book has shared current research on how teacher education vis-à-vis pre-service and in-service teacher training programs are preparing teachers to integrate technology across subjects and grade levels in a meaningful way. This means educators from all levels need to acquire 21st-century skills and technology integration skills that would enable them to effectively teach and learn with and through digital technologies. The chapters from different parts of the world have provided ideas and strategies for teacher educators and a springboard for educational

DOI: 10.4324/9781003406631-18

researchers on how to prepare teachers to thrive in digital learning environments and provide equitable strategies for all learners.

The authors agree that the COVID-19 pandemic created the largest disruption of education in the entire world. The calamity affected students and educators worldwide. However, those in low- and lower-middle-income countries were affected the most (UNESCO, 2020). School-based, face-to-face teaching and learning was not always possible because of lockdowns and social distancing requirements to reduce the spread of the pandemic. There was a heightened attention to education technology to mitigate the disruption. Teachers at all learning levels were required to use remote instruction with technology, as part of a crisis response protocol to continue with curriculum delivery (Bozkurt & Sharma, 2020). However, authors have shown that teachers needed various supports, including digital pedagogical strategies, frameworks, digital tools, and mental wellness supports.

Nonetheless, the integration strategies shared throughout this book have provided practical guidance to educators seeking to harness the power of technology effectively. Emphasizing the importance of balance, these strategies have advocated for a holistic approach, blending digital resources with traditional teaching methodologies to create a harmonious learning experience (Singh et al., 2021). Furthermore, a strong focus on digital citizenship and responsible technology usage ensures that learners are equipped with the skills necessary to navigate the digital realm safely and ethically.

Authors from different parts of the world have highlighted both challenges and success stories in technology integration, illustrating its influence in various educational situations and drawing inspiration from distinct case studies. We uncover how technology functions as a catalyst for positive change, providing learners with equitable possibilities to prosper, from developed nations to impoverished regions. Chapters presenting case studies have been a testament to the universal applicability of technology in education. From classrooms in developed nations to those in remote and underserved regions, technology has proven to be a catalyst for breaking down barriers and fostering inclusivity. We have witnessed inspiring stories of educators utilizing technology to bridge gaps in educational access, empowering learners from all walks of life to realize their potential and contribute meaningfully to their communities and societies.

In this concluding chapter, we sum up the main results and contributions of the book and look at a unifying narrative navigating the intersection of technology and teacher education.

Contributions from Different Corners of the Globe

In the dynamic landscape of education, the infusion of technology has emerged as a transformative force, reshaping teaching and learning paradigms on a global scale. This book, *Global Perspectives on Teaching with Technology: Theories, Case Studies, and Integration Strategies*, presents a comprehensive exploration of the intricate interplay between technology and education. As we traverse the chapters, an overarching narrative unfolds, illuminating the multifaceted contributions of theoretical frameworks, case studies, and innovative teaching strategies. Here, we synthesize the essence of this journey through a lens that spans continents and contexts, offering a holistic perspective on the educational potential and challenges of technology. The chapter contributions have come from higher, upper middle, lower middle, and low-income countries from four continents (World Bank, 2022).

United States classrooms stand as microcosms of a digitalized society, where surveillance technology takes centre stage. The critical exploration within these pages urges educators to navigate the ethical dimensions of such technology, prompting conversations about the delicate balance between surveillance and privacy. A dialogue emerges, contemplating the profound implications for students' rights and digital citizenship – a resonant theme in an era of heightened surveillance.

Contributions from Japan have shown that there is a notable transformation in the educational landscape, as prominent universities specializing in teacher education lead the way in implementing ground-breaking methods for preparing educators. The integration of artificial intelligence, data science, and educational informatics in the curriculum exemplifies a harmonious fusion of technological advancements and pedagogical principles. The narratives of these establishments exemplify a worldwide pattern, in which educators are responsible not only for acquiring expertise in technical complexities but also for embracing the interdependent connection between technology and effective pedagogy (Fawns, 2022).

South African narratives highlight the journey of pre-service teachers as they navigate the process of integrating technology into their pedagogical toolkit. Over the course of the past two years, a notable transformation has taken place – a reflection of education institutions strengthening their technological infrastructures in response to the challenges posed by the pandemic (Shava, 2022). The authors have highlighted the ongoing global trend of educators enhancing their digital skills, emphasizing the importance of being ready for the changing educational environment.

The transformative potential of technology can greatly impact dialogues within classrooms worldwide. Authors have shown the connection between mathematics classrooms and foundational literacy, highlighting the importance of employing effective pedagogical strategies for successful technology integration. The stories come together to emphasize the importance of taking a comprehensive approach to fully harness the potential of technology (Shava, 2022), thereby bridging the gap between technology and teaching.

When exploring Uganda, an innovative program comes to light, which combines technology with essential skills and social-emotional learning, effectively addressing the needs of marginalized learners. The narrative effectively illustrates how technology, when integrated with pedagogical elements, addresses the unique requirements of a wide range of learners. The insights of facilitators reflect the mutually beneficial connection between technology and effective pedagogy, underscoring the importance of ongoing support and training (Chigona, 2018).

Kenya has been recognized as a valuable setting for exploring the potential impact of Design-Based Research (DBR), a methodological approach that holds great promise in studying educational technology. Collaborative innovation serves as a valuable bridge between theory and practice, providing valuable insights into how to effectively harness the potential of technology, while also recognizing and addressing the challenges that come with innovation. The flexible journey showcased here reflects the worldwide effort to utilize technology for impactful education. This is similar to what is happening in Malawi, where research-based approaches have also been embraced, providing valuable guidance for educators navigating the digital frontier. The effective integration of research and practice enables educators to adapt to the constantly evolving nature of technology, promoting resilience (Crompton et al., 2023). The studies have shown the importance of incorporating research-driven pedagogical transformations as educators take on the role of guiding the way towards a digital future.

In the face of infrastructural challenges in Zimbabwe, an inspiring story emerges that showcases the resilience and resourcefulness of individuals who have found innovative ways to incorporate e-learning despite the obstacles they face. The narrative highlights the importance of employing contextualized strategies (Mettis &Väljataga, 2021), emphasizing the collaborative contributions of different stakeholders in implementing curricula that are enhanced by technology.

A Unifying Narrative Navigating the Intersection of Technology and Education

The various narratives intertwine to present a comprehensive view of how technology is being incorporated into education. This book takes readers on a transformative journey that explores the diverse experiences and accomplishments of educators who have effectively integrated technology into their teaching practices, transcending geographical boundaries (Agarwal, 2021). The utilization of theoretical frameworks, case studies, and innovative teaching strategies can play a significant role in guiding educators towards a future where technology is used responsibly. This approach has the potential to empower learners (Tsai et al., 2020) and contribute to the development of an inclusive and digitally literate society. As we wrap up this exploration, it is evident that the collaboration between technology and education is a powerful force that requires flexibility, ethical awareness, and cooperative involvement (Mettis &Väljataga, 2021) as we navigate the unfamiliar territory of the digital era.

As we consider the path forward, it is important to recognize the obstacles that may arise. Challenges remain in ensuring equal access to technology and addressing disparities in digital literacy across various regions, which can impede efforts towards achieving widespread technological integration (Crompton et al., 2023). Nevertheless, by fostering collaboration and sharing best practices among educators and policymakers worldwide, we can effectively tackle these challenges and work towards creating a fairer and more inclusive technological environment in education.

This book offers an opportunity to explore the potential of technology in enhancing education through a collective vision. It encourages educators, administrators, policymakers, and stakeholders from around the world to come together, promote collaboration, and utilize digital innovations to create a more promising future for learners worldwide. As we adapt to the dynamic landscape of technology, let us stay resolute in our dedication to our overarching objective: to equip learners with the necessary knowledge, skills, and competencies to succeed in an interconnected and swiftly developing world (Kennedy & Sundberg, 2020).

Global Perspectives on Teaching with Technology: Theories, Case Studies, and Integration Strategies provides valuable insights that can help us navigate towards a future where technology and education work together harmoniously, enabling learners to fully explore their limitless potential. By wholeheartedly embracing this integration, we can demonstrate our strong dedication to fostering inclusivity, diversity, and equitable access to education. This will enable us to pave the way for a more promising world of learning and growth.

As we look to the future, it is imperative to acknowledge the challenges that lie ahead. Uneven access to technology and digital literacy disparities persist in many parts of the world, posing hurdles to achieving widespread technological integration (Crompton et al., 2023). However, through collaborative efforts and the exchange of best practices among educators and policymakers globally, we can address these issues and strive towards a more equitable and inclusive technological landscape in education.

This book serves as an invitation to embrace a collective vision of education empowered by technology. It calls upon educators, administrators, policymakers, and stakeholders worldwide to forge partnerships, foster collaboration, and leverage digital innovations to shape a brighter future for learners across the globe (Kennedy & Sundberg, 2020). As we navigate the ever-changing tides of technology, educators must remain steadfast in their commitment to the ultimate goal: to empower learners with the knowledge, skills, and competencies they need to thrive in an interconnected and rapidly evolving world.

Global Perspectives on Teaching with Technology: Theories, Case Studies, and Integration Strategies serves as a compass guiding us towards a future where technology and education coalesce seamlessly to unlock the boundless potential of learners. By embracing this integration with an unwavering commitment to fostering inclusivity, diversity, and equitable access to education, we can pave the way for a brighter, more promising world of learning and growth.

This book has taken a detailed look at the diverse world of technology in education, revealing its revolutionary power in altering the future of learning. The book has shared current research on how pre-service teacher and in-service teacher education programs have been preparing educators to teach with and through digital technologies in a meaningful way at different education levels in different world economies. Teaching with and through the digital tools requires a pedagogical shift from traditional ways of "chalk and talk" (Chigona, 2018). Theoretical papers and case studies have provided a snapshot of strategies and practices for technology integration across the globe. The 17 chapters written by different authors from 12 countries have provided various viewpoints highlighting different topics and different contextual perspectives. This breadth has made this book a must-read for everyone interested in technology integration in education.

In this book, we have highlighted global success stories in technology integration, illustrating its influence in various educational situations and drawing inspiration from distinct case studies. We uncover how technology functions as a catalyst for positive change, providing learners with equitable possibilities to prosper, from high-income economies to low-income economies (Bugaj, 2022).

The numerous case studies presented in this book have been a testament to the universal applicability of technology in education. From classrooms in high-income economies to those in remote and underserved regions, technology has proven to be a catalyst for breaking down barriers and fostering inclusivity (Bugaj, 2022). We have witnessed inspiring stories of educators utilizing technology to bridge gaps in educational access, empowering learners from all walks of life to realize their potential and contribute meaningfully to their communities and societies.

The integration strategies shared throughout this book have provided practical guidance to educators seeking to harness the power of technology effectively. Emphasizing the importance of balance, these strategies have advocated for a holistic approach, blending digital resources with traditional teaching methodologies to create a harmonious learning experience (Singh et al., 2021). Furthermore, a strong focus on digital citizenship and responsible technology usage ensures that learners are equipped with the skills necessary to navigate the digital realm safely and ethically.

Importance of Global Perspectives in Shaping the Future of Education

Although the impact of technology on education cannot be denied, its impacts are not consistent around the world (Soomro et al., 2020). The revolutionary power of technology extends well beyond national boundaries, breaking down cultural and geographical barriers. Educators and policymakers must acknowledge the importance of global viewpoints in influencing the future of education.

Adopting a global perspective allows us to learn from the accomplishments and problems of other educational systems around the world. Understanding how various countries use technology in the classroom and handle educational inequities provides us with useful insights that can shape our methods. Collaboration and cross-cultural exchanges promote a robust knowledge-sharing environment, fostering new solutions that resonate with learners from all walks of life.

References

Agarwal, A., Bansal, K. M., Gupta, A., & Khurana, R. (2021). Online education: A booming product for institutes post-covid-19? *Marketing Education Review, 31*(3), 262–272.

Bozkurt, A., & Sharma, R. C. (2020). Education in normal, new normal, and next normal: Observations from the past, insights from the present and projections for the future. *Asian Journal of Distance Education, 15*(2), I–X.

Bugaj, C. (2022). *The new assistive tech: Make learning awesome for all!*. International Society for Technology in Education. https://books.google.com/books?id=4L GFEAAAQBAJ&printsec=frontcover&dq=inauthor:%22Christopher+Bugaj %22&hl=en&newbks=1&newbks_redir=1&sa=X&ved=2ahUKEwjH-K2dn 7qCAxXNWUEAHYbKAtAQ6AF6BAgKEAI

Chigona, A. (2018). Digital fluency: Necessary competence for teaching and learning in connected classrooms. *The African Journal of Information Systems, 10*(4), 7.

Crompton, H., Chigona, A., & Burke, D. (2023). Teacher resilience during COVID-19: Comparing teachers' shift to online learning in South Africa and the United States. *TechTrends*, 1–14.

Fawns, T. (2022). An entangled pedagogy: Looking beyond the pedagogy – technology dichotomy. *Postdigital Science and Education, 4*(3), 711–728.

Kennedy, T. J., & Sundberg, C. W. (2020). 21st century skills. In *Science education in theory and practice: An introductory guide to learning theory* (pp. 479–496). Springer.

Mettis, K., & Väljataga, T. (2021). Designing learning experiences for outdoor hybrid learning spaces. *British Journal of Educational Technology, 52*(1), 498–513.

Shava, E. (2022). Reinforcing the role of ICT in enhancing teaching and learning post-COVID-19 in tertiary institutions in South Africa. *Journal of Culture and Values in Education, 5*(1), 78–91.

Singh, J., Steele, K., & Singh, L. (2021). Combining the best of online and face-to-face learning: Hybrid and blended learning approach for COVID-19, post vaccine, & post-pandemic world. *Journal of Educational Technology Systems, 50*(2), 140–171.

Soomro, K. A., Kale, U., Curtis, R., Akcaoglu, M., & Bernstein, M. (2020). Digital divide among higher education faculty. *International Journal of Educational Technology in Higher Education, 17*, 1–16.

Tsai, Y. S., Perrotta, C., & Gašević, D. (2020). Empowering learners with personalised learning approaches? Agency, equity and transparency in the context of learning analytics. *Assessment & Evaluation in Higher Education, 45*(4), 554–567.

UNESCO. (2020). *School closures caused by Coronavirus COVID19.* https://en.unesco.org/covid19/educationresponse

World Bank. (2022). *World Bank list of economies 2021–22.* https://msf.org.uk/sites/default/files/202202/World%20Bank%20list%20of%20economies%202022.pdf

Contributor Biographies

Navya Akkinepally is Head of Training and Impact at Learning Equality. Navya leads the training development and strategy at Learning Equality to support effective implementation of blended learning across low-resource contexts. She has a range of experience working with low-income communities as a teacher, an instructional designer, a teacher trainer, and an evaluator for school improvement programs across India, previously at Meghshala and Gray Matters India. She is a Teach for India alumna and is deeply passionate about bridging the gap in education.

Morgan C. Banville is Assistant Professor of Humanities at Massachusetts Maritime Academy located in Bourne, Massachusetts, USA. She received her Ph.D. in rhetoric, writing, and professional communication from East Carolina University in 2023. Her research interests include the intersection of technical communication and surveillance studies, often informed by feminist methodologies. You can find her recent work in the *Proceedings of the ACM International Conference on Design of Communication*, as well as *Programmatic Perspectives, Reflections: A Journal of Community-Engaged Writing and Rhetoric, constellations: a cultural rhetorics publishing space*, the *Journal of Technical Writing and Communication*, and more.

Agnes Chigona is the Head of Research in the Faculty of Education at Cape Peninsula University of Technology (CPUT), in Cape Town,

Contributor Biographies **291**

South Africa. She has extensively published research articles and supervised several master's and doctoral candidates to completion. Her research focus is on technology integration at school and on teacher education.

Janet Condy was the Director of the Literacy Development Research Unit at CPUT. She has been teaching for the past 42 years, including 19 years in mainstream schools and a Special School, and for the past 25 years she has been developing teachers at the Education Faculty of CPUT. She graduated with her doctoral degree in 2006 and in 2019 was inaugurated as a Full Professor with a C2 NRF rating. Her teaching and research focus has been primarily on literacy, including inclusive education, critical thinking, digital storytelling, and philosophy for children. She is currently co-leading three research projects: Reading-for-Meaning, Sisonke Supervision Mentoring Project, and a Critical Thinking Project. She has published over 60 articles and supervised to completion four doctoral students and 13 master's students.

Helen Crompton is Executive Director of the Research Institute for Digital Innovation in Learning at ODUGlobal and Professor of Instructional Technology at Old Dominion University, USA. Dr. Crompton earned her Ph.D. in educational technology and mathematics education from the University of North Carolina at Chapel Hill. Recognized for her outstanding contributions, Dr. Crompton is on Stanford's esteemed list of the Top 2% of Scientists in the World. Her exceptional work in technology integration has garnered her numerous accolades, including the SCHEV award for the Outstanding Professor of Virginia. Dr. Crompton's expertise extends beyond academia to practice, as she frequently serves as a consultant for various governments, bilateral and multilateral organizations such as the United Nations and the World Bank, leveraging her knowledge and experience to drive meaningful change in the field of educational technology.

Rebecca Daltry is a researcher at Jigsaw, a social enterprise that exists to build rigorous evidence for lasting change in education, and a founding partner of EdTech Hub. Rebecca's current research focuses on education technology and refugee education in low- and middle-income countries. She has experience conducting large-scale mixed-method and qualitative research, with a focus on developing participatory and youth-led initiatives with schools and communities. She holds an

MA in international education and development from the University of Sussex, where she formed a particular research interest in the intersections between faith, development, and education, as well as topics related to gender, youth, conflict, and citizenship.

Alice Dhliwayo is currently a postdoctoral fellow at the University of the Free State in South Africa. She specialized in English language and literature education. Her experience in education spans three decades of classroom practice in Zimbabwe, from primary school education to teacher training in higher education. Dr. Dhliwayo has been a postgraduate studies lecturer for the faculty of education at Solusi University in the area of English language and literature studies. She was also involved as one of the experts in curriculum development of Advanced Level literature in English for Zimbabwe's competence-based curriculum. Her research interests center around technology in education, especially teacher education.

N. Anne Gichuri is an associate professor and the Director of Research at the School of Education and Human Services at the University of St. Thomas in Houston, Texas. Dr. Gichuri's qualifications include three graduate degrees in education policy and administration, curriculum development, comparative international education, intercultural exchange, and international development. In addition to these areas of expertise, Dr. Gichuri has extensive research interest and professional experience in cross-national and interdisciplinary research, program evaluation, technology and instruction, and demonstrated leadership in doctoral dissertation committees as chair and methodological expert.

Foster Gondwe is Senior Lecturer in Instructional Design and Technology at the University of Malawi. His research focuses on the intersection of information technology and teacher education, especially technology professional development of teachers and teacher educators. Currently, he is also the Book Reviews editor of the *Journal of Interactive Media in Education*, Open University, UK.

Liddy Greenaway is Research and Evaluation Specialist at Learning Equality. Liddy works with Learning Equality to carry out research and evaluation activities across the organization's global programs, to evidence best practice, document learning, and support continuous improvement. Liddy has 10 years' experience in monitoring,

Contributor Biographies   **293**

evaluation, and learning in education, health, and humanitarian innovation. She holds a BA in philosophy from University of Bristol and a MPhil in development studies from University of Cambridge. Liddy is passionate about inclusive, participatory research and evaluation, and creative research communications and storytelling.

James Hughes is a newly qualified computer science and information and communication technology (ICT) teacher who has started his first job at Pentrehafod Secondary School in Swansea, Wales. He has extensive experience in IT, having worked for 25 years as a data scientist in BT and Openreach and then as an IT consultant for his own company. Having been part of a research group looking at the IT skills gap in Wales, he has taken an interest in this area, particularly in relation to the lack of female candidates for computer science courses, which is contributing to the skills gap.

Thuthukile Jita is Associate Professor and a program director for Teaching Practice or Work Integrated Learning (WIL) in the Department of Curriculum Studies and Higher Education at the University of the Free State (UFS) in South Africa. Professor Jita's research interests include curriculum studies, pre-service teacher education, use of information communication and technologies (ICT) in subject teaching, and digital transformation in higher education, with a focus on specific technology innovations for teaching in the undergraduate and postgraduate pre-service teacher education programs.

Sini Kontkanen works as a university lecturer at the University of Eastern Finland at the School of Applied Educational Science and Teacher Education. She is interested in how ICT can enhance learning and teaching in different educational contexts and especially in-service and pre-service teachers' digital professional development from the point of view of Technological Pedagogical Content Knowledge (TPACK). Dr. Kontkanen has published several articles on this topic, exploring how authentic learning experiences with ICT, social software applications, and digital learning environments can enhance teachers' intentions and readiness to use ICT for teaching and learning. She is also currently involved as a researcher in the FINSCI project (Funded by Academy of Finland, STN), which examines parents' science capital and children's science literacy. In teacher education, she teaches pre- and in-service teachers how to integrate ICT, media education, and literacy skills into their teaching.

294 Contributor Biographies

Lauren Lichtman is Head of Partnerships and Strategy at Learning Equality. Lauren has a passion for working together to support innovations to break down barriers, so all children and youth have their right to quality education realized. Her work has always been driven by upholding human rights, ranging from supporting the work of corporates engaging in education to fighting crime by investigating international financial movements. Lauren holds an M.A. in international educational development with a focus on Peace Education from Teachers College, Columbia University.

Qian Liu is Research Fellow at Institute of Education, University College London. She completed her PhD study at the University of Cambridge. Her research interests include teacher professional development, innovative pedagogy with digital technology, and learners' equitable engagement in STEM. She has diverse practical experiences working as a school teacher, a teacher educator, and an early entrepreneur in the education sector.

Caroline Magunje is an educational technologist with more than 10 years' experience in higher education academic development in Zimbabwe. Dr. Magunje is passionate about the involvement of women and girls in resource-constrained communities in the digital age. She is a proud alumnus of Canon Collins Trust (UK) and the USA Techwomen program. She is currently Postdoctoral Fellow in the Department of Information Systems at the University of Cape Town, South Africa. Her research interest includes the integration of technology in curriculum delivery and cybersecurity in education in developing contexts.

Louis Major is Senior Lecturer in Digital Education at the University of Manchester, UK. Working in the Manchester Institute of Education, he co-leads the Digital Technology, Communication and Education (DTCE) Research and Scholarship group. Louis's research focuses on digital technology's role in the future of education, in particular, how this can help to address educational disadvantage and support effective dialogue and communication. He has been part of the global EdTech Hub team since 2020, which aims to provide evidence-based advice to inform decisions about the use of technology in education. Louis is also an editor of the *British Journal of Educational Technology* (BJET) and founding member of the Cambridge Digital Education Futures Initiative (DEFI).

Contributor Biographies **295**

Takayoshi Maki is Associate Professor in the International Education Development Program and a Center Director at Asia Pacific and Africa Teacher Education Cooperation Center, Hiroshima University, Japan. His primary research interest is in teacher education reforms in Thailand, where he stayed at Chulalongkorn University, the Ministry of Education, and Mae Fah Luang University. He has been involved in various research projects related to Thailand, Southeast Asia, and Africa, such as teacher educators' professional development, disaster education, rural teacher education, implantation of KOSEN, university admission, and ICT integration into teacher education. His research laboratory consists of teacher educators worldwide and strives to be a collective entity of strongly motivated truth-seekers, operating by the motto "research as my daily meal."

Karishma Mhapadi is an education consultant. Karishma is a passionate advocate for equal education, fueled by her personal experience as a first-generation learner. She has worked with organizations such as UNICEF, the World Bank, and Teach for India to close the gap in access to education and information for underserved communities. She received her Ed.M. in international education policy from Harvard University.

Kevin Otieno has a range of experience implementing education-based programs that champion student participation and supportive teaching in Kenya. Kevin's interest is on foundational literacy and numeracy, where he has been instrumental in implementing programs aimed at improving skills at pre-primary and primary school levels. His particular focus is on training, curriculum and instructional material design and development, and education technology. Kevin works as a training and research consultant in Kenya, a member of Women Educational Researchers of Kenya (WERK), training manager at Kindergarten Experts International, and Director of Data Management (Kenya) at Inside Out Learning, where he is focused on creating evaluation tools to document the efficacy of IOL methodology. Kevin has been part of the EdTech Hub design-based research in Kenya since 2022 on behalf of WERK, which aims to provide evidence-based advice to inform decisions about the use of technology in education.

Mary Otieno is Senior Lecturer in Educational Planning and Policy Studies Research at Kenyatta University in Nairobi, Kenya. She has been a coordinator of the UNESCO Chair project in sub-Saharan Africa at York University on reorienting education systems to serve the youth and vulnerable communities. Mary's research focus is on strengthening education systems with respect to equity, quality, and improved learning outcomes. Mary has a particular interest in foundational learning, education and technology, gender education, as well as teacher education. This research takes place in both basic and higher education, where she works closely with ministries of education in advancing education policy and quality education in Kenya. Mary has been part of the EdTech Hub's design-based research in Kenya since 2022 on behalf of Women Educational Researchers of Kenya (WERK), which aims to provide evidence-based advice to inform decisions about the use of technology in education.

Wakio Oyanagi is Professor of Educational Technology at Faculty of Informatics, Kansai University, Japan. His research interests include the use of technology in teacher education. He has been conducting research on educational practices, including classroom research at schools. He is a former president of the Japan Association for Educational Media Study and currently serves as vice president of the Japan Society for Educational Technology.

Heather Nadia Phillips is a postdoctoral research fellow in the research directorate at Cape Peninsula University of Technology (CPUT) in Western Cape, South Africa. As of 2023, she has 43 years of teaching experience, having held positions of deputy principal and principal at a primary school as well as lecturer of under- and postgraduate programs in the education faculty of CPUT. Dr Phillips' research expertise falls within teacher education focusing on quality, professional development, pedagogy, critical thinking, and literacy. Her core responsibilities include publishing research articles, reviewing journal articles, supervising postgraduate students, creating literacy training to develop critical thinking and reading for meaning in schools nationally, and developing seminars focusing on research methodology. Dr. Phillips is the project director of the Sisonke Supervision Mentorship Program, an institutional project aimed at developing postgraduate supervisors, and assisted in the planning and implementation of the program since 2022.

Satu Piispa-Hakala works as a doctoral researcher in the University of Eastern Finland at the School of Applied Educational Science and

Teacher Education. She has been training in-service teachers in the Learning and Teaching in Digitalized Environments specialization program since 2018. In her PhD research she studies in-service teachers' use of educational technology from the perspective of teacher agency. She is enthusiastic about in-service teachers' skills and pedagogies and their development with digital technologies in education.

Daniel Plaut is Associate Director at Results for Development (R4D), where he works as a learning partner to education providers to help further the impact of their initiatives. Daniel also serves as Innovation Learning Lead at EdTech Hub, where he facilitates the use of iterative evaluation and design-based implementation approaches, to support tech-enabled interventions. His recent work focuses specifically on tech-enabled teacher professional development and digital personalized learning programs.

Susanna Pöntinen is a university lecturer at the University of Eastern Finland at the School of Applied Educational Science and Teacher Education. She has extensive experience in researching and teaching ICT in education. Her recent research focuses on digital professional development, digital assessment knowledge, and practices of student teachers in initial and in-service teacher education. She is also passionate about exploring digitally enhanced pedagogical practices to support students' digital literacy, inquiry learning, and self-assessment skills in primary schools. In initial teacher education, she teaches and mentors student teachers on topics related to the use of digital technologies in education. For more than 20 years, she has been involved in various research and development projects related to the use of digital technologies in education.

Hiba Rahim is Director of Impact and Evaluation at Learning Equality. Hiba leads the development and strategy of Learning Equality's monitoring, evaluation, and learning. She specializes in mixed-methods work, and her experience in monitoring and evaluation ranges from improving teacher professional development programs in Pakistan and the Galapagos Islands to longitudinal analyses of Montessori learning outcomes in Dallas, Texas. Hiba dreams that all children are empowered with high-quality, individualized, holistic education to fulfill their dreams and those of future generations to come. She holds an Ed.D. from Southern Methodist University, Ed.M. from Harvard University, and a B.Sc.Ed. from Northwestern University.

298 Contributor Biographies

Asad Rahman is Practice Lead at Brink, a behavioral innovation practice. Brink is a Founding Member of the EdTech Hub, a global partnership and movement for evidence-based decision making in educational technology. Asad is Experimentation Lead at the EdTech Hub, where he harnesses rapid and iterative approaches to gathering and applying evidence through the Hub's Sandbox methodology. He has led eight Sandboxes with the Hub, focusing on how educational technology tools such as telephone helplines, interactive radio instruction, personalized learning software, and virtual learning environments can mitigate the global learning crisis in low- and middle-income countries.

Michael Ribble is the Director of Technology for the Manhattan-Ogden School District in Manhattan, Kansas. Dr. Ribble's qualifications include graduate degrees in Educational Administration, Management Information Systems, and Educational Leadership. In addition to these areas of expertise, Dr. Ribble has authored several books and articles around the topics of digital citizenship and technology leadership in schools.

Masayasu Sakaguchi is a lecturer at Hyogo University of Teacher Education (HUTE) in Japan. Currently, he belongs to the Graduate School of Education (Human Development Education Major) at HUTE. He has been committed to research and education mainly on the topics of multicultural society and education from the sociological and comparative perspectives (he especially focuses on the cases of the Republic of South Africa and Japan). He has been primarily interested in exploring the possible ways for people to "live together" with others with diverse backgrounds in society. More specifically, he has been trying to find the possible contributions which education (school education) can make to achieve "unity in diversity" in multicultural society. Also, he has been collaborating with other researchers with various backgrounds in order to discuss the development of school teachers who can respond to globalization, Information and Communication Technology (ICT), etc.

Nozomi Sakata is Assistant Professor at the Center for the Study of International Cooperation in Education in Hiroshima University, Japan. Her research interests and expertise lie in comparative and international education, specifically on policy diffusion, pedagogical reform, policy interactions and negotiations at macro-, meso-, and micro levels, and a capability approach to educational development. Nozomi currently leads a research project exploring possible conceptual overlaps between historically nurtured pedagogies, currently valued pedagogies, and globally promoted learner-centered pedagogies across sub-Saharan Africa (Tanzania, Ghana and Kenya) and Latin America (Mexico). She has wide experience of working in African contexts, her home country of Japan, and of studying in the United Kingdom and the United States, enabling a nuanced understanding of south-north challenges.

Chikondi Sepula is an associate lecturer responsible for computer science education at the Department of Mathematics and Science Education, University of Malawi. Currently, Chikondi is pursuing postgraduate studies in the Faculty of Education at Rhodes University. Research interests encompass artificial intelligence and its application in education, the development and integration of computational thinking in teacher training programs, and the effective use of digital technologies in teaching and learning environments.

Asami Shimoda is Associate Professor at the National Institute of Technology, Hiroshima College (KOSEN), specializing in KOSEN, technical and vocational education, and comparative education. Her current research theme is "International Expansion and Actual Situation of KOSEN Educational System," examining Japan's strategy, system, and activities and its expansion to Thailand. With prior experience at the Japan International Cooperation Agency (JICA), she contributed to international education cooperation, notably in projects such as "The Improvement of Teaching Method in Mathematics" in Honduras and "SMASTE School-Based CPD Project Phase II" in Zambia. While stationed at JICA headquarters, she was a research member for comprehensive evaluations in technical education institutions, including King Mongkut's Institute of Technology (Thailand), Electronics Engineering Polytechnic Institute of Surabaya (Indonesia), Jomo Kenyatta University of Agriculture and Technology (Kenya), and Japan Senegal Vocational and Technical Training Center (Senegal). Ms. Shimoda's work integrates academia and practical field experiences.

Clement Simuja is Senior Lecturer in the Faculty of Education at Rhodes University. Research interests and areas include digital education, focusing on the real-life constraints and problems faced when technology-based education is implemented. He is currently working on a research project examining the complex roles of and interplay among three main components of learning environments: content, pedagogy, and technology.

300 Contributor Biographies

Lungi Sosibo serves as Adjunct Professor in the Faculty of Education at Cape Peninsula University of Technology, where she has previously served as Senior Lecturer, Head of Department, Assistant Dean, and Acting Dean. She is a NRF C-rated researcher who has published extensively in higher/teacher education, with a special focus on curriculum reform and transformation. Her research has been cited by scholars and postgraduate students nationally and internationally. She boasts international partnerships with Nova South-Eastern University, Fort Lauderdale, USA; Adeyemi College of Education, Ondo, Nigeria; and Tai Solarin University of Education, Ijebu-Ode, Nigeria. She has an extensive record of successful postgraduate supervision, master's and doctoral theses examination, international conference presentations, NRF proposal reviews, and research grants. As Adjunct Professor, she publishes papers, supervises postgraduate students, mentors emerging researchers, and facilitates writing-for-publication workshops. She has served on Umalusi Council, Council for Higher Education (CHE), Northlink College, and CPUT Councils.

Chantyclaire Tiba holds a doctorate in educational technology from the Cape Peninsula University of Technology (CPUT), obtained in 2019. She lectures on the Honors in Education program at CPUT, and supervises master's and doctoral candidates. Her research interests are educational technology, mobile technology, digital storytelling, social media in education, teacher education, and transformative pedagogies used for teaching.

Nyarai Tunjera is an accomplished educational technologist with 15 years of higher education expertise. She is an ICT Educator and Research Fellow in the Faculty of Education at Cape Peninsula University of Technology, South Africa. Dr Nyarai Tunjera research interest lies in technology integration within the pre-service teacher preparation programmes. Her work advances education and prepares teachers for the digital age.

Teemu Valtonen works as a professor at the University of Eastern Finland at the School of Applied Educational Science and Teacher Education. His research interests lie in the use of Information and Communication Technology (ICT) in education, targeting especially pre-service teachers' skills and readiness to use ICT in education. In addition, current research focuses also on learning analytics and artificial intelligence in education. Dr. Valtonen has received a Finnish Academy grant (2016–2021; Academy Research Fellow) for his longitudinal research work titled as "Nature and development of pre-service teachers' TPACK".

Index

Note: Page numbers in *italics* indicate a figure and page numbers in **bold** indicate a table on the corresponding page.

actor network theory (ANT) 8, 267–268
AI *see* artificial intelligence
Amal Alliance 180, 182, 196
Annual Status of Education Report (ASER) 188–190
anonymity 83, 99, 147, 269
Anticipation Guide 202, 205–206
artificial intelligence integration (AI) 11–14, 49; and data science 51; globalized nature of 20
arts and sciences and engineering 53
Association of African Universities 266
ASSURE model 134, 138–139
asynchronous online discussion forums (AODFs) 144

Bachelor of Education (B.Ed.) 128–129, 131
Bachelor of Education Foundation Phase (BEd FP) 111, 113, 116, 120–121, 123
big data 49
biometric data 4, 30–31

biometric identification 30, 37–39
biometrics 37–38
Blackboard 65, 143–144
British Educational Research Association (BERA) 83, 165

care 34–35; work 29, 31–32, 35–36
CBP *see* Customs and Border Patrol
Center of Teacher Education Program for Transformation (C-TEX) 50
ChatGPT 2–3
children 47, 53, 81–83
China *see* digital technology in Chinese primary mathematics
Chinese lesson study (CLS) 163
CK *see* Content Knowledge
classroom: behaviour in 222–223; contemporary 1; dialogue 160–162, 164, 167–168; engagement 13; management 162, 236, 240; practice 247; research 44; SDL and OTL 145; space 27–28, 30–34; teaching 97; technologies in 29

302 Index

classroom practice, applying ICT: educational policy development related to ICT 236–238; effective use of ICT in classroom practice at schools 241–242; Japanese education policy 233–236; teachers' attitudes toward ICT in schools 238–240, 239, 241

collaboration 28, 164; and co-design 246; effective 247; ethical 14; ideas and 20; peer 174

collective agency 164, 174, 175

community of learning (CoL) 153

community of practice (CoP) 4–5, 62; case study 63–64; characteristics 62–63; components 4; data collection and analysis 64; principle of 62–63; and teacher educators' professional growth 70–71

Computer Application and Technology (CAT) 94–96, 98, 100–106

confidence 18, 111, 221; sense of 117–118; substantial 123–124; in teaching 121

confidentiality 64, 147, 269

Content Knowledge (CK) 115, 204, 208–209

cooperative learning strategies 202

CoP *see* community of practice

COVID-19 pandemic: biometric technology decades 38; classroom space during 36–37; education into online space 2; elementary and secondary education 231–232; ICT in schools 232, 236; impacts of technologies and applications 34; outbreak of 146–147; SD learners 146; technological rush 27

critical inquiry 175

curriculum design 180

Customs and Border Patrol (CBP) 38–39

cybersecurity threats 18

data science 4, 283; educational 50–51

decision-making 183; cultural and political 33; evidence-based 251; student-informed 13

design-based research (DBR) 8, 161, 284; approach 174; combination of LS and 174; complexities undertaking 248; critique of 249; definition 163; dialogic approach to 252; features of 163–164; integrated DBR partnership approach 254–258, 254; intrinsic link between LS and 164; -led LS 167–169; teacher-researcher engagement in 247; understanding of practitioner collaboration in 249–250; user journey mapping 250, 256

dialogic design-based research partnership approach: complexities undertaking Design-Based Research (DBR) 248; dialogic theoretical foundations 252–253; foundational phase of integrated multidisciplinary methods 255–256; implementation iteration workshops 1 256; implementation iteration workshop 2 257; innovation sandbox 257–258; integrated approach to partnership 253–254; integrated DBR partnership approach 254, 254; intermediate theory building 253; iterative, co-learning phase of lesson study 257; meaningful engagement between teachers and researchers 248–249; practical and theoretical contributions 258; research aims and setting 250–251; research team 251–252; scoping and initiating dialogue 255; understanding of practitioner collaboration in DBR 249–250

dialogic space theory 252

digital citizenship framework: educators 21; essential resources 15; nine principles of 12, 14; online privacy 12; responsible use skills 16–18; safety 15–17; savvy 17–19; security issues 12; social 19–21
digital divide, breaking: challenges and limitations 190; evaluation of Flying Colors' effectiveness 188–190, 189; findings 190; Flying Colors 182–185, 184; limited education in Northern Uganda 181–182; methodology 188, 190; study context 180–181; technologies used within Flying Colors 185–188, 186–187; *see also* Flying Colors program, Uganda
digital learning 204; environment 28, 50–51, 218, 282; materials 215
digital literacy: definition 34; and technophobia 274; skills 14, 266
digital personalised learning (DPL) 247–248, 251–253, 255–257, 259
digital resources 143, 147, 165, 282, 287
digital technology in Chinese primary mathematics: context, participants, and technology 165–167, 166; DBR-led LS 167–169, 168; design-based research 163–165, 164; design principles of TPD for dialogic teaching with digital technology 170, 171–173; lesson study for teacher learning and pedagogy 162–163; teacher change and teaching practice 169–171, 170; technology-mediated dialogic teaching 161–162; TPD design 171–172; TPD implementation 172–173; TPD management 173
digital technology, global perspectives: contributions from different corners of the globe 283–284; global perspectives in

shaping the future of education 287; intersection of technology and education 285–287
discrimination 80
diversity 75–76

Early-Childhood Development Officers (ECDOs), 255
ED Puzzle 202–203
educational informatics 4, 283
educational institutions 1, 199, 223–224, 226, 275
educational technology (EdTech) 8, 111, 247–248, 257; integration of 8; pedagogies of 217–218, 225; systematic development of 248
Education Resources Information Center (ERIC) 231–233
Education Revitalization Executive Council 48
effective learning 55, 96, 102, 139, 145
e-learning department 269, 271–272
e-learning in HEIs, in resource constrained environments: acceptance of e-learning as a flexible mode of delivery 275–276; actor network theory 267–268; age as a hindrance to technology-enhanced curriculum delivery 273; establishment of an e-learning department 271–272; digital literacy and technophobia 274; enrolment stage 274; faculty resistance to innovation/need for e-learning professional development 268; ICTs in Sub-Saharan Africa 268–269; introduction and background of the study 265–266; methodological considerations 269; mitigating threats in the university network 275; network builder identifying e-Learning 270–271; stability in online programs 276–277; teacher educators' internet

access 272–273; threats in the interessment stage 273; *see also* actor network theory; digital literacy

Emergency Remote Education (ERE) 2

enrolment 274–275

equity 28, 32

equality 75, 79–80; of usage 258

facial recognition 30, 37–38

facilitators, teachers as 13, 172, 169; online 277

feedback 152–153

Finland *see* professional development programme, teachers' perspective

FLN *see* foundational literacy and numeracy

Flying Colors program, Uganda 180, 182; data collection for 182; effectiveness 188–190; pedagogical design of 182–185; technologies used within 185–188, *186–187*; training plan 184

focus group discussions (FGDs) 188, 255

foundational literacy and numeracy (FLN) 180, 182, 185, 188, 193, *194*, 194

Foundation Phase, exploration of: data collection and analysis 116–117; on integrating technology 117–118; methodology 115–116; pre-service teacher's ability to integrate technology in teaching 118–120; research context 113–114; technology integration in teacher training 111–113; theoretical framework 114–115; TPACK as crucial competency 120–122; *see also* pre-service teachers; Technological Pedagogical Content Knowledge (TPACK)

Fourth Industrial Revolution (4IR) 68

GCSE *see* General Certificate of Secondary Education

GenAI programs 2–3

gender equity 5, 76

General Certificate of Secondary Education (GCSE) 76

GIGA *see* Global Innovation Gateway for All-Schools Initiative

girls and computer science: background to the problem 77–81; Computer Science Take-Up 84, *85*; ethical considerations 83; at GCSE 76–77; grasp of equality 88, *89*; other patterns 86–88, *87–88*; research methodology 81–83; role models 85–86, *86*; women in computing 88

Global and Innovation Gateways for All (GIGA) 46, 48, 51, 53, 233–237

global perspectives *see* digital technology, global perspectives

Google Slides 202, 207

Harvard's EASEL Lab 190

HEIs *see* higher education institutions

'Hidden Figures' video 82, 88

higher education institutions (HEIs) 65, 68, 265; *see also* e-learning in HEIs, in resource constrained environments; information and communication technology (ICT); pre-service teachers education

Hopelink Action Foundation (HAF), Uganda 179, 188, 196

Hyogo University of Teacher Education 49–50, *52*, 56

information and communication technology (ICT) 44; community of practice and teacher educators' professional growth 70–71; community of practice framework 62; critical challenge of 68–70; methodology 63–64;

Index 305

objectives 53–55; on teacher education 61–62; teacher educators' choices of 65–68; *see also* community of practice (CoP)
information morality 4, 50–51
informed consent 27, 99, 239
Innovations for Poverty Action (IPA) 181, 196
in-service teachers 68, 77, 119, 218; education 2–3, 6–8, 89, 286; efficacy of 62; expertise of 217; gender training 77; training programs 281; *see also* classroom practice, applying ICT; dialogic design-based research partnership approach; digital divide, breaking; digital technology in Chinese primary mathematics; e-learning in HEIs, in resource constrained environments; professional development programme, teachers' perspective; technology integration, case study on 5th grade reading
instructional technology 127–132
instructors 26–32, 34–37, 144–145, 150–151, 234
intellectual property 20, 27; protections 12; rights 19
intermediate theory building 253
Internet 3, 273
Internet of Things 49

Jamboard 33, 55
Japan *see* pre-service teachers education (Japan)
Japan Association for Educational Technology (JAET) 236–238

Kenya *see* dialogic design-based research partnership approach
key informant interviews (KIIs) 255
'knowledge, virtue, and body' 45
Kolibri Learning Platform 7, 179–180, 185

Learning Equality 7, 180, 183, 185, 188
learning management systems (LMS) 28, 36, 50–51, 65, 144, 269
LEGO Foundation, The 180, 196
lesson study (LS) 161–165, 168, 174; adaptations of 163; DBR approach to 175; implantation 173
lesson study groups (LSGs) 163
low and middle-income countries (LMICs) 248, 253, 258, 260

Malawi *see* technology-enhanced education
media for learning 129
MEXT *see* Ministry of Education, Culture, Sports, Science, and Technology
Ministry of Education, Culture, Sports, Science, and Technology (MEXT) 44–46, 232, 234, 236, 240
modelling 112–113, 139
municipalities 221, 223–226

National Council for Higher Education 132
national networks 224, 226
National Planning Authority (NPA) 182
National Science Foundation (NSF) 78

Office of National Statistics (ONS) 77
online learning 30, 119, 146, 270, 272, 276
online teaching and learning (OTL) 142, 148–149; synchronous and asynchronous 144, 146, 153–154
open educational resources (OER) 183
Osaka Kyoiku University 49

parallel lesson study (PLS) 163, 167–169, 175
participants 71, 99, 119–120, 269; racial identity of 147
PBL *see* project-based learning

306 Index

Pedagogical Content Knowledge (PCK) 115, 204, 214–216, 226–228

Pedagogical Knowledge (PK) 115, 204, 208, 209

PK *see* Pedagogical Knowledge

Post Graduate Certificate of Education (PGCE) 4, 5, 75, 95, 97–98, 107

pre-service teachers (PSTs): education 4–6; Foundation Phase 66; importance of 44; information and communication technology in 44; integrate technology in teaching 118–120; Intermediate Phase 200; journey of 283; majority of 117; perceptions 5, 114; PST2 121; PST3 119; PST4 119–121; PST5 118–121; PST6 118; PST7 119; struggle 94; thoughts and feelings 111; TPACK framework 114–115; within Computer Application and Technology 94; *see also* Foundation Phase, exploration of; girls and computer science; information and communication technology (ICT); pre-service teachers education (Japan); pre-service teachers' pedagogical awareness; self-directed learning, barriers to; technology-enhanced education

pre-service teachers' pedagogical awareness: data analysis 99; methodology 98–99; overview of literature 95–97; research context 95; researchers' perception of participants' technological, pedagogical, and content knowledge 103–105; significance of technology in fostering student active and engaged learning interest within the classroom 102–103; theoretical framework 97–98; utilizing technology purposefully in classroom settings 100–102

pre-service teachers education (Japan): curricula in Japan 45; digital human resource development 52; education 44; five qualities about teachers 47; future of school education in Japan 46–48; Hyogo University of Teacher Education 49–52; ICT-Based Education 53–56, 54, 55; present and future of education in Japan 44; school education in Japan 45; *see also* teacher education universities

privacy 18, 20, 27; invasion of 30; offline 17; online 3, 12, 17

problem-solving 96, 105, 183; collective 215; innovative 105; skills 162, 204

professional development programme, teachers' perspective: behaviour in classroom 222–223; behaviour level 222–224; characteristics of a high-quality PD programme 215–216; confidence 221; data and analysis 218–219, 219; knowledge and beliefs 220–221; Learning and Teaching in Digitalized Environments 216; learning level 220–221; reaction level 220; research context 216–218, 217; research questions 216; results level 224–226; sharing one's own expertise and networks 223–224; *see also* classroom

Programme for International Student Assessment (PISA) 44

programming education 4, 45–46

Progress in International Literacy Study (PIRLS) 198–199

project-based learning (PBL) 180–181, 183, 185

Provincial Education Department 99

PSTs *see* pre-service teachers

Index **307**

Rainstorm 43
reading-for-meaning (R4M) 198,
201; strategies integrated with
technology 205–210
'Reiwa' 46
remote proctoring technologies 27, 30
resource limited environments *see*
e-learning in HEIs, in resource
constrained environments
robotics 49
rubrics 134, 210

safe, savvy, and social (S3) guiding
principles 15–21
Scholarship of Teaching and Learning
(SoTL) 128, 131–132, 137–139
Science, Technology, Engineering
and Maths (STEM) 75–77, 79–81,
89–90
Science, Technology, Engineering,
Arts and Mathematics (STEAM)
4, 48, 50–51
secondary education 26; elementary
and 231–233, 243; in Malawi 128;
primary and 46, 61, 112; situating
within 28–32; *see also* students
security education 50–51
SEL *see* social emotional learning
self-directed learning, barriers to
(COVID-19): context of study
143; discussions 152–154;
lack of sense of community
149–150; methodology 146–147;
poor online course design and
implementation skills of lecturers
150–152; students' personality
traits 148–149; synchronous and
asynchronous online teaching
and learning 144; synergy
between social constructivism,
self-directed learning and online
teaching and learning 145;
theoretical framework 145–146;
see also online teaching and
learning (OTL)
self-esteem 206–207, 221

semi-structured interviews 98,
116, 218
sharing circle 116–118
Social Ecological Technology
Integration (SETI) 2
social emotional learning (SEL)
180–183, 185, 188, 190, 195
'Society 5.0' 46–49
South Africa 106, 112; public schools
in 61; universities 67, 95, 98;
see also community of practice
(CoP); pre-service teachers'
pedagogical awareness; self-
directed learning, barriers to
stakeholders 250, 271; active 252;
education 251; government 190
STEAM *see* Science, Technology,
Engineering, Arts, and
Mathematics
STEM *see* Science, Technology,
Engineering and Maths
students: access for 28, 32; -centered
teaching 101, 183; -centred
learning 272; -centred pedagogy
227; -centric education 94; critical
thinking skills 18, 103; data
privacy 16; -directed learning 183;
engagement 107, 232; feedback
102; guidance 236; rights 283;
safety 17; in secondary education
30; surveilling 35; tablets for 69;
work 167
students' personality traits 148–149
student teachers 128–130, 132–133,
137–139, 265
Sub-Saharan Africa (SSA) 63, 265;
ICTs in 268–269
Substitution, Augmentation,
Modification, and Redefinition
(SAMR) 2
surveillance 27, 34–35; apathy 29
surveillant impacts of technology:
CBP Case for Integration 36–37;
class and critical examination
39; critically examining
technologies 32–33; keyword

report 37; layered surveillance and transparency as strategy 35–36; situating within secondary education 28–32; surveillance, care, and digital literacy 34–35; thoughts and implications 39–40

Tayari structured pedagogy (SP) 250
teacher education: challenges faced by 68–70; choice of ICT apps 66–68; choices of ICT tools 65–66; curriculum 154; Hyogo University of 49–50; information and communication technology in 61–62; in-service 6–8; internet access 272–273; preparedness and ability of 112–113; pre-service 4–6; professional growth 70–71; programs 107; research-based 130–132; training of 272
Teacher Education Programme (TEP) 143, 146, 153
teacher education universities 48–56; Designing the City of the Future 51; Hyogo University of Teacher Education 49–52; ICT-Based Education 53–56, 54, 55; major roles of 49; redefining of learning 55; STEAM education 51
teacher professional development (TPD) 77; DBR approach to 163–164; for dialogic teaching with digital technology 170, 171–173; design 171–172; implementation 172–173; management 173
Teachers' Licence Law 48
technical communicators 26–29, 32–35
Technological Content Knowledge (TCK) 115, 204
Technology Knowledge (TK) 115, 204, 206, 209
Technological Pedagogical Content Knowledge (TPACK) 2, 5, 7, 60, 95–98, 105, 153; content, pedagogy and technology 114–115; as crucial competency 120–122; model of 97–98, 138; seven constructs in 115; theoretical framework 95–98, 114–115, 199, 204
Technological Pedagogical Knowledge (TPK) 115, 204
technology-enhanced education (Malawi): context of study 128–129; instructional problem analysis 132–133; instruction design 134, 135; problem statement 129–130; reflective question 133–134; research-based 130–132; selecting instructional media 136–137; SoTL Case Study 132–137; see also teacher education
technology integration: in classrooms 97, 106, 124; content knowledge 104; and infusion 242; skills 60, 281; into STEAM education 4; in teacher training 111–113; in teaching 107, 114, 119
technology integration, case study on 5th grade reading: benefits of using technology in developing reading for meaning skills 203–204; context 199–200; employing teaching strategies using technology 202–203; lessons learnt 206–210; problem 200–201; R4M strategies integrated with technology 205; teachers' role in integrating technology 203; technology and reading for meaning 201; theoretical framework 204; see also reading-for-meaning (R4M)
TEP see teacher education programme
Tokyo Gakugei University 49
Toolkit for Systematic Educational Dialogue Analysis (T-SEDA) 164, 167–168
transparency 4, 18, 29, 35–36

Index   **309**

Uganda *see* digital divide, breaking understanding equality, 88, 89
UNICEF 247
United Nations Educational Scientific Cultural Organisation (UNESCO) 199, 275, 282
United States 26, 32–33, 283; *see also* surveillant impacts of technology
University of Fukui, the 49, 53, 56
University of Malawi (UNIMA) 128

Wales, UK 5; *see also* pre-service teachers

Women Educational Researchers of Kenya (WERK) 251
World Bank 183, 268
World's Best Schools 199, 210
World War II 78

Zimbabwe 8, 265–266, 268, 270, 277, 284; *see also* e-learning in HEIs, in resource constrained environments
Zoomabc 167

9781032524245